Language and Being

Language and being

Language and Being

Joseph Conrad
and the
Literature of Personality

Peter J. Glassman

Columbia University Press/New York and London
1976

Library of Congress Cataloging in Publication Data
Glassman, Peter J   1945–
    Language and being: Joseph Conrad and the lit-
    erature of personality.
    Bibliography: p.
    Includes index.
    1. Conrad, Joseph, 1857–1924.   I. Title.
PR6005.04Z727   823'.9'12   75-29092
ISBN 0-231-03999-9

To my father,
and to the memory of my mother.

Contents

Preface

Joseph Conrad had no personality in the sense which we normally intend the word. Supported in only the most vague ways, framed by virtually no external sanctions, Conrad's character could not have felt to him a discrete and secured entity upon which, as it were, he might rely. Conrad seems to have conducted his entire life as might a desperately unindividuated child: threatened by what seemed to him the endless incoherence of the not-himself, protected by no set of reliable persuasions about his personal resources or rights, he appears to have lived each instant of his life under the urgent and terrible necessity to define what was his, what was the world's, and what relation was possible between the two.

In this unenviable enterprise, the legacy of his complex and repellent experience, the writing of fiction came to replace for Conrad the normally inherited or chosen personality structures of family, nation, sexuality, love. In a letter to Edward Garnett, perhaps his closest friend, Conrad wrote:

> I seem to have lost all *sense* of style and yet I am haunted, mercilessly haunted by the *necessity* of style. And that

story I can't write weaves itself into all I see, into all I
speak, into all I think, into the lines of every book I try to
read. . . . You know how bad it is when one *feels* one's
liver, or lungs. Well I feel my brain. I am distinctly conscious of the contents of my head. My story is there in a
fluid—in an evading shape. I can't get hold of it. It is all
there—to bursting, yet I can't get hold of it no more than
you can grasp a handful of water.

(Garnett,135)

It is one of his most revealing communications, suggesting
as it does the intense and fascinating correspondence
Conrad evolved between his literature and his character,
between his capacity to write narrative prose and his power
to experience emotion. In the chapters which follow I try
to define the history of this, the essential economy of
Conrad's life.

I have faced a number of difficulties in this undertak-
ing which perhaps it should be best to discuss here. In particular it has been difficult to devise a satisfying approach
or access to Conrad's private sensibility. For although, from
one point of view, Conrad perhaps wrote nothing but autobiography, each of his novels presents nothing more, I
should think, than a momentarily gratifying or a momentarily necessary version of himself. It is the principal point
of my book, in fact, that Conrad wrote fiction largely because he required a way to become honorably multiple in
his identity; because he wished and needed to offer to the
world and to himself what in 1900 he called "a simulacrum"
of inner life. His correspondence is similarly unreliable as
an absolute index of his character. Conrad wrote letters as
he wrote novels—to propose a self or a set of selves to
men and women toward whom he looked for sustenance
and sanction. Nor are the several biographies of Conrad al-

together instructive. For all of their excellence—and each of the biographical works which I have consulted seems to me within the limits of its ambition and genre quite distinctly excellent—none offers a full understanding of the connection between Conrad's life and his literature. As I try to suggest, there was no discrimination between the two for Conrad and therefore there ought to be none for us.

I have felt compelled, then, to work from rather complicated, often individually inflected, grounding points. I borrow freely, for example, from Jocelyn Baines' superb and now standard biography for the details of what one might call Conrad's absolute experience. Yet, I do not offer my book as biography. For however often I am led to consider the sheer materials of his existence, I chiefly am interested not in Conrad's actual history but in his attitude toward his history and in his systems of escape from it. Too, although I frequently consult his letters, I never suppose that Conrad's correspondence defines his "real" or complete state of mind. I have hoped, rather, that by simultaneously engaging his fiction, his letters, and his life one may accrue information about Conrad's inner assumptions and moods substantial enough to support not wholly speculative judgments about his character. In the end, this is to say, my approach to Conrad's tortuously hidden personality has been objectively—I hope not merely objectionably—personal. I interpret upon what have seemed to me to be persuasive bases; certainly, though, I do interpret.

Whether or not one may extend the methodology of literary criticism, the discipline in which I have been trained, to the examination of a novelist's conscious and subconscious life is a question which cannot be argued adequately here. This much, however, one might say.

Conrad's literature exactly fixes no boundary about itself: he wrote to live, and lived to write, in a way which lends meaning to the hackneyed phrase. In the case of Conrad my experiment appears to me not simply honorable or interesting but, as I hope to establish, necessary. I should add that one thinks of a number of other authors who invite similar attention.

I have drawn upon the kindness of many of my colleagues and friends in preparing this study. While expressing my indebtedness for the assistance which I have received, I should like to emphasize that any infelicities of assumption or judgment which survive in the text are my own responsibility; indeed, I have undertaken certain procedures in the book specifically against advice. That my work is not more difficult or problematic is largely to be attributed to the attention of Professors John D. Rosenberg, Karl Kroeber, and Daniel B. Dodson, all of whom read and commented extensively upon draft versions of the text. Professors Homer Brown and Herbert Leibowitz were particularly generous and helpful to me. Professors George Stade and Steven Marcus, and Professor and Mrs. Michael Rosenthal, have shaped and gentled my book as they have shaped and gentled my life. Professor Edward W. Said has behaved toward me more as a brother than as a teacher and friend. My principal debt is to the late Professor Lionel Trilling, who formed my sensibility.

I am grateful, too, to my parents-in-law, Mr. and Mrs. Albert Piccolo, and to my godparents, Mr. and Mrs. Joel Glassman, for their innumerable kindnesses and their loving support. To my father, James Glassman, to my stepmother, Robin Glassman, to my wife Claudia, to Emily and to Nicholas, my thanks shall be more private, as has been their sustaining gift of patience, peace, and love. I should add that I am very grateful to Mr. William F. Bernhardt and to Mr. David Diefendorf of Columbia University Press for their patient and superb editorial guidance.

Permission to quote from Joseph Conrad, *Complete Works*, and from G. Jean-Aubry, *Joseph Conrad, Life and Letters*, has been granted by the Trustees of the Joseph Conrad Estate. Permission to quote from Jocelyn Baines, *Joseph Conrad: A Critical Biography*, has been granted by George Weidenfeld & Nicolson, Ltd. Permission to quote from *Letters from Joseph Conrad, 1895–1924*, edited by Edward Garnett, copyright 1928 by The Bobbs-Merrill Company, Inc., R. 1955 by David Garnett, has been granted by the publisher and by Mr. David Garnett. Permission to quote from *Letters of Joseph Conrad to Marguerite Poradowska, 1890–1920*, translated and edited by John A. Gee and Paul J. Sturm, copyright 1940 by the Yale University Press, has been granted by the publisher. Permission to quote from *Conrad's Polish Background: Letters to and from Polish Friends*, edited by Zdzisław Najder, translated by Halina Carroll, published by Oxford University Press, has been granted by the publisher. Permission to quote from *Joseph Conrad: Letters to William Blackwood and David S. Meldrum*, edited by William Blackburn, has been granted by the Duke University Press. Permission to quote from *Joseph Conrad's Letters to R. B. Cunninghame Graham*, edited by C. T. Watts, published by the Cambridge University Press, has been granted by the publisher. I am grateful to each of the above for their generosity.

PETER J. GLASSMAN

Columbia University
November 15, 1975

Abbreviations

Joseph Conrad, *Complete Works*, 26 vols. (Garden City, New York: Doubleday, Page and Company, 1925), volumes cited are as follows:

III.   *Notes on Life and Letters*
VI.   *A Personal Life*
XI.   *Almayer's Folly*
XIV. *An Outcast of the Islands*
XVI. *Youth* ("Youth", *Heart of Darkness,* "The End of the Tether")
XVII. *The Shadow-Line*
XX.   *Typhoon*
XXI. *Lord Jim*
XXIII. *The Nigger of the "Narcissus"*

Baines   Jocelyn Baines. *Joseph Conrad: A Critical Biography* (London: Weidenfeld and Nicolson, 1960; fourth impression, with corrections, 1967).

Blackwood   *Joseph Conrad: Letters to William Blackwood and David S. Meldrum,* ed. William Blackburn (Durham: Duke University Press, 1958).

Garnett   Joseph Conrad. *Letters from Joseph Conrad, 1895–1924,* ed. Edward Garnett (Indianapolis: Bobbs-Merrill Company, 1928).

Last Essays   Joseph Conrad. *Last Essays,* intro. Richard Curle (London: J. M. Dent and Sons, 1926).

LL,I. or II.   G. Jean-Aubry. *Joseph Conrad, Life and Letters,* 2 vols. (Garden City, New York: Doubleday, Page and Company, 1927).

Najder   Zdzisław Najder. *Conrad's Polish Background* (London: Oxford University Press, 1964).

Poradowska Joseph Conrad. *Letters of Joseph Conrad to Marguerite Poradowska, 1890–1920,* tr. and ed. John A. Gee and Paul J. Sturm (New Haven: Yale University Press, 1940).

Watts   Joseph Conrad. *Joseph Conrad's Letters to Cunninghame Graham,* ed. C. T. Watts (Cambridge: Cambridge University Press, 1969).

Language and Being

Language and Being

Chapter One

Nothing new as to events. As to feelings, nothing new
either. And herein lies the trouble; for if one could get
rid of his heart and memory (and also brain), and then
get a whole new set of these things, life would become
ideally amusing. As this is impossible, life is not so; it is
abominably sad!

(*Poradowska*, 12)

Write it, damn you, write it! What else are you good for?

—James Joyce

All That World of Bodiless Souls
1857-1895

The details of Conrad's early life are becoming almost as
well-known as his novels, for his actual biography is as tex-
tured, alien, and alluring as any of the fictions he wrote.
And yet, if we feel drawn to Conrad's experience, we know
little about its actual consequences for him. We know almost nothing, for instance, about his attitudes toward himself or toward the world during his childhood. We know
not nearly enough about his sensibility during his bizarre
and desperate months at Marseilles. We know more, but
not what we would wish, about his responses to Malaysia,
the Congo, England, and his life at sea. All that we do
know, though, suggests that Conrad suffered intensely
from his early engagement with the world. I believe, indeed, that the values and forms of Conrad's fiction are con-

nected inseparably with the demands of his experience and with the structures of his personality from 1857 to 1895. It is with that experience, then, and with his responses to it, that this study begins.

One: 1857–1869

Conrad's childhood is remarkable even among the many instances in the nineteenth century of deprived boyhood. Motherless at seven, bound for four years to an exiled, fanatic, and grotesquely inept father, orphaned at eleven, Conrad conducted an existence of such bleakness that, years later, he was able to express surprise that he had remained sane.[1]

Conrad's father seems by all accounts to have been a charming and good man who loved his wife and only child. But he loved as well literature and his country—a dangerous combination of affections in any man, and in Apollo Korzeniowski a disastrous one. Apollo began his career as a farmer. By the fourth year of his marriage, though, he had managed to bankrupt his small Ukrainian estate.[2] Released in this emphatic and perhaps deliberate way from his quotidian responsibilities, he felt free to indulge the chief passions of his life. Thus, in 1861, amidst a general atmosphere in Poland of expectancy and fervor,[3] he moved

1. Cf. III.168.

2. Cf. Jocelyn Baines, *Joseph Conrad: A Critical Biography* (London: Weidenfeld and Nicolson, 1960; fourth impression, with corrections, 1967), p. 6–7; Zdzisław Najder, *Conrad's Polish Background* (London: Oxford University Press, 1964), p. 5.

3. The outbreak of the Crimean War seemed to many patriotic Poles to offer signal encouragement in the long struggle against Russian oppression. Cf. Baines, 8–9; Najder, 3–5.

his family to Żytomierz, a provincial center of insurrectionist literature and politics. In May Apollo left his family with Conrad's maternal grandmother at Terechowa and joined the extremist revolutionary party in Warsaw; [4] in October, in spite of the threatening conditions of tension in the Polish capital, he sent for his wife Evelina and son Konrad. Weeks later, after forming in his home a clandestine revolutionary council, Korzeniowski was arrested and imprisoned for seven months. In May, 1862, Apollo and Evelina were convicted of treason and sentenced to permanent exile in Perm, a remote Russian province.[5]

Conrad passed his third year, then, in an atmosphere of extraordinary disruption and distress. His first letter, "written" to his father from Żytomierz, sounds quiet and sweet with unexceptional love. But it is tinged, too, with all the mystified confusion of an abandoned child:

> Daddy, I like it here, I run about the garden, but I don't like it when the mosquitoes sting. I will come to Daddy when it stops raining. . . . Were you at that Barbara's where Grannie? [sic] (Baines, 10)

So young a child obviously cannot know that a father who absents himself may continue to love his son and to feel interest in what he experiences and does. Four "I's" from a three-year-old, as if Apollo must be made to rediscover his deserted son as a self, and so feel impelled to return home to reclaim him. So too, perhaps, that sad effort of the child

4. Apollo spoke of publishing a literary review. In fact, though, he went to Warsaw to organize the revolutionary campaign. Cf. Baines, 10; Najder, 5.

5. Cf. Baines, 11–12; Najder 6 and 6n. Najder suggests that Evelina Korzeniowski may have been imprisoned with her husband. She certainly was co-accused with Apollo and was *sentenced* to share his exile from Poland. (Throughout his life Conrad mistakenly believed that his mother voluntarily accompanied Apollo. Cf. VI.23.)

to define precisely what has attracted his father more imperatively than himself. "Were you at that Barbara's where Grannie?" Where *were* you, Daddy? Can you explain what engages you so much that you do not mind leaving me behind? When shall I come to you, then? When it stops raining?

Conrad's life at Terechowa was complicated further by his mother's perfervid behavior. No doubt Evelina, too, had needs: in the absence of her husband she seems to have encouraged her son to enter into her own attitudes of ardency. Consider, for example, the implications of the following note to Apollo:

> I am tired: I have spent the whole day sewing a mourning dress for Konradek. It is so black here—children too—that the boy asks for the mourning himself. (Najder, 6)

A pretty picture: the mother playing at martyrdom, the child asking for the robes of mourning—trying bravely, it would seem, to make a species of game from the materials of his confusion and pain. Conrad's grandmother adds to one's sense of the child's desolation:

> Words cannot describe the sweetness of this child. He is very friendly with the poor, telling them family news and asking them to pray for the return of his father from Warsaw. I discovered this from the beggars at the church. (Baines, 10)

"I discovered this from the beggars. . . ." The women who superintended Conrad's childhood appear to have been unsophisticated indeed about the grim apparatus of his trauma.[6]

6. No reliable record survives of Conrad's reaction to his father's (and, possibly, his mother's) arrest and incarceration. One may speculate,

On 8 May 1862 the Korzeniowskis were escorted to Vologda.[7] The journey was a long one and conditions were severe—so severe that Conrad contracted pneumonia and Evelina pulmonary tuberculosis. Vologda itself, as described by Apollo, was bleak, barren, cold beyond endurance:

> What is Vologda? A Christian is not bound to know this. Vologda is a great three-verst marsh on which logs and trees are placed parallel to each other in crooked lines; everything rotting and shifting under one's feet; this is the only means of communication available to the natives. . . . The climate consists of two seasons of the year: a white winter and a green winter. The white winter lasts nine-and-a-half months and the green one two-and-a-half. We are now at the onset of the green winter: it has already been raining ceaselessly for twenty-one days and that's how it will be to the end.
>
> During the whole winter the frost remains at 25–30° [Réaumur; 24–30° below 0° F.] while the wind from the White Sea, held up by nothing, brings constant news from the polar bears. . . . The population is a nightmare: disease-ridden corpses. (Baines, 13–14)

In such a place as this, in the company only of his parents and twenty-one other exiled adults,[8] Conrad passed the winter of 1862–1863. He was five years old.

---

though, that a four-year-old child does not survive a police raid upon his recently regained home or the permanent disruption of his family life with impunity—particularly when, as Conrad may have thought, he just has been reclaimed by his father; when, as he may have put it to himself, he just has *rewon* his father.

7. The governor at Perm, the Korzeniowskis' original destination, had been at school with Apollo. He seems to have taken pity on the family, and to have arranged for their transfer to Vologda—which the Korzeniowskis did not reach until 16 June. (Cf. Najder, 6.)

8. G. Jean-Aubry, *Joseph Conrad Life and Letters*, 2 vols. (Garden City: Doubleday, Page and Company, 1927), vol. 1, p. 8.

Life at Vologda was so frightful that Conrad and Evelina deteriorated rapidly. Evidently their state was serious indeed, for the normally severe Russian officials permitted the transfer of the Korzeniowskis to Chernikhov, an exile community substantially more comfortable than Vologda; [9] and in the summer of 1863 Evelina's family secured permission for herself and her son to visit her brother, Thaddeus Bobrowski, at his Novofastov estate. Here, for the first time in his life, Conrad had to do with children of his own age (if of dissimilar experience!). As important, at Novofastov—again for the first time in his life—Conrad lived within the supportive structures of a family committed to uncomplicated domestic existence. But for three months only, for in the autumn of 1863, in spite of a radical decline in his mother's condition, Conrad and Evelina were ordered to rejoin Apollo.[10]

In Chernikhov Evelina's health irreversibly declined. Her doctors had given up hope and so, apparently, had her husband:

> My poor wife has been dying, for several years, from her sickness and from the repeated blows which have been falling on our family. During the past four months she has been cruelly ill, confined to her bed, with barely enough

9. Cf. Najder, 8.

10. Obviously one should like to know something about Conrad's response to his life at Novofastov; unfortunately no record survives. If the fervor and immediacy of his adult recollections may be taken as sample, though, the months at his uncle's home with their emphatic intimations of alternative affected Conrad in a permanent and intense way. It can come as no surprise that, fifty years later, he described the visit as "the very happiest period of my existence" (VI.24). [Conrad recalls the furlough in A Personal Record. Cf. particularly VI.23–25; 31–37; 46f.] Certainly Conrad retained throughout his life a vivid memory of the seriousness and sorrow occasioned by his return to Chernikhov. (Cf. VI.63–64.)

strength to glance at me, to speak with muted voice. . . .
May God be with us—for people can do little for us now. I
am everything in the house—both master and servant. I do
not complain of this as a burden; but how often it has
been impossible for me to help the poor, unhappy woman
or bring her relief! Our little Conrad is inevitably neglected in the midst of all this.[11]

Two days later Apollo confirmed his diagnosis and detailed
the various bleaknesses of the Korzeniowskis' life:

I believe, best of friends, that two or three days ago I sent
you a letter. . . . I think I did, as I don't know what I'm
doing—what I feel—and I remember nothing. You will understand when I tell you: my wife is very, very ill—there is
hope only in God. . . . Her mind alone remains unshaken.
I ask myself, is this courage or does she not know how ill
she really is? Who could read the answer in her eyes, if I,
to whom they have ever been an open book, cannot see
what is written there? And yet, I cannot read her eyes.
Only, sometimes, a stronger pressure of her hand in mine,
or in little Conrad's, testifies to her courage. . . . We are
wretched and unhappy indeed, but thank God that we
have been allowed to bear this fate together. . . .[12]

It is a brave and masculine letter, much the best that Apollo
ever wrote. And with its talk of solidarity in crisis the letter
does much to explain how the members of the family managed to sustain themselves amidst their many calamities.
But how much Apollo and Evelina seem to have required of
their child in this regard! Conrad evidently was asked to sit
for hours with his moribund mother. More distressing, he

11. Baines, 16. Slightly different versions of the letter appear in LL,I.11–12
and in Najder, 8.

12. Baines, 16. Jean-Aubry records a slightly different version of the letter
in LL,I.12.

obviously was expected to share in and to ratify his father's gratitude that the family had been "allowed to bear this fate together." Allowed, indeed: it is a difficult notion for a seven-year-old to engage. Certainly no such adult mechanism of support could have made his mother's suffering or his own quite comprehensible or bearable to the child— particularly when his father's state of mind was as distracted and hysterical as the letter's first lines suggest it was. Apollo was close to the truth, no doubt, when he confessed that Conrad was badly "neglected" during his mother's last illness.

On 18 April 1865, Evelina Bobrowska Korzeniowski died. After seven years of frequently furtive and fragile family life, after three years of actual exile, endured in appalling climates amidst an atmosphere laden with disease, grief, and foreboding, Conrad lost, in his phrase, the one "loving, . . . silent, protecting presence" (VI.24) of his life. No wonder his photographs from 1863 and 1865 present such a stark, sad, stiff impression, as if the sublimely anxious textures of his life, so long unrelieved by even the possibility of pleasure, at last had made an absolute condition for the child.[13]

Never before had Conrad had so compelling a claim upon his father—and never before had Apollo been less available or strong. Impoverished, ill, worn-upon, Apollo decided on the day after his wife's death that he, too, should die, and that his son already was effectively orphaned.[14] On this occasion of crisis for Conrad (and for his own paternity) Apollo was able to perceive his son's needs; but, characteristically, he preferred to indulge his own:

13. The photographs are reprinted in LL,I.22.

14. Cf. Apollo's letter to Casimir Kaszewski, LL,I.13.

The poor child does not know what it is to have a companion of his own age. He sees the sadness of my old age, and who knows, perhaps that sight may freeze and wither his own young heart; that is one of the chief reasons which makes me wish to send him away from me. (LL,I.,15)

A more responsive father might have understood that his son precisely did not need to be sent away from him at such a time. As I have said, though, Apollo responded during this emergency not to Conrad but to himself:

I have passed through heavy and even terrible days of brooding on God's blessings and, if I survive, it will not be thanks to my own, but God's strength. I know I have not suffered and never could suffer like our Saviour, but then I am only a human being. . . . Whatever remains for me to do in life, I cannot either sacrifice or give anything, for I have nothing to sacrifice or offer up. (LL,I.,16)

One imagines that he might have "sacrificed" or "offered up" something of his mawkish self-indulgence. But the twin supports of Apollo's identity evidently had evolved into just this vague pietism—and into a shameless dependence upon his son's strengths ("Since autumn my health has not a little declined and my little one has had to take care of me" [LL,I.,15]). Occasionally, indeed, he conjoined the two macabre strategies:

I shield [Conrad] from the atmosphere of this place, and he grows up as though in a monastic cell. For the *momento mori* we have the grave of our dear one, and every letter which reaches us is the equivalent of a day of fasting, a hair shirt or a discipline. We shiver with cold, we die of hunger. We are overwhelmed by the destitution of our fellowmen, our brothers, but prayer remains to us, and in our prayers, I call God to witness, there is scarce a word about ourselves. Should I describe this place I would say that on the one hand it is bounded by locked doors behind which the being dearest to me breathed her last, without my being able to wipe the death sweat from her brow, while on the other, though there the doors are open, I may not cross the threshold, and I see what Dante did *not* describe, for his soul, appalled though it was with terror, was too Christian to harbour inhuman visions. Such is our life.[15]

Apollo, then, would seem to have schooled his son less in ordinary syllabi than in his own banal investment in isolation and adversity.[16] "Fasting, hair shirt, discipline"; "shiver, die, overwhelmed"; "bounded, locked, inhuman." Apollo appears to have taught his son to conceive of himself as a corporation of distress, to declare his personality by assuming an adversary and aggrieved stance toward the conditions of his experience. It shall be seen that Conrad never altogether recovered from the consequences of his father's unfortunate pedagogy.[17]

A year after Evelina's death, Apollo at last decided that his son should be freed from his "monastic" existence. Conrad was sent to his grandmother in Novofastov, with whom he spent the summer and part of the following win-

15. LL,I.16. I follow Baines's minor corrections of Jean-Aubry's transcription (Baines, 20).

16. Apollo had intended to tutor his son at home. He did ask cousins and friends to provide syllabi and texts; and he encouraged Conrad to share in his own wide reading. It does not appear, though, that Conrad received anything like a systematic education during these months. (Cf. Baines, 17–19; LL.I.15; Najder, 8–9.)

17. Apollo's behavior after the death of Evelina closely resembles the behavior of Kaspar Almayer in *Almayer's Folly*. I shall speak to the point in my discussion of the novel.

ter.[18] Conrad's health was poor in these months, and remained so throughout his childhood. He suffered, according to Apollo, from "gripes" in his bladder.[19] In fact, though, Conrad seems to have been afflicted with migraine headaches and perhaps even with epilepsy.[20] Whatever, his symptoms of extreme shyness, "fits" of one sort or another, and general susceptibility "to feelings and thoughts which are not really proper"[21] suggest that Conrad had not survived his father's ministrations without severe cost to his stability.

Apollo, too, was declining—enough so that in December 1867 the Russian government commuted his exile. Conrad rejoined his freed father and the two settled in Lwów. Apollo suggests that both father and son continued to support themselves by luxuriating in their misfortune: "Both wandering exiles, we need each other; he needs me as his miserable guardian and I him as the only power that keeps me alive" (Baines, 21–22). Conrad still was too ill to attend school or, apparently, often to leave home.[22]

In February 1869 Apollo moved to Cracow. Conrad at last was able to attend school, but his father's behavior had become, if possible, more bizarre. Stanislaus Czosnowski

18. In spite of—or, by now, because of—the greatly increased possibilities of normalcy and pleasure extended to him at Novofastov, Conrad acutely missed his father (Cf. particularly LL,I.17). No doubt he believed by 1866 that nothing else so demonstrably confirmed him in his existence as his father's sad dependence upon him.

19. Najder, 9.   20. Najder, 9–10; 10n.

21. Najder, 9; 36. Apollo later described Conrad's symptoms as "painful cramps in the stomach" (LL,I.18).

22. Conrad may have been invalided. But it appears that Apollo kept him at home primarily because he disapproved of the miscegenation of the Polish schools in Lwów. (Cf. Najder, 10; Baines, 22.)

reports, for example, that he discovered Apollo "sitting motionless in front of his wife's portrait; he did not move and little Conrad . . . put his fingers on his lips and said: 'Let's go quietly through the room, because father always looks intently at Mother's portrait on the anniversary of her death—all day, saying nothing and eating nothing' " (Baines, 23). How nice for "little Conrad" that, as his father lay dying, he was able to reveal to his son new modes of the grotesque.

When no longer little, Conrad described in tones of undiminished wonder this latest period in his extraordinary history of disruption and pain:

> I was rather indifferent to school troubles. I had a private gnawing worm of my own. This was the time of my father's last illness. Every evening at seven, turning my back on the Florian Gate, I walked all the way to a big old house in a quiet narrow street a good distance beyond the Great Square. There, in a large drawing-room, panelled and bare, with heavy cornices and a lofty ceiling, in a little oasis of light made by two candles in a desert of dusk I sat at a little table to worry and ink myself all over till the task of my preparation was done. The table of my toil faced a tall white door, which was kept closed; now and then it would come ajar and a nun in a white coif would squeeze herself through the crack, glide across the room, and disappear. There were two of these noiseless nursing nuns. Their voices were seldom heard. For, indeed, what could they have had to say? (III.167)

The mechanism by which Conrad sustained himself during this time of silences, shadows, and shades closely resembles his adult strategy of support. Intolerably pressed by the world, he learned imaginatively to withdraw from it:

I don't know what would have become of me if I had not
been a reading boy. My prep finished I would have had
nothing to do but sit and watch the awful stillness of the
sick room flow out through the closed door and coldly en-
fold my scared heart. I suppose that in a futile childish way
I would have gone crazy. But I was a reading boy. There
were many books about, lying on consoles, on tables, and
even on the floor, for we had not had time to settle down. I
read! What did I not read! Sometimes the elder nun, glid-
ing up and casting a mistrustful look on the open pages,
would lay her hand lightly on my head and suggest in a
doubtful whisper, "Perhaps it is not very good for you to
read these books." I would raise my eyes to her face
mutely, and with a vague gesture of giving it up she would
glide away. (III.168)

Even as a child, then, Conrad discovered that one may
preserve one's personality—or perhaps even establish
it—by entering into extreme communion with created
linguistic worlds.[23] For reasons which I shall describe, the
tactic was to become indispensable to Conrad's adult imagination of himself.

No amount of reading, though, nor any other strategy, could protect Conrad from the grief and terror occasioned by his father's lingering illness:

In the evening, but not always, I would be permitted to
tip-toe into the sick room to say goodnight to the figure

23. Conrad indicates in *A Personal Record* that he had been reading to this
purpose from the age of five (VI.70–71). It should appear that virtually
from the first he understood the crucial importance of his instinct: the
resistance which he describes himself offering to the interfering nun
seems for all its inarticulateness to have been fierce indeed; and on no
earlier occasion are we told that Conrad attempted to impose his own will
upon others. In fact, all previous descriptions of Conrad echo his grandmother's encomium: "Words cannot describe the sweetness of this child"
(Baines, 10).

prone on the bed, which often could not acknowledge my presence but by a slow movement of the eyes, put my lips dutifully to the nerveless hand lying on the coverlet, and tip-toe out again. Then I would go to bed, in a room at the end of the corridor, and often, not always, cry myself into a good sound sleep.

I looked forward to what was coming with an incredulous terror. I turned my eyes from it sometimes with success, and yet all the time I had an awful sensation of the inevitable. I had also moments of revolt which stripped off me some of my simple trust in the government of the universe. (III.168)

Helpless as always either to understand or effectively to resist the demands of his experience, Conrad could do nothing during this latest assault against his childhood certitudes but keep his grief to himself in an impressive but desolating display of dignity.

Apollo Korzeniowski died at last on 23 May 1869. Mrs. Bobrowska reports that Conrad was demonstrably inconsolable: "With bitter tears, he prayed for the soul of his father . . . until at length Mr. Buszczyński took him away and pressed him to his heart" (Baines, 24). Conrad himself, though, recalls that he offered a radically different response:

When the inevitable entered the sick room and the white door was thrown wide open, I don't think I found a single tear to shed. I have a suspicion that [our] housekeeper looked on me as the most callous little wretch on earth.[24] (III.168–69)

24. The child's impression of moral isolation must have been severely reinforced by his actual isolation during Apollo's funeral procession. Many years after the event Conrad wrote: "[I can] see again the small boy of that day following a hearse; a space kept clear in which I walked alone, conscious of an enormous following . . ." (III.169).

The two accounts do not necessarily conflict. The child no doubt was forlorn; but perhaps he grieved for himself and for his understandably exhausted power of affect rather than, as his grandmother supposed, for his father. Certainly no child ever can have had greater reason to have felt mournful about his life. And yet, at the age of eleven how is one to know what is morally excusable and what is not? Clearly at work in Conrad at the time of his father's death was the suspicion that he might have become monstrous, that he had neither excuse nor right to permit his grief the form that it took. At one or another level of consciousness, that is, it surely was Conrad himself who believed that he was "the most callous little wretch alive"—and Conrad who earlier gave *himself* "a mistrustful look," who himself felt "doubtful" about his abnormal investment in reading. More sad than his grief, more sad than his stolidity, more sad than even his experience itself seems to me this incipient attitude of self-censure—an attitude which perhaps dates back to Conrad's first letter to Apollo, with its bewildered air of misunderstanding, inquisitiveness, and hurt. Why have you left me, Father? he asked then. Have I in some way deserved to be left? Here he has wondered, Why could I not cry for my father? Is it because I am heartless, insensible, not normally human?

This, then, was the dividend of Conrad's childhood, the portion of his patrimony. At the age of eleven, pressed already by isolation, loss, and disease, Conrad was left to meet the events and conditions of his experience with a personality further depleted in its resourcefulness by its own wearied instinct of self-hatred. Solitary, exhausted already by the exigencies of his parents' lives, Conrad began his orphanhood without the least trust that he had been blameless for all that had happened to his parents and to himself.[25] Had he been more acknowledged, had he been considered and treasured as a singular human presence, he might at least have buried his father with the faith that he was himself substantial and valuable. But for eleven years he had been educated to regard himself as not a person at all. For eleven years he had been trained to consider himself less authentic or appealing than his parents' passions or pains—to consider himself parenthetical in fact to them, to his country, and to history. Apollo and Evelina doubtless had little to give to their only child. But they might have given him more than this; they might have left their son with more than a disposition to detest himself.

Two: 1869–1874

About Conrad's life in the months immediately following his father's death we know very little. Initially Conrad was cared for by his maternal grandmother and by Apollo's friend, Stephen Buszczyński; in time his uncle, Thaddeus Bobrowski, became his effective guardian. Because he had not been taught Latin or German, Conrad apparently could not be sent to gymnasium. He did attend private classes in Cracow, though, and in 1870 was sent for the first time in his life to a legitimate school. A year later he was enrolled in a gymnasium at Lwów.[26]

25. Dr. Bernard C. Meyer suggests that Conrad suffered throughout his life from the subconscious persuasion that "he had been in some way responsible for his mother's death." (Bernard C. Meyer. *Joseph Conrad: A Psychoanlytic Biography* [Princeton: Princeton University Press, 1967], p. 68.) It is likely that Conrad felt "responsible" for his father's death as well: an orphaned child commonly supposes, of course, that, had he been more lovable, his parents should not have elected to die.

26. Baines, 27. Najder is not convinced that Conrad attended school at all after 1870. He argues persuasively that if Conrad did enroll formally in an

In some respects the conditions of Conrad's life
ought to have improved dramatically after 1869. He had
been released, after all, from the gestures of his father and
from the bedouin unparticularity of their shared wander-
ings. Too, his grandmother and uncle extended to him opportunities for comfort and repose which never before had
been permitted to him. And yet, each adjustment in the
textures of his life must have seemed to Conrad less an accommodation to his character than a further assault upon it.
For if Apollo had been in so many ways an inadequate father, he nevertheless had conditioned Conrad into a sensibility and a pattern of expectation which within his history
of emotion seemed normal. His uncle's pieties, though,
precisely opposed his father's. Bobrowski imposed upon
Conrad, indeed, a burden of injunction which called into
question the whole ethos of his previous experience:

> Without a thorough education you will be worth nothing
> in this world, you will never be self-sufficient, and a thor-
> ough education is gained only by thoroughly mastering the
> beginnings of every subject which is necessary for every
> cultivated man—which we hope you wish to become and
> we hope to see you become; therefore, my dear boy,
> apply yourself to mastering thoroughly their first princi-
> ples. I know that all beginnings seem tiresome to a boy,
> but every effort must be made to master them by work and
> determination. . . . In a word, one thing follows from an-
> other, one thing is built upon another. Therefore, not that
> which is easy and attractive must be the object of your
> studies but that which is useful, although sometimes dif-
> ficult, for a man who knows nothing fundamentally, who
> has no strength of character and no endurance, who does
> not know how to work on his own and guide himself,

---

institution during this period, he was able to meet his classes only ir-
regularly (Nadjer, 12). No reliable records exist of Conrad's academic career from 1870 to 1874.

ceases to be a man and becomes a useless puppet. Try therefore, my child, not to be or to become such a puppet, but to be useful, hard-working, capable and therefore a worthy human being—and thereby reward us for the cares and worries devoted to your upbringing.[27]

Bobrowski's values of self-sufficiency and perdurable practicality must have seemed to Conrad not only unadult and dull when compared with his earlier experience, but morally perplexing as well. He never before had been required to be "thorough," or to be determined, or even to work hard; he never before had been urged to admire "strength of character"; nor had he ever been asked to discriminate between "useful" and unuseful, "worthy" and unworthy, human life. Above all, he never before had been exposed to such an assured attitude of authority, or to such a resolute, pedagogic impulse. Bobrowski doubtless caused Conrad to feel orphaned not only from his parents but from his entire climate of assumption.

Worse, Bobrowski imposed upon his ward a wholly new set of responsibilities. Not only was Conrad asked to satisfy external criteria of value; he was required to legitimize as well the "cares and worries" he had caused his guardians by simply having, as Bobrowski phrased it, existed. Already disposed to believe that he had no independent personality, Conrad now was obliged to understand that he might permit himself no projects, impulses, or appetites of his own:

Your education has been thought out by us, your needs supplied; it remains for you to learn and to be healthy and even in that matter (although it chiefly depends upon God)

27. Najder, 35–36. Najder admirably describes the antagonism between Korzeniowski and Bobrowski. (Cf. Najder, 11; 17–18.)

if you take heed of the advice of your elders you may
become completely well—not giving way to feelings and
thoughts which are not really proper to your age. (Najder,
36)

Indeed, the boy who had damned himself because he
could not cry for his father, the boy who all his life had
been taught to conceive of himself as an appendage to everyone and everything exterior to himself, now was
required to offer his existence to the memory of his
parents'—and to the new claim of his guardians'—lives:

It has pleased God to strike you with the greatest misfortune that can assail a child—the loss of *its* Parents. But in
His goodness God has so graciously allowed your very
good Grandmother and myself to look after you, your
health, your studies and your future destiny. You know
that the whole affection we felt for your Parents we now
bestow upon you. You know too that your Parents were
always worthy of that affection—so you as their son should
be doubly worthy of being their son and become worthy
of our love. Therefore you must try to take full advantage
of all they taught you, and also of the instructions given to
you by the friends chosen by your father and by us, such
as Mr. Stefan B. and Mr. A. Georgeon, and in all things to
follow their opinions and advice. (Najder, 35; my emphasis)

And for all of this looking after, for all of this further dimi-
nuition of his autonomous identity, Conrad was obliged to
feel grateful to God!

In fact, though, the situation did require of Conrad
an emotion of great thanksgiving. For Bobrowski openly
loved his nephew and wished him nothing but strength,
success, and peace. A boy who had suffered so much for
so long could not well feel ungrateful for such a generous,

if conditioned, display of advice and support. Bobrowski doubtless galled Conrad; but in his letters and conversation he invariably called him "my dear Boy," and throughout their life together he extended to his ward that phrase's lovely intonation of respect, affection, and assumed mutuality.

Afflicted as he must have felt by deeply contradictory reactions toward his uncle of gratitude and chafing, love and suspicion, Conrad had to confront as well a grim situation at school. Every surviving record of his academic performance speaks of his inadequate training and sullen refusal to work.[28] Educated indifferently by his father, conditioned primitively in the habits and customs of his own generation, Conrad naturally felt himself at an immense distance from the circumstances of his new situation. At school, after all, he was treated not as the confidant of his mother or as the coeval of his father, but as an unformed person. His classmates no doubt seemed to him untested and yet egregiously sure of their worth, inexperienced and insignificant and yet unaccountably more confident than himself in sensibility and style. No wonder that Conrad made few friends in those years—or that, as do so many unliked children, he accommodated his inability to inspire affection by electing to become despicable.[29] He may have elected as well to become infirm: certainly he suffered during the first years of his orphanage from a perplexing array of illnesses usually associated with states of pyschic distress.[30]

28. Cf. Najder, 13; Baines, 27; LL,I.22. Conrad himself remembers that "the antagonism" between himself and his teachers "was radical" (Last Essays, 12).

29. Cf. Najder, 12–14.

30. Cf. Najder, 12–14; Baines, 27–28; Meyer, 29.

Everything in his new life, then, conjoined with everything from his old to produce in Conrad the persuasion that he was an abnormal child. He might have submitted to the impression, offered no exception to his uncle's or to his schoolmates' fierce censure of what little particularity he still possessed. Mysteriously, though, he did not. For in 1872, when the various affronts to his needs had become too threatening to endure, he demanded of Bobrowski permission to leave Poland for a career at sea.

There were practical invitations to flight which may have informed Conrad's decision. The material prospects of any young Pole were not encouraging in the 1870's; as the son of a convict he was liable to lengthy service in the Russian army; too, his health had been severely compromised during his parents' exile, and doctors probably had advised him that air and exercise should be restorative.[31] Clearly, though, none of these motives operated so strongly for Conrad as his own determination to establish himself, regardless of risk, as a persisting and autonomous entity. For if in some respects he too felt bewildered by his desire to leave Poland, he at least considered that he must

31. Both Baines and Najder argue that Conrad's decision to leave Poland was largely impulsive—or, if his decision were directed rationally, that it was motivated chiefly by one or all of the "practical" reasons which I cite above (Baines, 31–32; Najder, 13–14). It seems to me, though, that Conrad had a much more precise understanding of the implications of his act. I shall suggest, indeed, that it is appropriate to regard Conrad's decision as an extension of those mechanisms of survival which he had constructed for himself during his father's final illness, and which he revived throughout his life during occasions of extreme stress.

It should be noted as well that Conrad apparently suffered during the months in question from at least one and possibly several disappointments in love. (Cf. LL,I.24–26; Baines, 28–30.) Jean-Aubry sensibly speculates that Conrad may have wished to go to sea at least in part because he hoped to flee from the scene and the agents of his humiliation (LL,I.24).

effect a clear break between himself and the crushing modalities of his future:

> I understood no more than the people who called upon me to explain myself. There was no precedent. I verily believe mine was the only case of a boy of my nationality and antecedents taking a, so to speak, standing jump out of his racial surroundings and associations.[32] (VI. 121)

Even if Conrad were as mystified by his action as he suggests, he at least was intuitively aware that he must resist his "antecedents" and "associations" if he were ever to become a discriminable self. By going to sea, he may have imagined, he could *insure* his release from the whole topography of his frustration and constraint. He may have supposed, that is, that by going to sea he should compel himself to become beholden for his experience and quality not to his "racial surroundings" but to his own imaginative resourcefulness and to the pleasantly unconditioned textures of an ungovernable—and therefore noncoercive—situation. By opening himself in this way to a landscape of limitless possibility, he no doubt thought to discover a range of imaginative opportunity inconceivable within the tight little arc extended by Thaddeus Bobrowski and the secondary school system of Poland. Conceived of in this way, then, the sea for Conrad "was not an element. It was a stage, where was displayed an exhibition of valour, and of such achievement, as the world had never seen before" (III.53).

32. In his Preface to *A Personal Record* Conrad characterizes his decision to go to sea as an impulse "[to break] away from my origins" (VI. Preface, xiv). He later remarked: ". . . A man setting out on a sea voyage broke away from shore conditions and found in the ship a new kind of home" (*Last Essays*, 35).

Such impulses as these are affecting enough in a boy not yet sixteen. More interesting even than the matter of his motivation in leaving Poland, though, is the fact that, as he suggests in several of his adult reminiscences, Conrad seems to have been persuaded to take his "standing jump" primarily by his reading; the fact, that is, that Conrad's adolescent commitment to the sea operated as a function of his larger commitment to literature. Conrad insists, indeed, that he first began to conceive of himself as a personality only after reading Sir Leopold McClintock's memoirs: "The great spirit of the realities of [his] story sent me off into the romantic explorations of *my* inner self . . ." (*Last Essays,* 12; my emphasis). He repeatedly indicates that he was drawn in this way to "the realities" of fictional or recalled lives—because, as he suggests, linguistic experience invariably seemed to him more actual and attractive than his own. Particularly was this so, he tells us, of his responses to certain novelistic imaginations:

> History preserves the skeleton of facts and, here and there, a figure or a name; but it is in Marryat's novels that we find the mass of the nameless, that we see them in the flesh. . . . His women, from the beautiful Agnes to the witch-like mother of Lieutenant Vanslyperken, are . . . like the shadows of what has never been. His Silvas, Ribieras, his Shriftens, his Delmars remind us of people we have heard of somewhere, many times, without ever believing in their existence. . . . They do not belong to life; they belong exclusively to the Service. And yet they live; there is a truth in them, the truth of their time; a headlong, reckless audacity, an intimacy with violence, an unthinking fearlessness, and an exuberance of vitality which only years of war and victories can give. His adventures are enthralling; the rapidity of his action fascinates. . . . (III.53–54)

At work here is the impression that the imagined world of Marryat extends more opportunity for vigorous and authentic life than could the actual people or places of Poland. Implied, too, is the suggestion that Conrad made a variety of *contract* with Marryat; that he had elected as an adolescent not only to believe in but actively to imitate the "enthralling," "fascinating" authority of Marryat's fictional modes of being rather than to consent to the skeletal forms of life proposed by "history."

As with Marryat so with McClintock, Garneray, Mungo Park, Bruce, Livingston, Victor Hugo—and James Fenimore Cooper: [33]

> In [Cooper's] sea tales the sea inter-penetrates with life; it is in a subtle way a factor in the problem of existence, and, for all its greatness, it is always in touch with the men who, bound on errands of war or gain, traverse its immense solitudes. His descriptions have the magistral ampleness of a gesture indicating the sweep of a vast horizon. They embrace the colours of sunset, the peace of starlight, the aspects of calm and storm, the great loneliness of the waters, the stillness of watchful coasts, and the alert readiness which marks men who live face to face with the promise and the menace of the sea. (III.55–56)

Cooper's fiction, this is to say, compelled Conrad because it seemed *itself* to enclose—and to proffer to its audience—whatever occasion for authenticity and pleasure the world may be understood to extend. Cooper's "descriptions" evidently seemed to him more "magistral" and "ample"

---

33. Baines, 30. Conrad recalls in *A Personal Record* that he also read *Gil Blas*, *Don Quixote*, Dickens, Scott, Thackeray, and Shakespeare (VI.70–71). Najder establishes the extent of Conrad's rich involvement with traditional Polish literature (Najder, 15–17; 29–31).

than the stolid realities to which they putatively refer; he received Cooper's linguistic "colours," "peace," and "aspects" more powerfully than the world's. And Cooper's semantic people seemed to him to engage their lives in more genuine and attractive ways than had the actual men whom he had known. In fact, Cooper's fiction seemed to Conrad absolute in its appeal: "The truth is within him. The road to legitimate realism is through poetical feeling, and he possesses that . . ." (III.56).

I emphasize the economy which Conrad establishes here not only because it proposes itself as an obvious and important portion of his motivation in leaving Poland but because it was becoming the principal conviction of his life. If earlier Conrad had read literature to quiet his grief, he now read to describe the world and to situate himself within it. Perhaps at one time or another every literate young man has supposed that one's authenticity is to be extracted from literature, not from life, or that "legitimate realism" is a dividend of language, not of actual experience. But how many should be able to say with Conrad that they have trusted absolutely to this peculiar and demanding assumption, that they have committed their entire existence to the fragile shapes of created linguistic worlds? How many should be able to declare with Conrad that language is more genuine in its forms than the landscape to which it responds?

> Life is life, and art is art—and truth is hard to find in either. Yet in testimony to the achievement of both [Marryat and Cooper] it may be said that, in the case of [myself] at least, the youthful glamour, the headlong vitality of the one and the profound sympathy, the artistic insight of the other— to which [I] had surrendered—have withstood the brutal shock of facts and the wear of laborious years. (III.57)

In September 1874 Conrad completed his "surrender" to language by leaving Cracow, his uncle, and his otherwise tedious future. At the age of sixteen, he had determined to create for himself a personality as, in literature, others had created a world. He never abandoned the impulse—nor, as he tells us, did he ever regret it.[34]

Three: 1874–1878

Conrad appears for a time actually to have made his bold strategy work. The seamen of Marseilles, to which port Conrad removed, evidently enjoyed and accepted him (IV.122–23); and Conrad enthusiastically—if illegitimately —linked himself with them:

> The very first Christmas night I ever spent away from land was employed in running before a Gulf of Lions gale, which made the old ship groan in every timber as she skipped before it over the short seas until we brought her to, battered and out of breath. . . .
> We—or, rather, they, for I had hardly had two glimpses of salt water in my life till then—kept her standing off and on all that day, while I listened for the first time with the curiosity of my tender years to the song of the wind in a ship's rigging. . . . (IV.152–53)

Whether or not Conrad yet had established his right to connect himself in this way to the qualities and skills of his fellows, he clearly was able to imagine that he had. One may suppose, indeed, that in this respect the first sea voyage of his career extended to Conrad the initial social experience of his life. For on no earlier occasion had

34. Cf. III.57; cited p. 25, above.

Conrad discovered an instinctive emotion of communion with the purposes or passions of a community of men; on no earlier occasion had he felt moved to respond toward a group of actual beings as toward "brothers in craft and feeling" (IV.149).

In fact Conrad seems in this year to have carved a place for himself within several communities. A success, apparently, as a sailor, he as well made himself a bright figure about the city's quays and cafés. Particularly does he seem to have impressed himself upon a colorful, if unlikely, set of adventurers who knew Conrad as "Monsieur George" and esteemed him as a man of wide experience, culture, and courage. The companion of a fellow "keen of face and elegantly slight of body, of distinguished aspect, with a fascinating drawing-room manner and with a dark fatal glance," the comrade of a Scandinavian "fair and six feet high, . . . authoritative, incisive, wittily scornful," the confidant, too, of an engaging and poetic outcast (IV.158–59), Conrad for the first time in his life had friends—stirring, instructive friends, as he must have thought, not mere schoolboys.[35] Especially important to Conrad in this regard was his intimate relationship with one Dominic Cervoni, "a great voyager on the inland sea"

35. Cf. G. Jean-Aubry, *The Sea-Dreamer: A Definitive Biography of Joseph Conrad,* tr. Helen Sebba (New York: Doubleday, 1957), p. 63; Baines, 35–36.

    The Arrow of Gold (1919) and portions of *The Mirror of the Sea* (1906) draw heavily but unreliably upon Conrad's experiences in Marseilles. Both works were written during a later era in Conrad's imaginative life than that which I discuss in this volume; and both present versions of Conrad's personality which for severely complicated reasons he felt impelled to proffer to his friends, to his public, and, in particular, to himself. I shall not speak to either account here, therefore, but shall return to the two "memoirs" in a separate volume which I am preparing on Conrad's later career.

(IV.163). Cervoni became the model for several of Conrad's fictional heroes and doubtless proposed himself as the very incarnation of that vigorous and authentic mode of being for which he had so hungered.[36] It is likely, too, that Conrad established himself during these busy months with a woman. Whoever she may have been, and whatever the extent of their intimacy, someone in Marseilles apparently operated upon Conrad with painful but intoxicating sexual effect.[37]

During his first months in France, then, the isolate and unformed Conrad made himself into quite another entity. In fact he seems to have become, as one might say, an extraordinary combination of Korzeniowski and Bobrowski, an odd and no doubt difficult admixture of laborer and boulevardier, sailor and soldier of fortune. Suddenly a member of communities profoundly disparate in style and assumption, a character at once mundane and mysterious, now workmanlike, now frivolous, Conrad at any rate managed in Marseilles to turn himself into a person pronouncedly more potent in personality.

36. Conrad recalls Cervoni in *The Mirror of the Sea* and *The Arrow of Gold*. (Cf. especially IV.162f; I.106.) In *The Mirror of the Sea*, indeed, Conrad twice describes Cervoni as a second Odysseus (IV.163; 183). Meyer offers commentary upon the possibly psychoneurotic sources of Conrad's attraction to Cervoni (Meyer, 31–33).

37. It has not yet been possible to identify Conrad's mistress, nor to suggest with confidence the extent of his emotion for her. *The Arrow of Gold* describes a passionate and complex relationship with a woman called Doña Rita, but the novel's imagination of the affair is difficult to credit. Baines conducts a full discussion of the matter (Baines, 46–51; 54–57). Meyer also writes at some length about Conrad's sexual life in Marseilles. He suggests that Conrad may not have had an actual mistress, but that he rather concocted an elaborate fantasy of sexual love which we may take to have expressed his intense desire to recover and to possess a number of women, his deceased mother in particular (Meyer, 40–53; cf. especially pp. 50–51).

Conrad's means of economic support during these
months were as complicated and contradictory as his newly
replenished gestures of personality. He represented himself to his uncle as a novice sailor; and between 1874 and
1875 he did make at least two voyages on a ship owned by a
family friend.[38] But after returning to shore in December
1875 Conrad idled for a full six months, during which time
he spent his allowance, devastated his inheritance, and
borrowed heavily from his guardian.[39] Moved either by
conscience, necessity, or Bobrowski's exhortations, Conrad returned to sea in July 1876. He told his uncle that he
had signed on with an ordinary commercial expedition; it is
likely, though, that he rather had joined in a criminal speculation.[40] In March 1877 the conglomerate seaman-
smuggler-sophisticate was scheduled to sail again. But he
contracted an infection of the anus—unhappy man!—and
was unable to board his ship.[41] In August he quarrelled
with his uncle's helpful friend and left his employment.[42]
Bobrowski felt understandably worried; [43] but Conrad tem-
pered his guardian's concern by promising to rejoin on its
next voyage the ship which he had been forced to abandon
in March. Indeed, he secured 3000 francs from poor
Bobrowski with which to prepare for the new journey.[44]

However Conrad supported himself between March
1877 and February 1878 it is certain that he no longer lived
as, nor any longer imagined himself, an apprentice seaman.
Conrad himself has indicated that he invested all the

38. Baines, 34–35.   39. Baines, 36.   '40. Najder, 36–38.

41. Baines, 42.   42. Baines, 43.

43. Cf. Najder, 36–45; 47–9; 183–202. I shall discuss shortly the probable
effect upon Conrad of Bobrowski's severe letters.

44. Baines, 44; Najder, 46–47.

money he had cajoled from Bobrowski in a barque called The *Tremolino*, in which he, a number of his Marseilles companions, and Dominic Cervoni ran guns for the Carlist Pretender to the Spanish throne.[45] In fact, though, Conrad seems to have formed his "astonishing" (IV.157) syndicate and to have undertaken his smuggling for purely commercial reasons.[46] Or, if he indeed felt sympathy with the Carlist cause, it at least is likely that he ran his guns long after the Carlist war itself had ended.[47]

Brilliantly successful in a first venture, in any case, Conrad apparently invested his entire capital in a second, this time disastrous, expedition. The *Tremolino* was wrecked; his colleagues appear to have skipped; and Conrad himself was left penniless.[48] Deeply in debt to his uncle, to whom he hardly could confess the terrible reverses of his new career, and embarrassed, too, by his obligations to several of his new friends, Conrad tried to restore his fortunes—or perhaps to flee from the consequences of his extravagantly bad judgment—by rejoining

45. IV.155–83. Cf. Baines, 46f.

46. Cf. Baines, 52–53. Bobrowski believed that Conrad's activities during this period were unambiguously sordid—apolitical, commercial, egregiously foolhardy. Bobrowski offers this version of his nephew's brief career in a letter to his close friend, Stephen Buszczyński. (Najder, 176–77) Bobrowski writes the letter from an attitude of such obvious and burdened pain that it should be unreasonable to suspect his account of the matter.

Baines is probably correct to conclude, though, that Bobrowski did not discover that Conrad had taken a mistress during this period. It is likely that Conrad invested a considerable portion of his capital in the affair—and that his mistress, whoever she may have been, encouraged him in his confused politics. (Cf. Baines, 54–7.)

47. Cf. Baines, 52. Conrad repeatedly insisted that he had served Don Carlos when the war was at its height. (Cf. I.4; IV.159.)

48. Cf. Najder, 176–77.

his providentially returned ship. But the port authorities at Marseilles somehow had managed to discover enough about Conrad's Polish background to disqualify him from further appointment to the French marine services.[49]

Pressed, as should be so many of his fictional heroes, by this set of sudden and wholesale repudiations, victimized at once by his own failures of prudence and the apparently hostile confluence of external circumstances, Conrad no doubt felt himself without resources for recovery. He did borrow 800 francs from a friend, Richard Fecht, with which he financed an attempt to enlist in the American navy at Villefranche. But the Americans, like the French, would have nothing to do with him. Obviously at a last gasp, he made the desperate gesture of risking—and losing—the entire loan at Monte Carlo.[50] Destitute again, and having defiled every adolescent imagination of himself, Conrad returned to Marseilles in a grim terror of Bobrowski. In late February or early March of 1878 he invited Fecht to tea, set his sparse table, and shot himself through the chest.[51] Like Tuan Jim, he was not yet twenty-one.

It often has been suggested that Conrad's suicide attempt ought not to be regarded as a considered repudiation of life. Because Conrad shot at his chest and not at his head,[52] because he presumably arranged to be found by Fecht[53] and prominently displayed for his rescuer his guardian's name and address,[54] it frequently has been assumed that Conrad shot himself in an emotion of great

49. Aliens who were subject to military service in a foreign nation were not permitted to ship in a French vessel (Najder, 176). Conrad of course was liable still to induction into the Russian army.

50. Najder, 177.   51. Najder, 177.   52. Baines, 55.

53. Meyer, 38; Baines, 55.   54. Meyer, 39.

distress but not of legitimate despair.[55] Certainly Bobrowski himself believed that his nephew's action should be taken as a mere gesture or peccadillo. He hurried to Marseilles, to be sure, and in spite of his previous admonitions he arranged to satisfy Conrad's many creditors.[56] But never did he acknowledge either to his nephew or, apparently, to himself that Conrad had exhausted his instinct of life. Indeed, Bobrowski behaved—and instructed Conrad to behave—as though the attempt had not even occurred. He insisted, that is, that Conrad propagate the story that his chest wound had been sustained not in a collapse of affect or in an extravagant displacement of personality, but in a duel fought for the sake of a woman.[57]

Because Conrad never confessed to his public or friends that he did attempt to destroy himself in 1878, it is not possible to suggest with certainty what the source and quality of his desperation may have been. One does not doubt that, at one level of consciousness, Conrad *did* shoot himself by way of making display to his uncle, that he might make the more persuasive his appeal for forgiveness and, perhaps as important, for a further advance against his long-exhausted "allowance." [58] But one finds it

55. Cf. Baines, 54–55; Meyer, 38–39.

56. Najder, 175; 196–97. In a series of harsh letters Bobrowski earlier had declared that he should not make funds available to Conrad beyond his fixed quarterly allowance. When pressed Bobrowski invariably did extend support; but he behaved on each occasion as though he should not again take pity. (Cf. Najder, 38; 40–45. Bobrowski's letter to Conrad dated 26 October 1876 is particularly important in this regard.)

57. Najder, 177. Bobrowski's distortion—supported by Conrad's own false memoirs—had been accepted as factual until recently.

58. Baines offers this as one of Conrad's chief motives. He speculates, too, that the attempt may have been intended as a demonstration to his mistress (Baines, 54–55).

difficult to suppose that Conrad was so purely manipulative as this, or that one fires a bullet into one's chest merely from an impulse of, as it were, public relations. It seems to me more likely that Conrad wanted and expected to be saved but that he desired, too, to devastate the personality which in its twenty years of life had constructed so complicated and unsupportive a set of roles for itself. It seems to me, that is, that in 1878 Conrad acted not only to destroy "the desperate and chaotic condition of his immediate situation" in Marseilles,[59] but to engage and to obliterate his entire experience of being; that Conrad wished in firing his pistol not to evade a particular accumulation of circumstances but to annihilate himself and his whole vile history.

If this were his motive, the attempt established or corrected nothing. Indeed, in a life already marked by a profuse succession of stringent ironies, the pathos of Conrad's new situation must have felt barely endurable. For in this most primitive attempt of his life to be taken seriously, to be knowledged as an authentic and autonomous (albeit emptied) personality, Conrad met not with certification or support, but with a further diminution of his scant authority. Bobrowski travelled to Marseilles and he paid his nephew's debts. But he did so, as he wrote to Buszczyński—and doubtless informed Conrad himself—less because he loved Conrad than because he cherished the memory of his own sister, Conrad's mother. He went so far as to declare, in fact, that he interpreted Conrad's suicide attempt not as an aggression against his guardianship (or even against Conrad's personality!) but as an assault against nothing less than the reputation of the Polish people:

59. Meyer suggests that Conrad's attempt was "prompted largely" by this impulse (Meyer, 39).

Apart from the 3,000 fr. which he had lost, I had to pay as much again to settle his debts. Had he been my own son I wouldn't have done it but—I must avow—in the case of my beloved sister's son, I had the weakness to act against the principles I had hitherto held. Nevertheless, I swore that even if I knew that he would shoot himself a second time—there would be no repetition of the same weakness on my part. To some extent also I was influenced by considerations of our national honour, so that it should not be said that one of us had exploited the affection, which Konrad undoubtedly enjoyed, of all those with whom he came into contact. He is lucky with people. (Najder, 177)

Conrad was less lucky, certainly, with guardians: for who else could have offered less in response to his crude and terrible need? By refusing to certify his pain ("even if I knew that he would shoot himself a *second* time," indeed!), by describing him once again not as a sovereign personality but as merely the offspring of his parents and the chattel of his nation, Bobrowski no doubt managed to devalue for Conrad even his self-detestation, even *this* extreme and sad evidence of his authenticity as a self. Or perhaps it hurt and unsettled Conrad more that his uncle found it appropriate on this occasion to mock the whole project of his life by referring to him with such cheap and cruel sarcasm as "the Individual." [60]

60. Bobrowski also referred to Conrad during this period as "the delinquent" (Najder, 176) and freely suggested that Conrad was not "a real man" (Najder, 178). It is not even clear that Bobrowski joined his nephew with appropriate alacrity; to a friend he wrote: "I was absolutely certain that [Conrad] was already somewhere in the Antipodes, when suddenly, amidst all the business at the Kiev Fair in 1878, I received a telegram: 'Conrad blessé envoyez argent—arrivez.' Naturally I could not fly to him straight like a bird; but having settled my business and having received a reply that Konrad was already better I set off at once from Kiev . . ." (Najder, 176).

Obviously Bobrowski supposed that he had acted in Marseilles in

Ultimately much more damaging to Conrad's identity structure, though, was Bobrowski's insistence that he suppress the fact itself of his attempted suicide. For by concealing from others the unsavory origin of his wound, Conrad perhaps learned to deny to himself what actually had taken place in Marseilles: certainly the "autobiographies" which he wrote in 1906 and 1919 are alarming in their wholesale and apparently *self*-deceived distance from fact.[61] Conrad's earlier efforts to vivify his desiccated experience were harmless enough, for never before had he behaved as though one might directly and deliberately repudiate reality. It is one thing to programme one's personality, as Conrad did at Cracow and Marseilles. But it is another to disown one's absolute actions and needs, as his guardian instructed him to do in March 1878. If always before the outside world had interfered with Conrad's authenticity, he now had begun to subvert it himself.

Conrad, then, had tried in Marseilles to accommodate the burden of being who he was first by disguising his personality, then by attempting to extinguish it. Bobrowski leveled such a brutal attack against the strategy that Conrad never again could consider suicide seriously. But for the next seventeen years of his life he imitated certain of the imaginative effects of self-destruction in two apparently discrete but closely connected ways: by accepting the insti-

---

Conrad's best interest. And certainly he loved and protected Conrad, in spite of the fact that his nephew had given him repeated cause for concern. I have wished to suggest here not that Bobrowski was a monster, but that he often behaved toward Conrad in ways which did not address Conrad's needs. A man who is twenty doubtless cannot expect to be coddled by his guardian. But surely he may ask that he be extended support and succor on an occasion of disabling distress.

61. Conrad wrote the chapter in *The Mirror of the Sea* entitled "The Tremolino" in 1906, *The Arrow of Gold* in 1919.

tutional impersonality of a commercial seaman, and by embracing the multiple identities of a novelist when he no longer could respond to the sustaining and normalizing anonymity of a life lived at sea.

A month after attempting suicide, however, Conrad's impulses would have been less complex. Whatever his motivation—perhaps simply because he had to earn an income and no longer could sail with a French vessel [62]—Conrad bade farewell to his uncle and joined the English merchant ship *Mavis* on 24 April 1878.[63] In his second marine service, at odds with his guardian, reality, and himself, the creature who had tried to assassinate himself at twenty accidentally commenced the century's great adventure of asserted personality.

Four: 1878–1886

Conrad began his recovery inauspiciously enough. Some weeks after joining the *Mavis* he quarrelled with his captain and left the ship when it docked at Lowestoft on 18 June 1878. Knowing no one in England and speaking only broken phrases of the language, he made his way to London, where he spent nearly all the money his uncle had given him.[64] Obviously Conrad had not yet neutralized his urge to destroy himself.

His tolerance exhausted, Bobrowski fired off an appropriately devastating letter:

62. Conrad has written that even before leaving Poland he had intended to join the British marine service (VI.122). Baines properly insists that "it was largely circumstances outside Conrad's control and unconnected with any long-term design that persuaded him to decide to embark on a British ship" (Baines, 58).

63. Baines, 58.   64. Najder, 54; 198.

Really, you have exceeded the limits of stupidity permitted to your age! and you pass beyond the limits of my patience! . . . I don't want and am not going to chase after you to the ends of the world—for I do not intend nor do I wish to spoil all my life because of the fantasies of a hobbledehoy.

I shall help you, but I warn you that you must persevere in your decision, work, as upon this your whole future depends. I will not allow you to be idle at my expense. . . .

This much Conrad often had been told before. But never before had he experienced the full range or extremity of his uncle's contempt:

You know that you have lost the trust I had in you—you must feel that you had it once and that my withdrawal of it was justified. Try to retrieve it, not by words, but by deeds.
. . .

Don't idle, learn, and don't pretend to be a rich young gentleman and wait for someone to pull your chestnuts out of the fire—for this will not happen. If you cannot get a ship, then be a commission agent for a time, but do something, earn something, for one cannot be a parasite. Many of your age are helping their families and work for them, while you, if you examine yourself scrupulously and impartially, will see that you are on the way to becoming a nuisance to your family.

Lest Conrad characteristically evade his meaning, Bobrowski put the matter to him as baldly as possible:

I wonder if you ever considered how much you have cost me? . . . It is a tidy sum, about 30,000 fr., and up till now, what has it produced—nothing!!!

Reform yourself—work—calculate—be prudent and

doggedly pursue your aim and with deeds, not with
words—prove that you deserve my blessing.[65]

A dangerous letter to write to a certified despondent. And
yet, its very brutality seems to have worked an extraordinary therapy upon Conrad. Perhaps, now that he had failed
each of his own criteria of value, he was delighted to be
able to believe that he had only to satisfy his guardian's. To
"retrieve" Bobrowski's "trust," to "prove" that he "deserved" Bobrowski's blessing, may have proposed itself to
Conrad in his condition of moral exhaustion as the sole
self-justifying project still available to him. Too, he may
have felt drawn to an enterprise so measurable in its expectations. Having discovered, that is, how difficult it may be
to legitimize oneself by amorphous graphs—prestige, élan,
manner—Conrad may have supposed that his uncle offered
an attractively specific and simple system of sanctions. To
gratify one man, to "do something, earn something," to
"doggedly pursue" an aim—*any* aim—may have excited
Conrad by the straightforwardness and reportability of its
design. And what, indeed, could be more cooperatively
exact than the exactions of the sea? What could offer themselves more simply or more knowably to a man in distress
than that set of qualities, proprieties, and skills required of
a merchant sailor?

Something, at any rate, either frightened or attracted
Conrad into compliance. For the next eight years he behaved, with singularly few interruptions, as a model of
practical resolution.[66] By 1886, in fact, he had risen to be-

65. Najder, 54–56. Baines quotes Bobrowski's letters, but omits crucial
portions (Baines, 60–61).

66. Baines chronicles Conrad's movements during the years in question
(Baines, 61–83). Bobrowski's letters from the period make it clear that, al-

come both a qualified Master Mariner and a naturalized citizen of Great Britain.

Conrad's letters to Bobrowski regrettably have been lost. But his published recollection of his state of mind during these years of achievement is significant in its relieved sense of project:

> I was elated. I was pursuing a clear aim, I was carrying out a deliberate plan of making out of myself, in the first place, a seaman worthy of the service, good enough to work by the side of the men with whom I was to live; and in the second place, I had to justify my existence to myself, to redeem a tacit moral pledge. Both these aims were to be attained by the same effort. How simple seemed the problem of life then. . . . (III.151)

If he had not before been "good enough" to satisfy himself, he seems to have determined that he now should "make out of himself" a creature at least good enough to please Bobrowski, the marine service, and his colleagues. If he had not been able successfully to programme himself, he might at least yield his wearisome identity to the "clear" and simple" ministrations of his uncle.

How happy, then, Bobrowski must have made his anxious nephew by his initially dumfounded, then increasingly relaxed and certain joy in his new productivity and resourcefulness. In 1879 Bobrowski informed Conrad that he was "delighted" with his "restraint" (Najder, 59). In 1880 he described Conrad's first successful examination as "a profound pleasure and my first reward" (Najder, 64). In 1882

---

though restoratively active, Conrad paid an extreme price in loneliness and depression during this "era" of his self-advancement (Cf. Najder, 56; 59; 62; 63). I have not wished to imply that Conrad's newest strategy was easily enacted.

he wrote of his "inexpressible pleasure" that Conrad had been "so full of energy, so full of exuberant ideas and the desire to work" (Najder, 84). By 1883, when Conrad and Bobrowski met at Marienbad after a separation of over five years, their relations had become warmly close, unwary, even tender.[67] Three years later Bobrowski felt himself able to inform his nephew that his "tacit moral pledge" almost had been redeemed:

> I hope [your Master's examination] went off successfully. This, together with the completion of your naturalization, would mean the fulfilment of all my desires for you, leaving everything else to you! (Najder, 111)

When in November Conrad was able triumphantly to announce his Captaincy, his guardian was exultant:

> Long live the "Ordin. Master in the British Merchant Service"!! [68] May he live long! May he be healthy and may every success attend him in every enterprise both on sea and on land! You have really delighted me. . . . (Najder, 113)

Bobrowski went so far, indeed, as officially to reverse his terrible judgment of 1878:

> As the humble provider of the means for his enterprise I can only rejoice that my groats have not been wasted but have led you to the peak of your chosen profession. . . .[69] (Najder, 114)

67. Cf. Bobrowski's lovely letter of 31 August 1883 (Najder, 93).

68. Najder reports that Bobrowski wrote the phrase in quotes in English (Najder, 113n). It should seem, then, that he was responding to a phrase supplied by Conrad in his lost letter.

69. Bobrowski was entitled to credit as more than "the humble provider of the means" for Conrad's success. He repeatedly had urged Conrad to

No wonder, then, that in 1886 Conrad felt himself fully sanctioned at last:

> [My Captaincy], satisfactory and obscure in itself, had for me a certain ideal significance. It was an answer to certain outspoken scepticism, and even to some not very kind aspersions. I had vindicated myself. . . .[70] (VI.120)

He had proven himself to be neither "nuisance," fantasizer, nor "hobbledehoy"—and had done so without the unearned assistance of "luck, opportunity, or any extraneous influence" (VI.120). After twenty-nine years of search, effort, and anguished isolation, Conrad at last had defined himself as an autonomous moral being.

And yet, in spite of his momentary contentment, Conrad's identification of himself continued after 1886 to be alarmingly vague. At the simplest level, his dissatisfaction had to do with the fact that he never had been so intensely engaged by the sea as a professional seaman ought to be. Between 1880 and 1886, for example, he seriously had considered leaving the merchant service to become the confidential secretary to a Canadian businessman,[71] an independent whaler,[72] and even an importer of

---

sit for his examination; indeed, he had made it virtually a condition of his continuing good will that Conrad become a British citizen and a qualified Master. (Cf. Najder, 100; 101; 103; 105; 106; 111; 113.)

70. Conrad purports to refer in this "public" passage to the "arguments and charges" leveled against him by his guardian and acquaintances when he originally announced his intention to go to sea (VI.120–21). In fact, though, he speaks privately—and primarily, I think—to *Bobrowski*'s "not very kind aspersions" of 1878 (see my p. 36–38), about which he could not write openly in 1912 lest he expose the fact that he once had attempted suicide. Taken together, the two "vindications" unquestionably provided Conrad with his first fully pleased adult attitude about himself—an attitude which, as I shall suggest, was conspicuously short-lived.

71. Najder, 63–64.   72. LL,I.80–83; 85; Baines, 79–80; 81–82.

flour and sugar.[73] In his congratulatory letter itself, indeed, Bobrowski implies that Conrad was uncertain whether he ever should return to sea again.[74] It is true that in one of his only surviving letters from the years in question Conrad speaks of his "love" for his profession.[75] But in *Notes on Life and Letters* (1921) he suggests how precarious the economy of that love had been:

> It was a special life, and the men were a very special kind of men. . . . I have looked upon them with a jealous eye, expecting perhaps even more than it was strictly fair to expect. And no wonder—since I had elected to be one of them very deliberately, very completely, without any looking back or looking elsewhere. The circumstances were such as to give me the feeling of complete identification, a very vivid comprehension that if I wasn't one of them I was nothing at all.

Throughout the passage Conrad discriminates in an absolute way between himself and his putative colleagues:

> What was most difficult to detect was the nature of the deep impulses which these men obeyed. What spirit was it that inspired the unfeeling manifestation of their simple fidelity? . . . It was very mysterious. (III.182–83)

This being so, one cannot imagine that Conrad ever had felt himself altogether connected by sensibility to the sailing life. The profession had helped to restore his vitality,

73. Baines, 82; Najder, 101; 105; 106–8; 110; 112; 113.

74. "Not being an Admiral," Bobrowski wrote, "I have no right to give orders to a newly created Master and I leave to his own discretion the solution—whether he is to change his O.M. into E.M.? . . ." (Najder, 113). Najder suggests that "E.M." probably referred to "Emeritus Master" (Najder, 113n). "O.M.," of course, refers to the British Order of Merit.

75. LL,I.83.

had exercised his curiosity and intelligence, and for several years more should feed and ambiguously please him. But now that he was a Captain of her service, Conrad responded toward the sea with frightened incompleteness. Estranged from genuine seamen's "deep impulses," mystified by their "simple fidelity" when his own was so complex and external, Conrad must have felt intensely alarmed by the prospect of committing the rest of his life to the secured pursual of a "spirit" which even in 1921 bewildered as much as it attracted him.[76]

For in fact Conrad's whole strategy of reconstruction after 1878 had relied in an extravagant way upon the direction and approval of his uncle. Because he had shaped his life at sea less by the actual character of the profession than by the nature of his guardian's imposed expectations, Conrad had failed to equip himself for the time when those expectations should become satisfied. Thus, although he had been relieved in 1886 of the necessity to "retrieve" Bobrowski's esteem, Conrad had not prepared himself to deal with the long-postponed burdens of his *own* personality: in the act—by the act—of fulfilling one "tacit moral pledge" Conrad had introduced into his life another. As the suddenly perspicacious Bobrowski put the matter: "You are, my dear Sir, now 29 years old and have mastered a profession; it is now for you to know and understand what you must do further" (Najder, 114).

Between 1878 and 1886, then, Conrad had shaped an edifice but had not yet discovered a calling: if he had been certified as a Master Mariner, he could not feel himself to be one. However "vindicated," he suffered in the year of

76. This attitude informs The Nigger of the "Narcissus" (1897); it is possible to suggest, indeed, that the novel was written to express it. I shall discuss The Nigger and return to Conrad's imaginative relationship with his first profession in a later chapter of this study.

his triumph from the "very vivid comprehension" that he may still have been "nothing at all." Perhaps Bobrowski meant to express this distressing possibility when he ended his testimonial letter with such wistful melancholy: "Set off, Panie Bracie,[77] once more on your journey over the seas, as apparently there is nothing for you to do now on land. Let me know when, where, which way, and for how long?" (Najder, 115).

Five: 1887–1889

As if persuaded with his uncle that it made little difference where or for how long he sailed, Conrad agreed in February 1887 to ship as first mate aboard a freighter bound for Java.[78] For the entire winter, though, he was caught in port at Amsterdam; when his ship finally did sail, he was struck by a falling spar and forced to become a patient for seven weeks at a hospital in Singapore.[79]

77. Literally "Sir Brother," "*Panie Bracie*" was Bobrowski's usual term of endearment for Conrad (Cf. Najder, 40n).

78. Jean-Aubry and Baines both remark that Conrad was desperate for money in 1886–87, and that he therefore should have felt obliged to accept whatever offer of employment might present itself (LL,I.91; Baines, 85). If this were so, Conrad no doubt might have required less than fourteen weeks in which to find himself a ship. I suspect that he rather felt himself immobilized for a period of two months or more by his uncertainty about himself and his career, and that he then, in a mood of panic lest the edifice which had supported him for the past eight years collapse outright, impulsively accepted the first position which offered itself. It is difficult to suppose that during these weeks of anxiety and doubt Conrad made a systematic effort to secure a command.

79. Meyer argues that Conrad suffered on this occasion from no "organic symptomatology" but from a "posttraumatic neurotic reaction" common to victims of "an anxiety neurosis" (Meyer, 56 and 56n). He suggests that Conrad responded during this period to a disabling fear of the responsi-

After his release from hospital in August 1887 Conrad surprised his uncle [80] by impulsively accepting a position beneath his qualification on an Arab-owned ship based in Malaysia. Certainly the decision was peculiar: for the sake of a position as mate on a squalid little ferrying vessel Conrad had elected to leave Britain, the British marine service, and the accumulated continuities of his entire maritime career. Clearly the imaginative economies which had supported his existence during the past nine years of his life were breaking down. Fearful that he was not a legitimate seaman, he scarcely could seek a command; a citizen of England more in circumstance, evidently, than in consciousness, he could discover no urgent reason to serve with "his" country's fleet rather than with another's.

Perhaps, then, Conrad accepted the otherwise unattractive opportunity to join the *Vidar* simply because he welcomed the undemanding nature of the ship's duties.[81] It should have agreed with his bewildered state of mind in 1887, that is, that the position offered him income without imaginative investment, a guarantee of leisure which might well promote his ability to recast the still-uncharacterized

bilities of command, and that he produced his symptoms from the wish at once to avoid those demands and to punish himself for his temerity (Meyer, 57–58). It is a persuasive argument, although I do think that Meyer somewhat misrepresents the sources of Conrad's anxiety. It seems to me, that is, that Conrad could not wish to command a ship at sea in 1886 and 1887 because he understood that, for the reasons which I have suggested above, he had not yet achieved command of himself. If he did suffer during these months from an anxiety neurosis, its sources probably were connected more intimately to his generalized anxiety about himself than Meyer suggests.

80. Cf. Najder, 199.

81. The *Vidar* conducted repetitive three-week journeys about the Malayan archipelago. Conrad describes the unexacting nature of the ship's duties in "The End of the Tether" (1902). (Cf. XVI.165–67.)

shapes of his personality. Or perhaps he was engaged rather by the novelty and multiplicity of impressions extended by the Malayan landscape.[82] Whichever, he wandered about with the *Vidar* for nearly five months in a doubtless apprehensive, if exhilarated, condition of consciousness. Indeed, so free was Conrad's time and so complex were his responses to Malaysia, his unwelcome autonomy, and the hard necessities of the future that he apparently kept a journal as his ship shuttled between its iterative ports of call.[83]

On 4 January 1888 Conrad abruptly left the *Vidar*.[84] He later recalled that, amidst a succession of "moments of boredom, of weariness, of dissatisfaction" (XVII.4), he had grown suddenly and overwhelmingly disgusted with the whole listless tenor of his seagoing life: "It was as though all unknowing I had heard a whisper or seen something. Well—perhaps! One day I was perfectly right and the next everything was gone—glamour, flavour, interest, contentment—everything" (XVII.5).[85]

82. Conrad often declared that his experience in the Eastern seas had provided him with "the greatest number of suggestions" for his "writing life." (Cf. XVI. Author's Note, vii.) During his voyages on the *Vidar* Conrad encountered many of the characters and settings which inform particularly his early fiction. Especially important in this regard were his acquaintances with William Charles Olmeijer and Tom Lingard, the prototypes for Kaspar Almayer and the fictional Tom Lingard. (Cf. Baines, 88–90; LL,I.95–98.)

83. The Captain of the *Vidar* reported to Jean-Aubry that he frequently discovered Conrad writing during their voyages together (LL,I.,98). It is not known whether Conrad wrote merely letters, a journal, or fiction in 1887 (although Baines sensibly speculates that he most likely was keeping a diary [Cf. Baines, 90]). At whatever he worked on board the *Vidar*, the voyages Conrad undertook on the ship either concurred with or in some fashion produced a formative era in his emotional and creative life.

84. Baines, 91.

85. *The Shadow-Line* (1917) examines Conrad's experience during

Since his successful examination he had passed—or endured—nearly eighteen months rich in spectacle but anarchic in structure. "Discontented, disgusted, and dogged" by the inexorable vacancy of his career at sea, Conrad felt in the mood to repudiate his entire experience as an independent moral agent:

> The past eighteen months, so full of new and varied experience, appeared a dreary, prosaic waste of days. I felt—how shall I express it?—that there was no truth to be got out of them.
>
> What truth? I should have been hard put to it to explain. Probably, if pressed, I would have burst into tears simply. (XVII.7)

Dissolute and purposeless, on the very edge of an hysteria, Conrad retired to the Officers' Sailors' Home in Singapore. Just past thirty, the qualified Master Mariner meant to rest, rock on the porch, and wait for a passage home (XVII.8).

By happy accident he discovered instead a command. Because he was the only certified officer unemployed and on hand, Conrad was offered temporary command of the *Otago*, a Scottish ship whose captain had died on a voyage from Bangkok to Melbourne.[86] At once confirmation and test, the unsought command struck Conrad as a presented opportunity to secure for himself an automatic and perhaps even permanent source of definition and peace. For months he had been paralyzed by his suspicion that he might be "nothing at all." Now, fortuitously, he felt

---

1887–88. I shall discuss this most important of Conrad's late novels in my second volume.

86. Conrad was offered his command on 19 January 1888 (Baines, 92n). Conrad details the peculiar circumstances of his appointment in *The Shadow-Line*.

able to suppose that he should have his mettle factually, as it were *externally,* defined by his performance as master of a vessel at sea—for such, as he later wrote, "is the prestige, the privilege, and the burden of command" (XX.39). He received his ship, indeed, not merely as an instrument of reprieve but as a virtual life-companion, the perfect replacement for Bobrowski in the tandem construction of his personality. Conceived of in this way, in fact, his unexpected and earlier feared captaincy seemed to Conrad to offer itself as an exquisite replacement for the ordinarily mean textures of time, place, and event:

> The shore to which [the Otago] was moored was as if it did not exist. What were to me all the countries of the globe? In all the parts of the world washed by navigable waters our relation to each other would be the same—and more intimate than there are words to express in the language. Apart from that, every scene and episode would be a mere passing show. (XVII.50)

For the first time in more than a year he felt animate and alive: "That feeling of life-emptiness which had made me so restless for the last few months lost its bitter plausibility, its evil influence, dissolved in a flow of joyous emotion" (XVII.49).

If it were test of himself that Conrad had desired, the voyage from Bangkok offered a whole rite of initiation. For with his command Conrad had inherited a dismal situation. The *Otago* had been poorly outfitted and incompetently captained; her crew was demoralized and incapacitated with fever; her officers were ill, inept, and surly.[87] As if this were not enough, the Gulf of Siam, a notoriously difficult

87. Cf. Baines, 93–94.

water, supplied first a protracted period of calm and then a fierce week of gale. In all the *Otago* required three weeks to manage the ordinarily quick passage from Bangkok to Singapore. By the time she reached port Conrad himself and one cardiovascular invalid were the only able-bodied men left aboard ship.[88]

Although Conrad considered the voyage to have been "maturing and tempering" (XVII.129) to his afflicted character, he thought it as well a dreadful reproach. Hardly at fault—a hero of resourcefulness, in fact—Conrad assumed that, as her master and intimate other-self, he had been in some mysterious way to blame for the *Otago*'s improbable catalogue of misadventures. Fifteen days out of Bangkok he described himself more forbiddingly than, in 1878, even Bobrowski had dared do:

> I feel as if all my sins had found me out. . . . My first command. Now I understand that strange sense of insecurity in my past. I always suspected that I might be no good. And here is proof positive, I am shirking it, I am no good.[89] (XVII.106–7)

It is undoubtedly a most unsatisfactory moment in Conrad's otherwise superbly courageous history. Ravened, wrung quite out by year upon year of struggle to justify and substantiate himself, Conrad succumbed on board the *Otago* to the most unmasculine posture of his career. And yet, how could he have done otherwise? Pathology may be induced as well as discovered: if in 1888 Conrad at last had

88. Baines, 95. Baines somewhat underestimates the difficulties of the voyage, which Conrad represents in full detail in *The Shadow-Line.*

89. Conrad indicates in *The Shadow-Line* that he reprinted this grim judgment upon himself from a diary which he had kept on board the *Otago* (XVII.105–6).

found it necessary gratuitously to despise himself, the relentlessly macabre textures of his experience surely had invited him to do so.

Shipping agents, though, are not required to participate in their employees' private systems of judgment. The *Otago*'s owners were warmly satisfied with Conrad's performance and invited him to continue in command of their ship to Australia and then to Mauritius. But Conrad no longer was able to respond to others' testimonials of support or trust. It is a measure of the extremity of his distress with himself that, like an adolescent on a dare, he felt compelled to sail the *Otago* to Mauritius through the Torres Strait, one of the world's most hazardous narrows. Able in no other way to affirm his—what? tactical skill? potency?—Conrad permitted himself deliberately to risk his life, his men, and his ship in a sad gesture of purposeless bravado:

> It was not without a certain emotion that, commanding very likely the first and certainly the last merchantship that carried a cargo that way—from Sydney to Mauritius—I put her head at daybreak for Bligh's Entrance and packed on her every bit of canvas she could carry. (*Last Essays*, 29)

And this in the midst of a severe southwest gale.[90]

The *Otago* survived her captain's reckless and artificial "test" of himself. But no fantasy construction any longer could provision Conrad against the inroads of his own self-censure. He arrived in Mauritius still in the throes of his crippling disposition to doubt and detest himself. And if he did not again actually attempt suicide, he did display a nearly equivalent level of self-destructive compul-

90. LL,I.112. Conrad casts the unsavory incident in a more pleasant, if specious, light in "Geography and Some Explorers" (*Last Essays*, 26–31).

sion first by securing the rejection of his abrupt proposal of marriage to a woman whom he barely knew,[91] and then, some weeks later, by brusquely resigning his command.[92] Conrad's long and impressive campaign to sustain himself by going to sea had come to an effective end.

Six: 1889–1890

Again at wits' end, Conrad returned to Europe in early summer, 1889. As he had eleven years before, he probably meant to appeal in his straitened emotional circumstances to Thaddeus Bobrowski; he intended in any event to effect a final reunion with his uncle at his estate in Poland.[93] Conrad discovered, though, that his naturalization had not yet been fully acknowledged by the Russian government.[94] Still liable to induction into the Czarist army,

91. Baines, 97–99. Meyer conducts a protracted discussion of Conrad's behavior in Mauritius (Meyer, 71–86). Many of his conclusions seem to me forced; but he is persuasive in his insistence that Conrad behaved in Mauritius as might "a man who is courting disappointment and seeking out hurt at the hands of a woman" (Meyer, 86f).

92. Conrad was ordered in 1889 to make a second voyage to Mauritius, but he understandably felt reluctant to encounter again the woman who so sensibly had refused him. Rather than comply with his instructions, he resigned his command in March or April (Baines, 100). In any case he certainly was unable emotionally to continue as Master of the Otago.

93. Baines, 100; 101. Bobrowski had advised Conrad of the terms of his will in January, 1889 (Najder, 128). Bobrowski previously had written a series of letters in which he spoke of the deaths of a number of his cherished contemporaries and expressed fears for his own life. (Cf. Najder, 124; 126; 127.) It seems likely, then, that Conrad's curious behavior in 1889 was directed at least in part by his fear that he soon should lose his uncle.

94. Baines, 101.

he could not consider entering Poland—nor, after the debacles of the past winter and spring, could he think of returning to sea.

Confronted by an impasse which seemed to offer no satisfactory resolution, Conrad rented rooms in London and took "solitary leisurely walks" (VI.68). He wallowed for a full "thirty of forty days" (VI.69) in a state of "utter surrender to indolence" (VI.74). But then, as if "some idle and frivolous magician . . . had cast a spell" (VI.68) over him, Conrad got up from breakfast one morning in autumn, 1889, and began to write a novel about William Charles Olmeijer,[95] a man whom he had encountered while serving on the *Vidar*.[96]

Perhaps he felt pressed by the need to convey to himself something of the imposing jostle of sensations he had discovered in Malaysia.[97] Or perhaps, as one of his biographers has remarked, he hoped to enjoy "a release of feeling and an unmasking of himself rarely permitted in his real life." [98] Conrad himself has indicated, though, that neither of these in some respect common impulses informed his own. He has suggested, indeed, that he did not begin to write fiction for any of the reasons which may be said normally to promote creative enterprise:

95. Cf. Baines, 89 and my p. 46*n*.

96. Baines, 103. Conrad describes the first day of his writing life in *A Personal Record* (VI.68 f).

97. Baines implies that this may have been the case (Baines, 102). He suggests, too, that as the son of a man of letters Conrad probably always had supposed that he might become a writer (Baines, 101–4). Meyer emphasizes Conrad's wish to emulate his father, which he describes as a compulsion (Meyer, 93). Certainly this impulse may have formed a part of the "obscure necessity" which Conrad describes in *A Personal Record* (VI.68; quoted above).

98. Meyer, 92.

It was not the outcome of a need—the famous need of self-expression which artists find in their search for motives. The necessity which impelled me was a hidden, obscure necessity,[99] a completely masked and unaccountable phenomenon. (VI.68)

Perhaps, this is to say, Conrad at some subrational level expected that by writing fiction he might discharge the "obscure necessity" which had hovered about him since 1886—the necessity, as Bobrowski had put it, to redefine for himself his whole imaginative relationship with the world. Or perhaps the "necessity" which afflicted him dated back further still, to those years in Cracow when, sickened by his own existence, he had invested so much in the confirming modalities discovered by others. He had not been able to construct in his own life the "enthralling" personality strengths which, as a child, he had admired in Marryat's fiction; nor had he been able to extract from his actual experience with the sea that set of gratifying certitudes supplied by Cooper's "magistral" tales. And yet, he evidently was able still to suppose—he had nothing else left in which he could believe, after all—that "the road to legitimate realism is through poetical feeling . . ." (III.56; my emphasis). He may have expected, then, that by reconstructing William Charles Olmeijer in language he might recover and make permanent the invigorating textures of his remembered experience with the man. For the actual Almayer had "touched" Conrad "deeply" (VI.77), had astonished and delighted him in a time of great trouble; [100]

99. It is significant that Conrad deploys virtually the same phrase to describe the uses of his certification as a Master Mariner (VI.120–21; cf. my p. 41). I shall go on to suggest that Conrad hoped to justify himself by becoming a novelist as earlier he had hoped to do by becoming a Captain.

100. Cf. VI.74–89.

indeed, Olmeijer once had seemed to Conrad to call into being "every condition of [his own] existence" (VI.86). By linguistically reinvoking this powerful but receding figure in all of his memorable particularity, Conrad may have hoped that he should recover that unconscious impression of authenticity and pleasure which, during an almost equally bleak period of his life, he had discovered in his association with the actual man. Should he be able to appropriate Olmeijer in this way, he assumed, he should supply not only himself but his involuntary coadjutor as well:

> "It is true, Almayer, that . . . I have converted your name to my own uses. But that is a very small larceny. . . . You came to me stripped of all prestige by men's queer smiles and the disrespectful chatter of every vagrant trader in the Islands. Your name was the common property of the winds: it, as it were, floated naked over the waters about the Equator. I wrapped round its unhonoured form the royal mantle of the tropics and have essayed to put into the hollow sound the very anguish of paternity. . . . You should remember that if I had not believed enough in your existence to let you haunt my rooms in Bessborough Gardens you would have been much more lost." (VI.87–88)

"All the toil and all the pains" (IV.88) of this cooperative enterprise were to be Conrad's. But it seemed a small price to pay; for he believed that, should he actually succeed, he might rescue both of the otherwise insolvent partners from that failure of "prestige," that sense of floating naked, which for so many years had devastated each of their cheerless lives.

For the moment, though, all of this presented itself to Conrad as impulse, not project.[101] He had idled for

101. Conrad later remarked that "the conception of a planned book was entirely outside my mental range when I sat down to write . . ." (VI.68).

weeks and now needed money even more than hope. Although he continued to work at *Almayer's Folly* and to take succor from its multiplying uses, he had, too, to find himself a job.

Unprepared as yet to return to sea, Conrad worked for a time in the offices of a shipping firm in which he had invested a small inheritance some years earlier.[102] He had not come this far, though, to become a clerk: by September he felt restless enough to ask a friendly broker to secure him a position as captain of a Congo River steamboat.[103] For three years Conrad had behaved in inconsidered and illogical ways, but never before during this time of distress and dissolution had he displayed less good sense. No reasonable man in his situation could wish to command a boat in the recently opened Congo. Disease was rampant and conditions of life for a European were radically unsafe. An ocean-going captain could not rationally hope to advance his career by commanding a freshwater puffer. Nor could an unlocated and perhaps

---

One cannot doubt that this was so. Conrad had returned to London on the verge of psychic collapse; without income, disaffected from his profession and more estranged from his own personality than ever before in his life, he should not have been likely during these weeks to experience a single self-flattering attitude about himself.

I shall suggest shortly, however, that Conrad increasingly came to trust to the economy which I describe above, and that after the death of Bobrowski he felt able—or forced—fully to empower the strategy.

102. Cf. Baines, 75; Najder, 94; 200.

103. Baines, 105. In early November 1889, Conrad secured the verbal promise of a command from the representative of King Leopold's improbable corporation, the *Société Anonyme Belge pour le Commerce du Haut-Congo* (Baines, 107). Before leaving in May 1890 to assume his new position Conrad was able to spend two months with Bobrowski at Kazimierówka. The visit is described in *A Personal Record* (VI.20f).

neurasthenic erratic sensibly look to equatorial Africa to promote his sources of confidence and ease.

Obviously, though, Conrad no longer possessed the power in 1889 successfully to discriminate among degrees of possibility or to gauge simple inflections of reality. Since none of his more sober gestures had been able to resupply his extravagantly uncertain sense of self, Conrad no doubt determined in 1889, as he had in Monte Carlo in 1878, to make an absolute investment in chance. Insofar as he was conscious about his intentions, that is, he probably decided that by detaching himself from each of the previous patterns and places of his existence, by deliberately risking all of his significant but unsatisfying career distinctions, he might gain for himself the great sanctions accorded to those heroes from his childhood reading who, as he thought, had done as much with their otherwise vacuous lives.[104]

Or perhaps his fantasy was less sophisticated. For more than a year the newspapers of Europe had expressed fevered excitement with Africa and its apparently noble explorers.[105] Conrad may have imagined that by joining the

104. When still a child, it will be recalled, Conrad had believed in the special "truth" of certain fictional lives. As he later put the matter: ". . . They live; there is a truth in them, the truth of their time; a headlong, reckless audacity, an intimacy with violence, an unthinking fearlessness, and an exuberance of vitality which only years of war and victories can give" (III.53–54; see my p. 23). Too, Conrad desired as a child to journey to what became the Belgian Congo. At the age of nine he imagined that the circumstance of Africa's openness and vastness should insure to a man of properly expansive spirit an automatic dividend of potency and personality. Conrad later wrote that he had gone to the Congo in order to test that childhood expectation (Cf. VI.13).

105. Stanley recently had rescued Emin Pasha; the Belgians were on the point of effecting a massive expansion of their seemingly selfless operation in the Congo. Everyone associated with the opening of the "new"

new crusade as an early and practically useful participant he might attach himself to the spectacular certifications achieved by Stanley, Livingstone, Emin Pasha, Leopold, and all the other celebrated agents of the African adventure. He implied as much, certainly, in a letter written shortly after he had departed for Boma:

> You will, I expect, wonder why I am writing to you. First, because it is a pleasure to talk to you; next, because, considering the distinguished person who is penning this autograph, it ought to be a pleasure to you too. You can bequeath it to your children. Future generations will read it, I hope with admiration (and with profit). In the meantime, *trêve de bétises!* (LL,I.,127)

Neither his levity nor his self-embarrassed irony can conceal his quickened hope. Obviously Conrad left for the Congo expecting to legitimize himself at last—to make himself as substantial and provocative a figure for future generations of Polish children as earlier heroes had been for him.[106]

One hardly need remark that the actual Congo extended to Conrad neither occasion nor opportunity: *Heart of Darkness* has made his savage disappointment with colonial Africa a condition of the modernist temperament.[107] As

---

continent had achieved tumultuous acclaim in Europe. (Cf. LL,I.121; Meyer, 94–98; Baines, 106–7.)

106. This is not to say that Conrad had abandoned or forgotten the potential uses of writing fiction. As he later remarked, he could not yet believe enough in that new mechanism of support to permit it to direct his life. Nor, though, could he quite free himself from its appeal: "It was never dismissed from my mind . . . Many things came in its way: daily duties, new impressions, old memories" (VI.68).

107. The account of Marlow's experience in the Congo offered in *Heart of Darkness* (1899) closely approximates Conrad's own. Baines provides a

the novel so memorably details, Conrad found in the Congo not heroes but hucksters, no sweet storehouse of possibility but a whole calamity of greed, vaingloriousness, and filth. Badly mistreated by his employers,[108] unnerved by the preposterous irrationality of his colleagues' purposes and behavior, feverish to boot, Conrad felt himself in the jungle quite ruined with despair:

> My days here are dreary. Make no mistake about that! I am truly sorry to have come here. Indeed, I regret it bitterly. . . .
>
> Everything is repellent to me here. Men and things, but especially men. And I am repellent to them, too. . . . As a crowning joy, my health is far from good. (*Poradowska*,[109] 16)

Even Conrad could not mistake the emphatic totality of his absurd misconception. As he sat in the "heavy night air of the last navigable reach of the Upper Congo," he directed against himself a single instinct of misery and regret which must have seemed to offer summary for his entire experience of life:

---

chapter-length description of Conrad's four-month misadventure (Baines, 105–19). Conrad further details the sordidness of the attitudes and activities which he discovered in the Congo in "Geography and Some Explorers" (1924) (*Last Essays*, 24–25). See, too, Conrad's journal of 13 June–1 August 1890 (*Last Essays*, 231–53). I shall discuss *Heart of Darkness* in a separate chapter of this study.

108. Conrad was mistrusted by the local manager of the *Société*'s interests. His command, such as it was, was delayed and at last withheld. (Cf. Baines, 116–18; LL,I.133; 139–40.)

109. In arranging for his position with the *Société*, Conrad had written to and subsequently visited a friend of his uncle, Marguerite Poradowska. The two became intimate correspondents; Conrad even may have believed himself to be in love with Mme. Poradowska. (Cf. Baines, 108–9; Meyer, 91; 98–99; 100–1.) I shall return to their correspondence and to the matter of their complicated and intense relation with one another.

Away in the middle of the stream, on a little island nestling all black in the form of the broken water, a solitary little light glimmered feebly, and I said to myself with awe, "This is the very spot of my boyish boast." [110]

A great melancholy descended on me. Yes, this was the very spot. But there was no shadowy friend to stand by my side in the night of enormous wilderness, no great haunting memory, but only the unholy recollection of a prosaic newspaper "stunt" and the distasteful knowledge of the vilest scramble for loot that ever disfigured the history of the human conscience and geographical exploration. What an end to the idealized realities of a boy's daydreams! (*Last Essays*, 25)

So extreme was his dissatisfaction with the Congo and with himself that he considered the previously unthinkable: "I feel rather weak physically and a little bit demoralized, and upon my word I think I am homesick for the sea . . ." (*Poradowska*, 17).

As soon as he respectably could, Conrad untangled himself from his contract and had himself floated downriver. Humiliated once more and by now seriously ill,[111] he "had the time to wish [himself] dead over and over with perfect sincerity" (VI.14).

Seven: 1891–1894

Conrad did not die in the Congo but his health had been permanently impaired and his character structure shattered. For the moment, of course, the latter felt of first consequence: fever and swollen legs [112] may be endured

---

110. Cf. VI.13 and my p. 56n.   111. Cf. Najder, 135.

112. Conrad had contracted gout in the Congo and suffered from recurrent attacks of the disease for the rest of his life (Baines, 119).

but a wish to be dead must be dealt with. Conrad evidently hoped to restore his desire to live by working a variation upon his customary tactic of yielding himself to the corrective authority of a personality more established than his own. Thus, in spite of his deteriorating physical condition he set off for Brussels immediately after his return to England in January 1891: he meant, presumably, to make his appeal not to his uncle but to Marguerite Poradowska.[113]

Mme. Poradowska did not possess the singular resources of Thaddeus Bobrowski. She could not counsel Conrad from Bobrowski's settled position of certitude and success, nor could she provision him on those frequent occasions of his purely pecuniary need. But during the course of his grotesque misadventure in the Congo she had come to discharge a perhaps more important function: she had encouraged Conrad to write to her, and in so doing had permitted him to release an uncontained intimacy of expressiveness which Bobrowski had considered inappropriate to a correspondence between men.[114] Too, in exchanging letters with Conrad she had exactly doubled the number of human beings who had professed themselves interested in his existence. Early in their correspondence he declared how much he treasured this gratuitous attention and concern:

> You have given my life a new interest and a new affection; I am very grateful to you for this. Grateful for all the sweetness, for all the bitterness, of this priceless gift. . . . For a long time I have been uninterested in the end to which my

113. See my p. 58n. It is possible, as Baines and Jean-Aubry remark, that Conrad wished as well to visit the actual Kurtz's fiancé. Conrad never indicated that he had made such a visit, however. (Cf. XVI.155f; LL,I.146; Baines, 120.)

114. Cf., for example, Najder, 137.

> road leads. I have gone along it with head lowered, curs-
> ing the stones. Now I am interested in another traveller;
> this makes me forget the petty troubles of my own road.
> (*Poradowska*, 12)

To one so lonely and uncertain of his own value as Conrad, the very fact that Mme. Poradowska occasionally should think of him seemed itself an unaccountable and joyous event: "What touches me is not merely the fact that you wish to be of service to me. It is above all knowing there is someone in the world who takes an interest in me, whose heart is open to me, that makes me happy (*Poradowska*, 21). Bobrowski was past sixty in 1891 and increasingly disturbed about his health; Conrad himself was more in need of support and shelter than ever before in his life. Requiring no actuary to advise him of the necessity to insure, Conrad made it his first order of business in Europe to solidify the tentative linguistic connection which he had established in the past eleven months with his unsuspecting "aunt."[115]

But Conrad could not so easily—or, for him, so traditionally—restore his character strength. For nearly thirteen years he had patched together an identification of himself; the artifice had been finely fought for and bravely desired, but it had splintered at last in the Congo and no longer could be merely mended or fixed.

After a scant three weeks with his "aunt" Conrad accordingly returned to London and was immediately sent to

115. Conrad invariably addressed Mme. Poradowska as "aunt" although he knew that she was not a blood relation. His odd habit confirms one's impression that he wished Mme. Poradowska to practice the same, as it were, obligated and permanent protection of himself that his guardian had been "compelled" to undertake after the death of Apollo Korzeniowski. (Cf. Meyer, 51.)

hospital.[116] He felt disturbed enough, as his uncle's reply indicates, to expose his depressed condition to Bobrowski:

> What can I say to your last letter of the 21st February / 5 March,[117] written from hospital? What else can I say but this: it grieved me deeply and gave me the impression that you are dispirited and weak. . . . [You] must co-operate by not yielding to lassitude or depression—for as you say: "le moral réagit sur la phisique" [sic]. And so my dear lad, let us be of good heart and keep our spirits up. . . . (Najder, 137)

Conrad no doubt had confessed his state of mind to his guardian by way of making appeal to his normally restorative power: his "aunt" may have been comforting and sweet, but she did not yet comprehend the full need of her "egoistic" [118] suppliant. And yet, Bobrowski could rally Conrad no more readily or simply than had Mme. Poradowska. It would seem that he had not understood how gravely his nephew's fragile economy had been affected in Africa. For more than "dispirited" or languid, Conrad apparently had become certifiably disordered:

> Nothing interesting to tell you. The older I get, the more stupid I become. I could not even invent any news. I am not very cheerful, cooped up as I am. I have books, but books are stupid, too. I think I shall be able to go to work in six weeks. Provided I find any!? (*Poradowska*, 19)

Obviously Conrad required from his uncle not the usual rallying of spirits, no ordinary pepping, but a wholesale

116. Cf. LL,I.141; Baines, 120; Najder, 137n.

117. Bobrowski usually dated his letters by both the Julian and Gregorian calendars. The second or Gregorian date corresponds to our calendar system. (Cf. Najder, 35n.)

118. Cf. *Poradowska*, 15; 21; 40.

shoring of his capacity to feel. It was not now, as Bobrowski had implied, a matter of his "yielding to lassi-
tude": after so many years of courageous and creative
struggle, Conrad had become controlled by his emotions
and no longer possessed the power to reassert his sovereignty over them.

For the next nine months Conrad was prostrated by
an incapacity which, as he later understood, was "neurasthenic" (*Last Essays*, 24). Offered work, he was too ill with
unbalance to accept it.[119] Confined to bed, he chafed and
wound himself with impatience and ire: "I have been in
bed for a month, and I believe it the longest month of my
life . . ." (*Poradowska*, 24). As the weeks passed and each
of his normally effective sources of rejuvenation failed to
restore his spirits, he became increasingly abject—and increasingly anxious to communicate his despair: "I view everything with such discouragement—everything darkly. My
nerves are completely disordered. . . . I am still plunged in
deepest night, and my dreams are only nightmares . . ."
(*Poradowska*, 25; 27). Even Bobrowski felt compelled to acknowledge the extremity of his nephew's condition: "I tormented myself a great deal after receiving your last letter
but one on the 2nd May, full of sadness and despondency . . ." [120] (Najder, 141).

119. Baines, 121–22; Najder, 143. Cf. *Poradowska*, 24.

120. Bobrowski felt so worried that, in spite of recent reversals in his af-
fairs, he sent two substantial sums of money to assist Conrad during his
convalescence (Najder, 136; 141). One is struck by the unusual frankness
of Bobrowski's concern. He wrote: "You know me not to be over-
generous, but if there is need for it I shall draw what's necessary to save
your health. Parsimony must give way!" (Najder, 141). Conrad was pitiably
anxious during his recovery to secure such demonstrations of acceptance
and affection from both Bobrowski and Mme. Poradowska. (Cf. *Poradowska*, 24; 25; 26.)

Himself thoroughly alarmed, Conrad tried a continental cure [121] and even worked on a chapter of *Almayer's Folly*.[122] Either the writing or the waters refreshed him: certainly his letters from Switzerland sound more relaxed and encouraged.[123] But during June and July he still felt sufficiently discomforted to avoid every opportunity for work and renewal which presented itself.[124] As if unable again to risk disappointment or humiliation, he seems to have spent the early summer cataloguing his past failures: "I am forming vague plans for the future: very vague! Yet what good is it to plan, since it is always the unforeseen that happens?" (*Poradowska*, 29). Flattened with shame and fear, he determined like a child who hides beneath his bedsheet to be in the future merely acted upon: "As soon as the said unforeseen does happen, I shall write you an account of it. I am myself rather curious to discover what it will be like" (*Poradowska*, 29). By early July he seemed anxious to cede ego function itself: "All my plans have miscarried. So I am making no more. One cannot avoid his destiny. We shall see what it brings" (*Poradowska*, 30).

For months Bobrowski had behaved with uncharacteristic patience. At last, though, he became exasperated: "I only keep asking myself the question: why, having decided to remain in London, you don't take a job with Barr, Möring, & Cie?" (Najder, 143). Conrad could not have expected his uncle very long to tolerate his maundering pas-

121. Baines, 121. Meyer describes the attraction of the baths for Conrad as "a condition of enforced idleness, where the luxurious submission to the play of supposedly magical waters and to soothing massage seems to effect beneficial results by re-invoking the passive pleasures of loving childhood care . . ." (Meyer, 102). Meyer curiously does not examine Conrad's apparent breakdown in 1891–92.

122. VI.14.   123. Cf. *Poradowska*, 28; 29; Najder, 145.

124. Cf. Baines, 121–22.

sivity. Perhaps, in fact, he had adopted his attitude of help-lessness exactly because he had *wished* Bobrowski once again to usurp his displaced and distasteful autonomy.[125] With remarkable alacrity, in any event, Conrad obediently accepted a position as warehouse manager with Barr, Moering almost immediately after receiving his instructions.[126] Presumably stirred by this first success in reactivating his uncle's superintending decisiveness, he seems to have pressed Bobrowski to undertake a still more sweeping administration of his identity function. Bobrowski replied:

> Today, you yourself ask me to indicate those shortcomings of your character that I have observed during the thirty-four years of your life, with the help of my "cold reason"; shortcomings that make your life difficult, as you yourself admit. You state in advance that you cannot perceive them yourself, and you therefore request me to conduct this operation upon your person. (Najder, 147)

Given his opportunity by the patient himself, the hard-nosed Bobrowski seized upon the chance to sermonize his fanciful and self-indulgent ward:

> I consider that you have always lacked endurance and per-severance in your decisions, which is the result of your in-stability in your aims and desires. You lack endurance, Panie Bracie, in the face of facts—and, I suppose, in the face of people too? (Najder, 147)

125. If this were Conrad's intention, it must be said that Bobrowski himself had encouraged his nephew's continuing dependency. He wrote to Conrad: ". . . You may tell me: it's a fine 'boy' indeed who is already 34 years old! However, I shall apparently call you this till my dying day for I have grown to like this expression and to me you always will be a 'dear boy'!" (Najder, 143; cf., too, Najder, 159.) Conrad actually was 33. Cf. my p. 70n.

126. Cf. *Poradowska*, 32.

Bobrowski warned Conrad, too, to reconsider his relationship with Marguerite Poradowska: "I advise you to give up this game, which will end in nothing sensible. A worn-out female, and if she is to join up with somebody, it will be with Buls . . ." (Najder, 148).

Conrad had been mistaken, evidently, about the uses to which he might put his uncle's secured character. He had been restored by Bobrowski in 1878; but on this occasion his guardian's co-optative severity did not revive him.[127] One cannot be jogged into permenent mental health by language, nor can one affect forever the gestures of another's personality. Conrad worked in his warehouse and doubtless tried to requisition for himself the quality of "endurance and perseverance in decisions." [128] But he soon found (at the age of thirty-three!) that he was not Bobrowski, and that he could not long abide the conditions of tedium and routine which his uncle had imposed upon him. From "the vast (and dusty) solitude" of the warehouse—or, as one might say, of his life—Conrad wrote a most dissatisfied letter to his worn-out female:

> After all, I am not so happy to be working as you seem to think. There is nothing very exhilarating in doing disagreeable work. It is too much like penal servitude, with the difference that while rolling the stone of Sisyphus you lack the consolation of thinking of what pleasure you had in

127. One imagines, in fact, that Bobrowski composed so harsh a letter—I have quoted only a small portion of its carefully calculated censure—because he, too, recalled the stunning effectiveness of his similar letter written thirteen years earlier.

128. Shortly after receiving his uncle's letter, Conrad wrote to Mme. Poradowska: "One admires what one lacks. That is why I admire perseverance and fidelity and constancy" (*Poradowska*, 34). Conrad's impulse to be instructed by his uncle obviously had become by now habitual, perhaps even instinctive.

committing the crime. It is here that convicts have the advantage over your humble servant. (*Poradowska*, 33)

Although he refers here to his work at Barr, Moering, Conrad clearly speaks as well of his entire experience of personality.[129] Denied childhood, never possessed of legitimate nationality, family, or home, on the whole friendless and unloved, Conrad had collapsed in 1891, it would seem, because he understandably had come to think of his whole character and life as a bewildering offense against nature. Completely estranged from the experience of normative human pleasure, he had imagined, that is, that in some mysterious, unintended, and certainly unpleasurable fashion he had defiled the terms of human existence and therefore should have to conceive of his life as an inexpiable "penal servitude":

> To speak truly I don't care a straw for happiness. I hardly know what it is. . . . We are ordinary people who have just the happiness we deserve; no more, no *less*. . . .
>
> There is no expiation. Each act of life is final and inevitably produces its consequences in spite of all the weeping and gnashing of teeth and the sorrow of weak souls who suffer as fright grips them when confronted with the results of their own actions. As for myself, I shall never need to be consoled for any act of my life. . . . (*Poradowska*, 35–36; Conrad's emphasis)

Brave and good words. But a few weeks later Conrad did require "consolation." [130] For, more than nine months after

129. In a later note to Mme. Poradowska, Conrad speaks of "the ball and chain of one's selfhood" (*Poradowska*, 72).

130. In a subsequent note to Mme. Poradowska, Conrad in fact refers to *himself* as an inveterate weeper and gnasher of teeth: " 'The Outcast, etc., etc., etc.' goes on its pretty way amidst the usual weeping and gnashing of teeth" (*Poradowska*, 92).

returning to England from the Congo, he still felt savagely unsettled—disabled, indeed: "I have absolutely nothing to tell you. I am vegetating. I don't even think; therefore, I don't exist (according to Descartes)." His whole power of affect in the balance, Conrad wrote to Mme. Poradowska the most pitiable appeal for help of his life:

> Good Heavens, could I be a Punch? The Punch of my childhood, you know, with his spine broken in two and his nose on the floor between his feet; his legs and arms stiffly spread, in that attitude of deep despair—so pathetically comic—of toys thrown in a corner. . . .
>   This evening I feel as if I were in a corner, spine broken, nose in the dust. Will you have the kindness to pick up the poor little devil, put him gently in your apron, introduce him to your dolls, let him play at dinners along with the others?

Be Bobrowski, he has asked his "aunt." Revive me as he could not; fix me, send me out into the world renewed once more. It is a mark of his desperation that he felt unable to believe that even a restored existence could be in any way more quick or pleasurable than his arid life ever had been before:

> I can see myself now at the feast, nose smeared with jam, the others looking at me with that expression of frigid astonishment characteristic of well-made dolls. I have many times been thus looked at by countless manikins! (*Poradowska*, 38–39)

Marked as it is by its harsh tone of disgust with his own character and experience, its brutal attitude of parody toward his own personality, the letter is distressed beyond anything Conrad ever before had written or imagined about himself. It is unsettling enough that he speaks of himself as a discarded and ridiculous doll—a "pathetically comic" caricature of an actual person.[131] More seriously disturbing is what one might term his narrative response to experience: Conrad behaves in his letter as if he does not himself conduct but merely *reports* his own existence.[132] The pronominal shift from first to third person makes metaphor in this respect for the calamity his experience always has threatened to provoke. He writes not "my," "I," "me," but "his," "his," "his"; "the poor little devil"; "him." The writer of so macabre, of so nearly autistic, an idiom borders upon the inability to regard himself as a discrete and self-activated entity. It is impossible to avoid the judgment that by mid-October 1891 the precious and powerful personality of Joseph Conrad had become very nearly insane.

Conrad must have composed a similarly shocking document to his uncle, because in late October Bobrowski dispatched an indignantly concerned warning:

> Unfortunately the tone of your letter—it is not difficult to read between the lines—shows that neither your state of

131. It is important to recall—as Conrad himself must have done when he wrote the phrase—that his uncle once had warned him against becoming a "puppet." ". . . A man who knows nothing fundamentally," Bobrowski had written, "who has no strength of character and no endurance, who does not know how to work on his own and guide himself, ceases to become a man and becomes a useless puppet. Try therefore, my child, not to be or to become such a puppet, but . . . reward us for the cares and worries devoted to your upbringing." (Najder, 36; cf. my p. 17n.)

132. One need hardly remark that this attitude toward his own experience should strongly have impelled Conrad to write "narrated" tales. As I shall suggest in later chapters of this study, *The Nigger of the "Narcissus"*, *Heart of Darkness*, and *Lord Jim* all evolve characters who learn from the act of narrating their respective novels to regard themselves with a derisive contempt similar to that which Conrad directs against himself in his frightful letter.

> health nor your state of mind is satisfactory. . . . At your
> age, "soit dit" at the age of thirty-four [133]—such a philoso-
> phy does not even enter the head of anybody young and
> healthy, and this worries me greatly, my dear lad; or
> maybe it is just a case of autumnal "spleen"? (Najder,
> 150–51)

Apparently it was not, for in November Bobrowski wrote
his fiercest letter in years:

> I begin as usual,—though I should perhaps begin with "My
> Dear Pessimist" because that at least suggests the aroma
> which your letters have for some time been bringing me.
> . . . I can't say that I am pleased with your state of mind,
> and having now recognized it for what it is, it is difficult for
> me to contemplate your future with equanimity. . . . (Naj-
> der, 152)

Bobrowski warned Conrad that he was becoming as
"troubled" (Najder, 152) as he had been in 1878 and that,
as in 1878, he must recover his balance by refusing to feel
conscious of himself as a personality with specialized wants
and needs:

> Perhaps my supposition is wrong, but I think that you had
> the same pessimistic disposition in Marseilles years ago
> . . . and this reinforces my point of view that being en-
> dowed with a melancholy disposition, you should avoid
> pondering on anything likely to bring you to pessimistic
> conclusions. . . . (Najder, 153)

Think of yourself, Bobrowski urged, "as a modest tiny ant
which by its insignificant toil in fulfilling its modest duty
secures the life and existence of the whole nest!" (Najder,

133. Conrad in fact was thirty-three.

154). One must diminish oneself, he insisted, if one ever is to become reconciled with the no doubt torpid but nevertheless acceptable textures of reality:

> Thus my assertion is: that although this world is not the best that one could imagine, it is nevertheless the only one we know and it is tolerable to the extent that we neither know any other nor are we able to create one. . . .
>
> I have developed in myself this calm outlook on the problem of life, whose motto, I venture to say, was, is, and will be "usque ad finem." [134] The devotion to duty . . . —this constitutes my practical creed which—supported as it is by the experience of my sixty years—may be of some use to you?—I shall probably learn the results from your next letters! (Najder, 154–55)

Before he could have received his uncle's ultimate and, as it happened, final directive, Conrad was offered a position as first mate of the *Torrens*, a still-celebrated sailing ship.[135] If it cannot be said that Bobrowski's peremptory demand that he return to work produced his willingness to accept the position, the fact that Conrad found himself able to remain with the ship for almost two years [136] in spite of continuing despondency [137] is without question to be attributed to the corrective influence of his uncle's Carlylean ministration. It might be argued as well that the methodol-

134. Baines remarks that Stein in *Lord Jim* closely resembles Bobrowski, and that Stein in fact is made to repeat Bobrowski's "motto" as his own in the course of his celebrated conversation with Marlow (XXI.215). (Baines, 126–27; cf. Najder, 19).

135. Cf. Baines, 127.

136. Conrad made two voyages with the *Torrens* between Plymouth and Port Adelaide during the period 25 November 1891 to 26 July 1893. (Cf. Baines, 127; 132.)

137. Cf. *Poradowska*, 43; 46; 47.

ogy of Conrad's recovery during those two years—and therefore, as I shall suggest, of his very survival as a self—may have been provoked at least in part by Bobrowski's unintentionally inspirational suggestion that he should "probably learn the results" of his advice from Conrad's "next letters." For Conrad seems to have been able to believe after receiving his uncle's impassioned lecture that he might restore himself to health by disinheriting absolutely that irksome and depleted entity, Konrad Korzeniowski, expatriate son of Apollo and occasional seaman, occasional novelist. He seems to have supposed that he might rather refer to himelf, as Bobrowski unconsciously had implied, as the largely anonymous writer of his sovereign letters, as an undefined Joseph Conrad knowable only in language and as changeable and multifarious in identity as language itself.[138]

Perhaps it was with this expectation in mind that Conrad felt free to return to *Almayer's Folly* while serving on the *Torrens*. So at least he seems to indicate in his lovely description of the relationship he was able to achieve with his manuscript during his tenure on the ship:

> What is it that Novalis says? "It is certain my conviction gains infinitely the moment another soul will believe in it." [139] And what is a novel if not a conviction of our fellowmen's existence strong enough to take upon itself a form

138. Conrad unquestionably supposed that he more forcefully presented himself in language than in fact to his "aunt." As has been seen, he *wrote* to Mme. Poradowska with great frequency and intimacy. But in spite of rather frequent opportunity, he permitted himself actually to meet with her only four times, apparently, between 1891 and 1895. (Cf. Meyer, 107–11.)

139. Conrad included the quotation as the epigraph to *Lord Jim* for reasons which I shall suggest in my discussion of the novel.

> of imagined life clearer than reality and whose ac-
> cumulated verisimilitude of selected episodes puts to
> shame the pride of documentary history? (VI.15)

The impulse upon which Conrad had begun *Almayer's Folly* had lain dormant during his year-long breakdown. After receiving his uncle's letter, though, he apparently was able to recover it—and to recover it as a vastly more purposive strategy of self-renewal. What is my manuscript, he has asked, but the sign and symbol of my inclusion in the whole scheme of existence? What is my novel but *itself* a personality "clearer than reality," itself an edifice more authentic in its selective presentation of character than one's mere (and infinitely more burdensome) "documentary" self?

Perhaps it was because Conrad could believe more in 1892 in this linguistic than in his "documentary" identity that while serving on the *Torrens* he took the drastic and superbly courageous step of submitting his incomplete manuscript to an external judgment.[140] The three questions he asked of his first critic were curiously charged—because, as I think, they were self-referring; taken together, they confirm one's impression that after his breakdown Conrad tried to confer upon the writing of fiction the entire structure and sanction of his severely depleted personality. He asked of his reader (a passenger named Jacques): Is it-I "worth finishing"? Is it-I interesting? Is it-I "quite clear"? (VI.17–18). Jacques' enthusiastically affirmative reply to each of Conrad's questions about himself extended to the first mate of the *Torrens*, who sorely needed it, the first genuinely fertile supply of pleasure and possibility he had discovered in his life:

140. Cf. VI.15–18.

> The purpose instilled into me by his simple and final [affirmation] remained dormant, yet alive to await its opportunity. I dare say I am compelled, unconsciously compelled, now to write volume after volume, as in past years I was compelled to go to sea, voyage after voyage. (VI.18)

This, too, is a species of "penal servitude." But here the convict may comprehend the nature and uses of his crime. Conrad should have to write "volume after volume" and to ask of each of his readers: Is my work and am I myself worth finishing, interesting, clear? But unlike Sisyphus he might derive comfort and dividend from his compulsive labor. For in exchange for his infinitely extending obligation he might achieve for himself, as he believed, what most other men seem simply to inherit or passively to receive as the indispensable, if unconsidered, quotient of human life: an emotion of "purpose" and the conviction, perhaps unearned, that one is actual and authentic.

You shall be defined by your letters, Bobrowski had suggested. But on what a scale! For he now should be certified, as Conrad theorized on board the *Torrens*, not only by Bobrowski, who was nearly sixty-five, nor by Mme. Poradowska, who wanted to marry Buls, but by everyone who could be persuaded to read his book—by, in a sense, the great world. Unstable and unpersuasive as an actual personality, no longer functional, indeed, as a "documentary" self, Conrad at last had shaped, however vaguely, that ideology of constructed linguistic identity toward which he had moved throughout his life.[141]

141. In this way Conrad may be understood to have shaped, too, a process by which he temporarily might reconcile the demands and claims of authorship with those of his seagoing life. The description which he provides in *A Personal Record* of his involvement of Jacques with *Almayer's Folly* and with himself is remarkable for the way in which it associates his

For the next two years Conrad elaborated the new architecture of his personality in virtually every letter he wrote. During his final voyage on the *Torrens*,[142] for example, he described to Mme. Poradowska the peculiar advantage in range and authority of experience which she enjoyed as a novelist:

> Your life is broadening. Your horizon is extended by all the possibilities of a great mass of human kind whose monotonous variety is measured by infinity; my vision is circumscribed by the sombre circle where the blue of the sea and the blue of heaven touch without merging. (*Poradowska*, 52)

The distinction between his own and his "aunt's" experience seemed to Conrad even more apparent after he had left the *Torrens*. For once he signed off his ship Conrad dis-

---

impressions and attitudes about the sea with his seemingly contradictory investment in his manuscript. As one reads the four-page account the demands of the two professions appear to merge into one embracing, if complicated, totality. For example: " 'I will read it tomorrow,' [Jacques] remarked. . . . In the moment of his exit I heard the sustained booming of the wind . . . and responded professionally to it . . ." (IV.16). This effect is repeated with conspicuous frequency: no doubt Conrad had experienced a similar conjunction of callings on board the *Torrens* which he wished in this way to describe—or perhaps even to reconstruct.

142. Conrad left the *Torrens* on 26 July 1893 in order to visit his uncle for what the two men feared must be a final exchange of communion and love. As Bobrowski put it: ". . . I do not want to forego this pleasure, which might be the last one . . .—for at my age any postponement might mean final defeat!" (Najder, 169; cf. Najder, 162; 163; 167–68; 170.) Conrad stayed at Kazimierówka from late August to late September 1893 (Baines, 132). While still at his uncle's estate he wrote to Mme. Poradowska in a way which confirms once again the uses to which he put Bobrowski: "As for myself, I have been in bed for five days. It is nice to be ill here (if one must be ill). My uncle has nursed me as if I were a little child" (*Poradowska*, 53).

covered that what little sense of external identification he possessed had been primarily a function of his life at sea. Minute and diffuse as it was, it could not fortify his shore existence:

> I am now unemployed and, since my return from Poland,[143] have spent my days in disheartening idleness. . . . It seems to me I have seen nothing, see nothing, and ever shall see nothing. I could swear that there is nothing but the void outside the walls of the room where I write these lines. (*Poradowska,* 54)

It is significant that in this mood of "very black melancholy" (*Poradowska,* 54) Conrad applied for help to neither his uncle nor his "aunt" but to his own inventiveness as a maker of words: however despondent he may have been, Conrad evidently was able in the act itself of describing his distress to establish a defense against it. Thus, as he identifies his "melancholy" as having to do with his persuasion that nothing in the universe has tangible substance or meaning, he is able to suggest to his "aunt" that his own and the world's particularity might be preserved from vacancy by the formulating act of inventing language to *describe* that vacancy. In his letter to Mme. Poradowska, for example, Conrad seems to imply that the Pacific Ocean has its distinguishing identity less from its own dimensions, which shock and overwhelm one, than from one's power to construct a semantic frame for its otherwise repudiating enormity. Conrad does not attempt in his letter to speak to the total reality of the world's great ocean. He undertakes rather to superimpose a linguistic pattern upon the bewildering authenticity of the sea, as if the graceful rhythms of

143. Cf. my p. 75n.

his own ordered speech might be understood themselves to make metaphor for the Pacific—or perhaps even to shape the Pacific into a comprehensible and characteristic, if unactual, geometry.

In the act of writing his letter, then, Conrad implicitly has argued that one may establish effective relationship with an ocean—with the outer world—precisely as he earlier had established relationship with Olmeijer. He has argued, that is, that if one is bold enough in what one demands of language, one may receive the Pacific itself as a species of sentence—as, in this case, "a sombre circle where the blue of the sea and the blue of heaven touch without merging." In fact one even may be able to suppose that, defined in this way, the exterior universe functions chiefly to certify oneself. Perhaps it is to this purpose that Conrad goes on in his letter to add: "Moving in that perfect circle . . . of which *I am always the centre,* I follow the undulant line of the swell . . ." (*Poradowska,* 52; my emphasis). Presumably this economy took firm hold of Conrad. For in his letter written from London, it will be recalled, he feels unable to imagine that anything actual exists beyond the shaping fecundity of his own language ("I could swear that there is nothing but the void outside the walls of the room where I write these lines.").

Given this state of mind, Conrad became increasingly certain that by virtue of his constant and professional engagement with language the legitimate novelist must be assumed not only to acquire a limitless extension in his frame of external reference [144] but also to achieve a pro-

144. It may be useful in this regard again to cite Conrad's letter of 17 May 1893. "Your life is broadening," he remarked to his novelist-"aunt." "Your horizon is extended by all the possibilities of a great mass of human kind. . . ." As a sailor, he continued, his own "vision is circumscribed"—

tected identity as a self. For it seemed to Conrad that in "producing" the landscape within which one moves and reacts, one also, at least in tendency, promotes a personality. It no doubt was with this supposition in mind that, when asked by his "aunt" to comment upon one of her novels, he replied: "I have read only the first chapter. I cannot, even if I dared to, judge. But with the very first pages I am in the presence of your charming personality. It is really you!" [145] (*Poradowska*, 60). Or, later: "I certainly love this book with an odd, wholly sentimental affection. I find you present on each page *as I love you best*" [146] (*Poradowska*, 82–83; my emphasis).

Satisfied to define Mme. Poradowska by her uses of language, accustomed after Bobrowski's practice to be himself defined by his own, Conrad without question imagined during the winter of 1893 that in completing work on *Almayer's Folly* he in fact was completing work on himself; that in producing "a hallucinated vision of forests and rivers and seas," in entering into an habitual "mood of visions and words" (VI.3), he was as well shaping and locating himself at last.

In developing this new economy, though, the creator of visions and words had not considered that he might lose his beloved uncle so suddenly as he did. In February 1894 Conrad learned that Bobrowski, still the mainstay of

---

and so too, accordingly, his authority as a self. In a later letter Conrad speaks in a similar manner about his response to Mme. Poradowska's novel, *Le Mariage du fils Grandsire:* ". . . It is very much alive, your little corner of the world, with its silent tumult of passions and its final cry of anguish. The *true* cry, that . . ." (*Poradowska*, 62; my emphasis).

145. One is reminded of Bobrowski's earlier suggestion that he should be able to define Conrad by the quality of his correspondence. Cf. my p. 71f.

146. Cf., too, *Poradowska*, 86.

his existence, had died after a brief illness at Kazimierówka. A week later he confessed the extremity of his grief to Mme. Poradowska: "I have just received a message from Poland. My uncle died the 11th [147] of this month, and it seems as if everything has died in me, as if he carried away my soul with him" (*Poradowska*, 63).

In his following letter to his "aunt," now the official repository of his precarious personality,[148] he explained the seriousness of his position:

> I am a little like a wild animal; I try to hide myself when I am suffering in body and mind, and right now I am suffering in both.
>
> The worst of it is that in the idleness to which I am now condemned I can hardly forget my suffering. (*Poradowska*, 63)

A few months earlier Conrad probably should not have survived the devastating loss of Bobrowski. But, as I have tried to suggest, he had created an alternative apparatus of self by writing *Almayer's Folly,* and to this alternative he turned in his time of great need. By late March the "wild animal" had invested his entire identity in that earlier experimental enterprise; so radically, indeed, had Conrad committed himself to the sweeping possibilities of authorship that Mme. Poradowska herself came to assume a place

147. Actually the tenth. Cf. *Poradowska*, 63n.

148. After the death of Bobrowski, Mme. Poradowska inevitably came to assume for Conrad an especially compelling stature. Conrad makes it a point to emphasize her newly increased importance to himself in his next letter. He writes: "You cannot know how precious your affection is to me." He later adds: "It is so gratifying to be understood, and you have always understood me from start to finish" (*Poradowska*, 64; 68). Whether or not Mme. Poradowska actually understood Conrad, it obviously was necessary for Conrad to believe that she did.

of conspicuously secondary importance in his excited hierarchy of value: "Forgive me for not having written sooner, but I am in the midst of struggling with Chap. XI; a struggle to the death,[149] you know! If I let up, I am lost!" (*Poradowska*, 64). Without question he means this literally. The last of Konrad Korzeniowski had perished, after all, with Bobrowski, the irreplaceable locus of his outmoded existence. "Everything has died in me," the obsolescent Korzeniowski correctly had remarked. "He has carried away my soul with him." Were Conrad to "let up," were he to fail to produce a linguistic topography which might shape both his novel and his own dissolute personality, he doubtless should have become "lost" from placed experience, "lost" from the last remaining strand of his imaginative connection with the world.

But the new mechanism of his self-generated character did not "let up." As he wrote—and he did little else in that first spring of his second life but write—Conrad began to uncover the full advantage and utility of his brilliantly audacious linguistic procedure:

> I begrudge each minute I spend away from paper. . . .[150]
> There are soaring flights; my thought goes wandering through vast spaces filled with shadowy forms. All is yet chaos, but, slowly, the apparitions change into living flesh, the shimmering mists take shape, and—who knows?— something may be born of the clash of nebulous ideas. (*Poradowska*, 64)

149. The phrase and its complex implications inform the action and the values of *Heart of Darkness* in what seems to me a crucial way. I shall return to the point in my discussion of the novel.

150. So much was this so that when he had completed one chapter of the manuscript Conrad immediately began work on the next: ". . . Chapter XI is finished. . . . I am beginning Chapter XII in a quarter of an hour" (*Poradowska*, 65).

Never before had he described himself or his life in such tones of excitement; never before had he characterized his existence from such an attitude of hope or delight. "Something" had been born, indeed. For as he completed his manuscript Conrad brought himself into being. As the various "apparitions" of his fiction declared and sustained themselves, Conrad engendered for himself all that he had been denied by his history—"soaring flights," a usable sense of world and self, that pleasured imagination of "flesh" and "shape" which more fortunate men unthinkingly inherit as the essential birthright of their pyschology.

This is not to say, though, that Conrad had completed his identification of himself in that busy spring, or that he had opened himself fully to the normal appetites and pleasures of human life. For the act of authorship, as he realized almost at once, could not produce either an instantaneous or a persisting emotion of recovery. He exactly should be compelled, rather, to write "volume after volume," to be always at work to inhibit that Korzeniowski sensibility which he never could outright overcome. Thus, after he had completed *Almayer's Folly* in April 1894 (and in so doing again had become a "documentary" self at large once more in the "documentary" world), Conrad experienced a violent new rush of vacancy and fear:

> It's finished! A scratch of the pen writing "The End," and suddenly that whole company of people who have spoken in my ear, moved before my eyes, lived with me for so many years, becomes a troop of phantoms, who are withdrawing, growing dim, and merging—indistinct and pallid—with the sunlight of this brilliant and sombre day.
>
> Since awakening this morning it seems to me that I have buried a part of myself in the pages lying here before my eyes. And yet I am happy—a little. (*Poradowska*, 66)

The shaping power of authorship, as Conrad acknowledges here, always should be for him tentative, potent only so long as actively engaged. Process rather than occasion, definitive only in the overview, the generative uses of language could not persist for Conrad beyond the act itself of writing language. Once concluded, *Almayer's Folly* instantly ceased to function as surrogate texture and place for its author. "Indistinct and pallid," the completed novel became for Conrad itself a part of the momentarily resisted universe of "phantoms" and dim forms. Once actually written, in fact, the book presented itself to its still-dependent artificer as a mere sheaf of "pages lying here before my eyes"; [151] for, as Conrad later remarked to Mme. Poradowska: "One must drag the ball and chain of one's selfhood to the end. It is the [price] one pays for the devilish and divine privilege of thought . . ." (*Poradowska*, 72).

Irrevocably estranged from the experience of secured selfhood, then, Conrad suffered during the summer of 1894 as he should suffer during similar periods of imaginative unemployment for the rest of his life. Thus, in the necessarily short interval between the completion of his first novel and the commencement of his second, Conrad felt afflicted by the full complement of the presumably contained Korzeniowski symptoms:

> Doubtless you have received my letter and think me crazy. I am so, very nearly. My nervous disorder torments me,

---

151. Conrad later wrote to Mme. Poradowska: "To tell you the truth, I feel no interest in what happens to 'Almayer's Folly.' That's finished. And in any case its fate could be no more than an inconsequential episode in my life" (*Poradowska*, 71). Of course Conrad exaggerates his attitude of unconcern. But however overstated, the letter's attitude is not simply affected: Conrad does mean to suggest that a *completed* manuscript can be of no service to him in his larger needs. (Cf., too, *Poradowska*, 89.)

makes me miserable, and paralyzes action, thought, everything! I wonder why I exist? It is a frightful condition. Even
in the intervals, when I am supposed to be well, I live in
fear of the return of this distressing ailment. . . . I no
longer have the courage to do anything. (*Poradowska*,
72–73)

Throughout his life Conrad should have to deploy language
to ward off "the return of this distressing ailment."
Throughout his life he should have linguistically to engage
and to deflect "the inseparable being forever at [his] side—
master and slave, victim and executioner—who suffers and
causes suffering" (*Poradowska*, 72). Throughout his superb, if anxious, existence as a novelist he should have either to write or, as during the terrible summer of his ap-
prenticeship, collapse into virulent and familiar self-hatred:
"I have done nothing, undertaken nothing, tried nothing,
risked nothing, and so have nothing—except the fever.
And even that went yesterday, leaving me very weak and
depressed. That is my report" (*Poradowska*, 73–74).

During the summer of 1894 Conrad at least possessed the strength of self to undertake two "things." He
submitted the manuscript of *Almayer's Folly* for publication; [152] and, in mid-August, he began to write *An Outcast
of the Islands*.[153] The gestures may have been mechanical,
perhaps even reflexive, but they were instantly restorative.
For in the very letter in which he reports his new enterprise
to Mme. Poradowska he declares that he shall recover:
"My health is returning, and as I obviously can't die I must
concern myself with living, which is very tiresome. (This is
not a pose; I really feel this way!)" (*Poradowska*, 77). A few
weeks later he more simply wrote: "I am almost entirely

152. Cf. Baines, 135; 137.   153. Cf. *Poradowska*, 76–77.

well. Must hope it will last" (*Poradowska*, 77). And on 4 October 1894 he was able to announce: "My manuscript has been accepted . . . I have taken what was offered, for really the mere fact of publication is important" (*Poradowska*, 86).

As if quieted by the imminent prospect of being brought out by Fisher Unwin "in a handsome volume" and of receiving "serious attention in the literary journals" (*Poradowska*, 81)—by the prospect of becoming, in a sense, externally legitimized at last—Conrad began the new year in the most composed frame of mind of his life:

> I think of you so often! Every day. And I imagine I see you, pen in hand, the lamplight on your pensive head, the white sheet of paper before you, and your imagination working as it causes to live in joy or suffering all that world of bodiless souls beneath your forehead! You must be very happy. You see your work; I, I grope about like a venturesome blind man.

Perhaps he did grope. But by January 1895 Conrad had constructed a personality which in spite of its continuing doubt and detestation of itself had become genuinely "venturesome." For in spite of his incertitude and incorrigible fear, fully aware that in so doing he could establish nothing permanent, Conrad worked on in 1895 to create for himself such qualities of purposefulness and pleasure as he could wrench from the obdurate materials of his history. So it is that in his New Year greeting to Mme. Poradowska he feels able to remark: "Well, here is Chap. VII finished. Four more to go! [154] Four centuries of agony, four minutes of delight, and then the end—an empty head, discouragement, and

154. Conrad later altered the chapter structure of *An Outcast of the Islands*. (Cf. *Poradowska*, 89n.)

eternal doubt" (*Poradowska,* 88–89). Not much of a dividend, perhaps. But as opposed to the bleak textures of his "documentary" experience, as opposed to "the discouragement which everyone knows but which knows me better—I think I do not say this out of vanity—than anyone else" (*Poradowska,* 90), those four quick minutes of peace and plenty must have seemed to Conrad a perfect paradise of pleasure.

The health and capacity of his self-promoted personality inevitably must feel, as he acknowledged, transient, delicate, deeply and perpetually uncomfortable. And he should have to repeat the remorseless sequence of his "agony" and "delight" throughout his life—he should have to conduct his life, indeed, in an unholy atmosphere of "eternal doubt." Yet, all of this doubtless proposed itself to Conrad, as it ought to propose itself to us, as merely the attending and endurable cost of a sublime human achievement. For against all odds and with what one should have thought intolerably slight ground for hope, Conrad had managed to extract from the fetid landscape of his brutally constrained character an unfeigned emotion of community with himself and the whole world of souls. The universe into which he had entered was peopled by "bodiless" creatures, to be sure, who enacted their careers not on the streets or seas of the world but beneath their creator's forehead or upon the stark pages of Fisher Unwin's printed prose. But they were tangible and authentic "souls" for all of that, alive "in joy or suffering" throughout the full, if brief, course of their subtle and lovely lives.

Conrad had managed by 1895, then, to describe a stance which most of us do not desire but which seemed to him perfect and pure. For early in his correspondence with Mme. Poradowska he had suggested that he should think his life attractive and complete could he only develop a way to confront his experience from shifting points of assumption and advantage:

> If one could get rid of his heart and memory (and also brain), and then get a whole new set of these things, life would become ideally amusing. As this is impossible, life is not so; it is abominably sad! (*Poradowska*, 12)

As he completed his second novel and entered the first year of the most distinguished decade of achievement in the modern history of English letters, Conrad had conceived a mechanism by which he might fend off the necessarily diseased demands of his "documentary" self and propose in their place "a whole new set" of preferred personalities. Orphaned, exiled, expatriated, he had created for himself what he took to be context and texture. Unknown and unconsidered, he had frought from the sterile confines of written language a usable instinct of identity for his unsatisfied "heart and memory (and also brain)." If his life subsequently did not become "ideally amusing," it at least became possible. If he had always to regard himself as "only the agent of an unreliable master," his own "power of expression" (*Blackwood*, 27), he nonetheless had construed for himself an imaginative promontory from which he could engage his experience in dignity and autonomy. No man may do more.

During the first months of 1895 the middleaged Polish seacaptain completed the last chapters of *An Outcast of the Islands*, dedicated *Almayer's Folly* to the deceased guardian of his abandoned identity, and set to work to wring from all the semantic topographies which lurked be-

neath his forehead "the vision of . . . a coherent, justifiable personality" (VI.Preface, xxi). In the chapters which
follow I shall speak to the five novel-length [155] autobiographies with which Conrad began that discreet and admirable adventure.

155. During the period which I address Conrad also wrote a large number
of short stories. The stories, though, have seemed to me (as they have
seemed to each of Conrad's critics) to propose themselves as a discrete
enterprise whose functions for their author are discriminable from the
novels' more considered and, I think, more interesting uses. I therefore
do not discuss here the short fiction which Conrad produced between
1895 and 1900. To interested readers one recommends Edward W. Said's
indispensable study, *Joseph Conrad and the Fiction of Autobiography*
(Cambridge: Harvard University Press, 1966).

Chapter Two

With eyes shut tight, his teeth hard set, he tried in a great effort of passionate will to keep his hold on that vision of supreme delight. In vain!

(XI.166)

A Great Effort of Passionate Will
Almayer's Folly

Almayer's Folly establishes more amply than could any biographical sketch how pressed Conrad felt by the harsh shocks and estranging patterns of his chthonic experience. The novel permits us—as it permitted its author—an often unguarded access into Conrad's habitual modes of perception. As we enter into the book's peculiar and, as I think, diseased sensory apparatus, we perhaps may feel more competent to imagine the full consequences for Conrad of his routine sensation of humiliation, loneliness, and self-loathing. For *Almayer's Folly* proposes itself as a version of its author's life, as a tense and tentative study of Conrad's own dismembered personality.

One

The external world presented in *Almayer's Folly* is marked by the extremity of its malevolent will. Murderous and murky, the landscape of Sambir is ordered upon a

principle of struggle so truculent as to make malignancy
virtually a condition of nature. On the novel's second page,
for example, Conrad finds occasion to speak of the "un-
necessary"—as it were, the *unnatural*—virulence of a tropical flood:

> The tree swung slowly round, amid the hiss and foam of
> the water, and soon getting free of the obstruction began
> to move down stream again, rolling slowly over, raising
> upwards a long, denuded branch, like a hand lifted in
> mute appeal to heaven against the river's brutal and un-
> necessary violence. (XI.4)

The Malayan jungle is no less malefic in its processes than
the river. Organized by its chaos, governed by its anarchic
deadliness, the dense overgrowth contends against itself in
a fierce internecine display:

> In a ring of luxuriant vegetation bathed in the warm air
> charged with strong and harsh perfumes, the intense work
> of tropical nature went on: plants shooting upward, en-
> twined, interlaced in inextricable confusion, climbing
> madly and brutally over each other in the terrible silence
> of a desperate struggle towards the life-giving sunshine
> above—as if struck with sudden horror at the seething
> mass of corruption below, at the death and decay from
> which they sprang. (XI.71)

The forest's shade, "so enticing in its deceptive appearance
of coolness," is said in fact to be an obscene cemetery
"where lay, entombed and rotting, countless generations
of trees, and where their successors stood as if in mourning, in dark green foliage, immense and helpless, awaiting
their turn." In this, a necrophiliac paradise,

> only the parasites seemed to live . . . in a sinuous rush
> upwards into the air and sunshine, feeding on the dead

> and the dying alike, and crowning their victims with pink
> and blue flowers that gleamed amongst the boughs, incon-
> gruous and cruel, like a strident and mocking note in the
> solemn harmony of the doomed trees. (XI.167)

More disturbing than the deadliness of this landscape is its apparent animation. "Strident and mocking,"
the viciousness of the jungle seems sentient and inten-
tional in *Almayer's Folly*, the expression not of neuter
chemical conditions but of an actual and certainly psychotic malice. "Enticing," apparently deliberate in its "incongruous and cruel" (XI.167) deception, the natural world
in *Almayer's Folly* evidently derives from its fierce duplicity
all the sad gratification of a possessed torturer. However
decorous in its sweet bits of pink and bright blue, the flow-
ering sadist of Sambir appears to achieve actual pleasure
in the novel by sapping the vast strength of the superb
Malayan timber:

> The big trees of the forest, lashed together with manifold
> bonds by a mass of tangled creepers, looked down at the
> growing young life at their feet with the sombre resigna-
> tion of giants that had lost faith in their strength. And in
> the midst of them the merciless creepers clung to the big
> trunks in cable-like coils, leaped from tree to tree, hung in
> thorny festoons from the lower boughs, and, sending
> slender tendrils on high to seek out the smallest branches,
> carried death to their victims in an exulting riot of silent
> destruction. (XI.165)

Destructive, then, more by disposition than by necessity,
nature proposes itself to Conrad and to his novel's characters as the very principle of violent mortality:

> He approached a place where the creepers had been torn
> and hacked into an archway that might have been the

> beginning of a path. As he bent down to look . . . . an acrid smell of dump earth and of decaying leaves took him by the throat, and he drew back with a scared face, as if he had been touched by the breath of Death itself.[1] (XI.167)

The awesomely empowered violence of the external world is even more hostile to men in *Almayer's Folly* than to mute rivers or trees. Conrad seems to suggest, indeed, that the deranged consciousness of nature feels itself to be directly challenged by the presumably defiant requirements of the human imagination; certainly the novel's people suppose that the ferocity of the natural landscape is directed particularly against their own appetites and needs. The Sambir River, for example, proposes itself to Almayer as the conscious opponent of his ineffectual will: "Years passed and the rare letters from Mrs. Vinck . . . were the only thing to be looked to to make life bearable amongst the triumphant savagery of the river"[2] (XI.28). The sun, too, appears to wage jubilant assault against his peace and prestige: "He followed their figures moving in the crude blaze of the vertical sun, in that light violent and vibrating, like a triumphal flourish of brazen trumpets" (XI.194).

But the chief weapon available to the external world in its psychopathic crusade against human contentment is neither the "crude" agency of meteorology nor the usually endurable processes of the tropical topography. Much more efficient and terrible is its manipulation of what in other men's novels might have been called fortuity or chance. It is a chief purpose of *Almayer's Folly* in this

1. I shall return to this important passage.

2. Conrad obviously should have made a similar investment in his own infrequent letters from Mme. Poradowska and Bobrowski. As I have suggested, *Almayer's Folly* was written and ought in part to be read as a species of autobiography.

regard to compel each of its important characters to receive the circumstances of his life as a frank assault against
his irreducible imaginative requirements. Mrs. Almayer, for
instance, treats her fortuitous capture by Tom Lingard as an
impossible circumscription of her life:

> She was conscious, and in the great peace and stillness of
> the tropical evening succeeding the turmoil of the battle,[3]
> she watched all she held dear on earth after her own sav-
> age manner, drift away into the gloom in a great roar of
> flame and smoke. . . . She realized that with this vanish-
> ing gleam her old life departed too. (XI.21)

"Perhaps had she known . . . where her destiny was lead-
ing her," Conrad adds, "she would have sought death"—as
once had he himself—"in her dread and hate of such a restraint" (XI.22). Nina Almayer is said to experience a similar
instinct of revulsion against the debilitating circumstances
of her destiny:

> [Nina] had lived a life devoid of all the decencies of civili-
> zation, in miserable domestic conditions; she had
> breathed the atmosphere of sordid plottings for gain, of
> the no less disgusting intrigues and crimes for lust or
> money; and those things, together with the domestic
> quarrels, were the only events of her three years' existence
> [in Sambir]. She did not die from despair and disgust the
> first month, as she expected and almost hoped for. (XI.42)

Little Taminah, too, feels crippled by the irresistible and
baffling adversities of her existence:

3. Conrad often represents such calamities as occurring against a back-
drop of sudden and incongruous calamity—as if it be a portion of the external world's perverse *modus operandi* to bewilder its victims by abruptly
surrounding them with paradoxical conditions of calm.

In the extremity of her distress she could find no words to pray for relief, she knew of no heaven to send her prayer to, and she wandered on with tired feet in the dumb surprise and terror at the injustice of the suffering inflicted upon her without cause and without redress. (XI.118–19)

Of all the novel's people, it is Almayer himself who feels most drastically assaulted by the apparent antipathy of the universe: " 'Dain dead, all my plans destroyed. This is the end of all hope and of all things.' His heart sank within him. He felt a kind of deadly sickness" (XI.122).

As "helpless" as the Malayan trees, the men and women of Sambir are joined, then, with the forests and streams of the jungle in an anguished community of victimization. But none of the novel's people are able to trade upon this potentially supportive fact; no one in *Almayer's Folly* experiences an emotion of fellowship or even of moral continuity with the physical setting in which his life is lived.[4] Far from entering into partnership with the natural world, no one in the novel—least of all the novel's narrative consciousness—feels able simply to *perceive* it. Light in *Almayer's Folly*, that is, does not appear to objectify or to inform. Shape does not seem structural or definite. Texture, color, odor, sound, each of the constituent ingredients of human cognition, fails to perform its essential locating function for the hapless people of Sambir. The very vagueness of the external topography prevents the

4. It might be said as well that only the narrative voice in *Almayer's Folly* successfully separates the operations of the forests and waterways of Sambir from the psychology of that largely undefined entity which actually orders the savage processes of life. Thus, it is the narrative's point of view, not the characters', that trees are sapped and waters churned in precisely the same way as human lives are ravaged. The people of Sambir characteristically take the overgrowth of the jungle and the machinations of the river to be merely isolated situations or conditions.

novel's characters from entering into communion with it, and seems itself a crucial inflection of the universe's general campaign against human confidence and ease.

As the novel opens, for example, Almayer hears the plash of paddles and a lilt of voices on the river; "but it was too dark to distinguish anything under the overhanging bushes" (XI.12). In that night of "appalling blackness" a cloud bank is said to have "crept down from the hills blotting out the stars, merging sky, forest, and river into one mass of almost palpable blackness" (XI.19). When Almayer confronts Dain and Nina in Bulangi's clearing he is troubled as much by the jungle's noncontextual arrangements of shape and light as by the shocking fact of his daughter's elopement:

> There was not a glimmer of light in the sky now, and the tops of the trees were as invisible as their trunks, being lost in the mass of clouds that hung low over the woods, the clearing, and the river. Every outline had disappeared in the intense blackness that seemed to have destroyed everything but space. Only the fire glimmered like a star forgotten in this annihilation of all visible things. . . . (XI.182)

As Nina conducts her courtship with Dain, she is no more able than her father to differentiate forms:

> The boat shoved off after a little while, looming large in the full light of the moon, a black shapeless mass in the slight haze hanging over the water. Nina fancied she could distinguish the graceful figure of the trader standing erect in the stern sheets, but in a little while all the outlines got blurred, confused, and soon disappeared in the folds of white vapour shrouding the middle of the river. (XI.56)

Occasionally "the deceptive light" (XI.165) produces comic rather than portentous distortions in aspect. A paddler's head, "covered with an enormous round hat," appears in the murky night "like a fantastically exaggerated mushroom" (XI.14). A sputtering lamp incongruously shapes the acutely vicious Mrs. Almayer: "Half a shell of cocoanut filled with oil, where a cotton rag floated for a wick, stood on the floor, surrounding [Mrs. Almayer] with a ruddy halo of light shining through the black and odorous smoke" (XI.66).

Haunted, then, by "vague shadows" and "indistinct forms" (XI.117), the troubled people of Sambir receive the universe in all of its variety and form as a monotonous landscape of assault in which nothing may be precisely characterized or discerned. Certainly many Victorian writers after 1859 felt distressed by the exposed reality of the natural process. But nature as it is represented in *Almayer's Folly* is surely much less a function of the contemporary climate of opinion in Europe than an expression of Conrad's temperament fully as inevitable as his first letter to his father or his exhausted attempt at suicide in Marseilles. *Almayer's Folly* conceives of the world in such peculiarly shifting hues of black and pallid gray because, given his history, that is how Conrad had been compelled typically to perceive it; the novel imagines the universe as a hostile and perhaps maniacally governed expanse less because Conrad grew up immediately after the publication of Darwin and Wallace's geography of unprincipled struggle than because Conrad reacted in a necessary and public way to his own experience of externally-imposed pain. As I earlier have remarked, we do not have a directly autobiographical account of Conrad's responses to Vologda, Marseilles, Mauritius, or the Congo. But as we wonder at the sustained suffering and vagueness of aspect which environ the squalid little jungle community of Sambir, we may understand that in the act of writing his first novel Conrad not only protected but as well defined his impoverished sensation of life.

Two

The initial response of the novel's characters to the uncompromising enmity of the exterior universe is to try to accommodate those conditions of violence and adversity which in any case they cannot alter. Immediately after her capture, for instance, Mrs. Almayer experiences "the dread of the unknown, but otherwise she accepted her position calmly, after the manner of her people" (XI.22). "Such things must be," she tells Nina. And she advises her daughter, as earlier Bobrowski had advised Conrad, that one must learn to suppress one's reactions to pain in order that one at least might meet the antipathy of the outer world from a stance of dignity and reserve: "Hide your anger, and do not let [Dain] see on your face the pain that will eat your heart" (XI.153). But Mrs. Almayer need not have feared for her daughter's dignity; it has been Nina's own instinct to engage in this way the privations of her experience:

> Nina adapted herself wonderfully to the circumstances of a half-savage and miserable life. She accepted without question or apparent disgust the neglect, the decay, the poverty of the household, the absence of furniture, and the preponderance of rice diet on the family table. (XI.31)

In fact Nina conducts her whole life in Sambir from an attitude of "outward composure" and "seeming detachment from the things and people surrounding her" (XI.38). "She might have been deaf, dumb, without any feeling as far as any expression of opinion went" (XI.40–41). Even Almayer attempts at times to control his confusion and pain. Although he cannot comprehend his daughter's episodic behavior, Almayer "accepted the situation, happy in the gentle and protecting affection the girl showed him, fitfully enough. . . ." He is more troubled by Nina's occasional "contemptuous look": but "he got used even to that" (XI.31).

Taminah, too, tries to reconcile herself to the privations of her life: "The girl . . . never complained—perhaps from dictates of prudence, but more likely through the strange, resigned apathy of half-savage womankind" (XI.37). Carrying herself with "stolid unconcern" (XI.114), she manages the many horrors of her existence by presenting to the world a posture of calm adjustment: ". . . From her springy step, erect figure, and face veiled over by the every-day look of apathetic indifference, nobody could have guessed of the double load she carried . . ." (XI.112). In fact, though, Taminah's apparent serenity *is* a posture. If her power to adjust extends to her otherwise unendurable experience a species of peace, it does so—as Conrad had felt while working at Barr, Moering—at the expense of her personality and pleasure: "Taminah had found peace." But "it was like the dreary tranquillity of a desert, where there is peace only because there is no life" (XI.116).

In one way or another everyone in the novel makes the same discovery. One may acquiesce to the conditions of life; as, in another context, Thomas Carlyle once remarked, One had better, by Gad. To make this obligatory assent to the terms of one's existence produces, though, a cession of that capacity to experience sensation which is all in *Almayer's Folly* that makes human life seem actual or attractive. And often the circumstances of life are sufficiently forbidding in the novel that, in spite of the common intention to appear impassive before the demands of their existence, the people of Sambir frequently cannot contain their instinct to express grief and need. Mrs. Almayer herself, certainly the novel's most self-controlled character, is finally no more disciplined in this regard than her bathetic husband:

> Mrs. Almayer rose with a deep sigh, while two tears wandered slowly down her withered cheeks. She wiped them off quickly with a wisp of her grey hair as if ashamed of herself, but could not stifle another loud sigh, for her heart was heavy and she suffered much. . . . (XI.154)

Even Babalatchi is compelled in the novel's penultimate passage publicly to confess his weariness and pain (XI.205–7).

Bobrowski, it will be recalled, had informed his nephew that "although this world is not the best that one could imagine, it is nevertheless the only one we know and it is tolerable to the extent that we neither know any other nor are we able to create one. . . ." [5] As had Conrad himself, the people of Sambir attempt to deploy their attitudes of strength in the way which Bobrowski had recommended. But as had Conrad, they find Bobrowski's strategy of accommodation too arid to endure. For they think the world intolerable; and they discover that one cannot conciliate its severity by suppressing the instinct to present

5. Cf. my p. 70–71.

oneself as a set of individual demands. Nina loves, Taminah yearns, and Mrs. Almayer cries. In so doing each of these women—and each of the novel's men, as well—testifies to Conrad's own persuasion that because the actual world is not "tolerable" one *must* "create" another.

Three

In however inarticulate a way, Kaspar Almayer understands more quickly than anyone else in the novel the necessity to produce a more congenial world. It is the principle of his existence, indeed, to impart upon the actual textures of his otherwise unrewarded life a climate of expectation which both excites his hope and, as he ingenuously trusts, sanctions his personality. Thus, in the novel's opening paragraph Almayer is "startled" by his wife's "shrill voice . . . from his dream of splendid [*sic*] future into the unpleasant realities of the present hour." He is said to detest his wife and to resent her interruption of his reverie. But he is able to disregard her intrusion—as it were to disenfranchise her existence itself—by making a virtually automatic gesture of imaginative regulation:

> An unpleasant voice too. He had heard it for many years, and with every year he liked it less. No matter; there would be an end to this soon.
> He shuffled uneasily, but took no further notice of the call. . . . He absorbed himself in his dream of wealth and power away from this coast where he had dwelt for so many years, forgetting the bitterness of toil and strife in the vision of a great and splendid reward. (XI.3)

Savagely pressed by "toil and strife," hopelessly lonely in his capacity as the only white man on an entire coast,

Almayer habitually "absorbs himself" and his great bitterness by producing in this mechanical way "the vision" of a more pleasant life lived amidst gentler conditions of climate and community.

Almayer's "vision" typically takes the form of a sudden exterior endorsement. He initially imagines, for instance, that he and Lingard shall extract a vast quantity of treasure from the jungle and that they shall employ the glittering stuff to certify themselves and Nina:

> They would live in Europe, he and his daughter. They would be rich and respected. Nobody would think of her mixed blood in the presence of her great beauty and his immense wealth. Witnessing her triumphs he would grow young again, he would forget the twenty-five years of heart-breaking struggle on this coast where he felt like a prisoner. (XI.3–4)

Consecrated in this external way, Almayer believes that he may begin "a new existence" (XI.5) of something like foetal authority: all that he desires, he supposes, shall be conferred upon him at once; and he shall be protected from the demands of the outer world by his "immense wealth." In this invincible condition of amniotic gratification, as he tells Nina, ". . . We shall be happy, you and I. Live rich and respected far from here, and forget this life, and all this struggle, and all this misery" (XI.18). In a sense, then, Almayer wishes to possess the world. And in fact he presumes, as must an embryo, that he does: ". . . He felt a sudden elation in the thought that the world was his" (XI.24).

In this Almayer doubtless describes Conrad's own early vocabulary of desire and need. For Conrad too, as a captain, an African explorer, and, above all, a novelist, no doubt imagined that he himself should present the secured cities of Europe with a similarly impregnable claim for admiration, endorsement, and respect—and that by so doing he should "forget" his own "heart-breaking" experience of misery and struggle.[6]

Unlike Conrad, though, Almayer has no Bobrowski to temper his excessive enthusiasm; nor has he any of Conrad's final susceptibility to reality, Conrad's redeeming reluctance to grant his will ultimate ascendancy over his reporting intelligence. Almayer in fact is oblivious to the practical difficulties implied by his "vision." "Dazzled by the greatness of the results to be achieved" (XI.62), he provisionally releases himself from the imposing obstacles of the jungle, the murderous Dyaks, and the probable treachery of Babalatchi and Lakamba—as earlier he blithely had dismissed the unpleasant actuality of his wife. He exists in such an efficient condition of enchantment, indeed, that he is not even aware of the larger impediment to his imperial fancy. "Bent upon forgetting the hated reality of the present" (XI.63), Almayer does not remark that the supposed partners of his visionary purpose, themselves solipsists, have developed equally forceful needs of their own which precisely conflict with his cooptative intention. He does not permit himself to perceive, that is, that Nina has become Malayan; nor does he acknowledge that Dain Maroola desires his daughter more than he does his gold.

And yet, Almayer is so resourceful in his power to shape reality and his own responses to it that he is able to shore the collapse of one imaginative edifice by instantly

6. As I shall suggest, Conrad puts to yet more extensive self-descriptive use the expectations of other characters in *Almayer's Folly*, and of the chief characters of *An Outcast of the Islands*, *The Nigger of the "Narcissus," Heart of Darkness*, and *Lord Jim*.

generating another. Thus, when he receives the inaccurate information that Dain has been drowned (and that, as a consequence, he shall be unable to secure the Dyak gold), Almayer reacts by immediately elaborating an alternative and more efficient "vision." Outraged by this hostile operation of his destiny, he with marvelous quickness and dexterity relocates himself *in* his pain. Expelled from his previous sense of mission and place, he tries to re-establish himself in the world—to repossess it, indeed—by declaring that, in one sense at least, the universe has confirmed his singularity by violating it:

> Fortune seemed to elude his grasp, and in his weary tramp backwards and forwards under the steady rain falling from the lowering sky, a sort of despairing indifference took possession of him. What did it matter? It was just his luck! (XI.73)

"It was just his luck!"—his and no one else's. If he has been afflicted by the universe, he at least has been assaulted more directly than has anyone else. If the world has repudiated him, it at least has been compelled to receive him as a particularized personality. Because, as he is able to suppose, he has been *uniquely* brutalized, he has found it possible to endure his adversity from a stance of dignified (if "despairing") "indifference." It is an impoverished imagination of self, no doubt, but a usable one—as Apollo Korzeniowski earlier had discovered.[7]

7. Cf. my p. 10. Almayer produces other, slightly less consequent, "visions." A momentary (and misinterpreted) improvement in his commercial situation encourages in him an outlandish access of hope and activity (XI.32). He builds his absurdly extravagant home (which gives title to the novel) in response to an inflated sense of the opportunities extended to him by the formation of the British Borneo Company (XI.33). The cruel and unctuous encouragement of the Dutch envoys generates a grotesque display of self-delusion and excess (XI.35–37).

After the putative death of Dain, Almayer deploys Apollo's complicated economy as the sole locus of his personality:

> "First one hope, then another, and this is my last. Nothing is left now. You think there is one dead man here? Mistake, I 'sure you. I am much more dead. Why don't you hang me? . . . I assure, assure you it would be a mat—matter of form altog—altogether." (XI.144)

Later in the novel he grandiloquently wonders, "Was he going to be tormented for ever, sleeping or waking, and have no peace either night or day?" (XI.160). And when he learns of his daughter's elopement, he remarks to himself:

> At the next beat it must stop. No heart could suffer so and beat so steadily for long. . . . Still beating unceasing and cruel. No man can bear this: and is this the last, or will the next one be the last?—How much longer? O God! how much longer? (XI.163)

These, of course, are all cries of a kind of ecstasy, of a deviant pleasure discovered in unpleasure. About the vocabulary of Almayer's pain there hovers an unsettling suggestion of satisfaction because, as I have suggested, Almayer has come to deduce the fact that he has personality from the fact that he experiences desolation. Like the stereotypic mother of Yiddish humor he has learned to center the primitive quality of his being in his intuition of suffering:[8] he embraces agony and makes of misery his relation with the world, as if to say, I do exist, must exist, because I feel such pain.

8. Almayer employs as well the linguistic gestures of the Yiddish convention. "Why don't you hang me?" he asks, precisely as the maligned Sophie or Sarie might be made to ask, Why don't you put a knife in my heart?

Almayer defines and certifies himself, then, by a process opposite to Bobrowski's. He imagines that one may
describe oneself by responding to the world as toward an
arc of pure, organic repudiation.[9] Certainly his father's
strategy, it as well may have been Conrad's own for much
of his life. His countless letters of plaint and stress, his
whole history of invalidism and collapse, suggest that
Conrad, like Almayer, had discovered the assertive uses to
which suffering may be put. Particularly must Conrad have
been close to this (Almayer's habitual) state of mind in
1878. Perhaps, that is, Conrad in part was led to assault
himself in Marseilles because at some sad level he
imagined that to signal such a condition of extremity
should be an act of self-description—or even of self-
generation. Perhaps as he fired a bullet into his chest it
perversely seemed to him, as here it seems to Almayer,
that by publishing his distress he might declare as well his
fecund singularity, and thus inhibit the source of his acute
disaffection from life in the very act of responding to it. I
am in such anguish that I must be actual, Conrad may have
thought: only an authentic and vigorous self could experience life so intensely as to require to obliterate it.

With Bobrowski's help and by the act of writing *Al-*

9. In this sense the moral independence of his daughter is to be understood as the most welcomed event of Almayer's life, for it seems to confirm, as Almayer imagines, his entire interpretation of existence. A "frightful catastrophe" (XI.192), Nina's elopement proposes itself to Almayer as
the perfect example of his singularity in misfortune: with his "sight . . .
dimmed by self-pity, by anger, and by despair" (XI.103), he is able to understand his daughter's behavior only by supposing that he has been victimized again—this time fatally—by his inexorable but curiously sanctioning destiny. Thus, as he laments Nina's treachery, he simultaneously is
able to feel substantiated by it. It has been Almayer's folly always to have
expected the world to support and to serve his conception of himself.
Perhaps he may assume that here it has.

mayer's Folly Conrad managed to avoid the final consequences of that "vision" which earlier he had shared with
Almayer, his first imaginative representation of himself. Almayer, though, is able to develop in the novel no such protection against himself. A weak man, he is delighted to discover that his strategy of asserted stress produces, as he
had intended that it should, a species of release from the
conditions and occasions of reality:

> They had his very last coin and did not care whether he
> went or stayed. And with a gesture of abandoned discour-
> agement Almayer . . . would abandon himself to the cur-
> rent of bitter thoughts, oblivious of the flight of time and
> the pangs of hunger, deaf to the shrill cries of his wife
> calling him to the evening meal. (XI.74)

By embracing his bitterness, Almayer not only effaces the
imprecatory demands of time, hunger, and his wife's shrill
voice. It appears that he extinguishes as well his personality
itself, the arbiter of his experience and, therefore, the ultimate source of his chronic pain. "He would abandon himself"—as if by ceasing to function as a free personality he
might make of himself a sweet sanctuary of selflessness,
and so repulse all distress at its font. Not happy but at least
markedly less mindful of his suffering, Almayer seems to
imagine that in this ingeniously self-destructive way he may
post himself against the violence of the outer world and
the anguish of the inner: No Trespassing, pain. This Is a
Preserve.

It is with this tactic in mind that, as he watches his
cherished daughter sail away with Dain Maroola, Almayer
consciously extends his crusade against consciousness.
Mutely aware that he has been reduced by Nina's flight to
the sum of his pain, he hits upon the curiously rational irra-

tionality of, as he puts it, "forgetting": "I shall try to forget. I have no daughter. There used to be a half-caste woman in my house, but she is going even now. . . . I will never forgive you, Nina; and tomorrow I shall forget you!" (XI.184; 191). In the belief that this programme of protective displacement must be enacted "systematically and on order" (XI.195), Almayer erases his daughter's footprints in the sand (XI.195–96) and burns his old home and office, the domiciles of his abandoned experience of identity (XI.198–200). As might a mad psychotherapist, Almayer has decided that "certain things had to be taken out of his life, stamped out of sight, destroyed, forgotten" (XI.199). A ludicrous stratagem, perhaps, but one which Bobrowski and certainly Conrad actually had enacted in 1878.

In fact, though, Almayer needs none of this literal devastation; for immediately upon his daughter's "treachery," this genuinely unbearable inflection of pain, he dies to personality as he long had wished and, from Conrad's previous point of view, perhaps even required to do.[10]

10. In his interesting discussion of *Almayer's Folly* Royal Roussel remarks that Almayer prefers "a kind of suicide" to that possibility of communion with life extended to him by Nina and Dain (XI.192). Roussel argues as well that Almayer makes his choice because he is attracted to "the fraudulent world of [European] civilization." (Royal Roussel, *The Metaphysics of Darkness* [Baltimore and London: The Johns Hopkins Press, 1971], p. 42.) Almayer unquestionably does commit a species of suicide in the novel; but I think that he does so primarily for the reason which I have been suggesting: because he hopes that by obliterating his personality he better may endure the demands of his experience. As I shall go on to suggest, each of the major characters in Conrad's early fiction attempts to do as much.

Perhaps Roussel's and my own reading of this, the novel's central, event do not conflict so much as they emphasize in different ways what Roussel describes as "the necessity" presented in *Almayer's Folly* to develop "external ground to the very existence of the individualized consciousness" (Roussel, p. 42).

Thus, as Nina deserts him Almayer's voice becomes "dispassionate" (XI.189) and "henceforth he spoke always in a monotonous whisper like an instrument of which all the strings but one are broken" (XI.192–93). His face becomes "immovable" (XI.192). He assumes, it is said, "the blank expression of those who live in that hopeless calm which sightless eyes only can give (XI.194). The one "string" of his welcomed misery is perfectly able to carry the whole tune of Almayer's depleted existence, then, because poor Kaspar at last has been confirmed in his "vision" that one may have one's personality exclusively in one's suffering:

> His features had lost all expression, and life in his eyes seemed to have gone out. The face was a blank, without a sign of emotion, feeling, reason, or even knowledge of itself. All passion, regret, grief, hope, or anger—all were gone. . . . Those few who saw Almayer during the short period of his remaining days were always impressed by the sight of that face that seemed to know nothing of what went on within. . . . (XI.190)

Almayer's Folly reserves for its willfully autistic "hero" a yet more powerful (albeit fatal) mechanism of self-suppression. Unable by the simple exercise of his will altogether to extinguish the hated actuality of his character, Almayer finally concludes his career by succumbing to the irreparable efficiency of a chemical "forgetting." An apparition hideous and empty, exactly—at last!—an entity external from himself and the world, he ends his life by smoking his pipes of mechanical peace in the recesses of his extravagant home. Conrad's version, perhaps, of what he might himself have become had he not written *Almayer's Folly*, Almayer completes his sorry arc by becoming pet to his monkey (XI.203) and slave to his fierce fear of self. "An immense man-doll broken and flung there out of the way" [11] (XI.204), he achieves "the inner meaning of his life" (XI.102) by dying, and thus releasing himself permanently from the unmanageable demands of experience received in personality.

Four

I have remarked that there is much about Almayer's behavior which suggests certain of Conrad's own attitudes and gestures. As much may be said about Nina. Indeed, it is probable that *Almayer's Folly* appealed to its author primarily because of the conflict which it establishes between Almayer and his daughter: [12] for by describing his characters' tensions Conrad no doubt felt empowered to investigate instincts of his own which in his non-linguistic experience had proposed themselves too indistinctly for use.

Almayer's Folly situates Nina, in any event, in Conrad's own condition of exclusion and vagueness of affect. Neither Malay nor Dutch,[13] Nina feels unlocated by

11. The phrase closely resembles, and I think was written privately to suggest, Conrad's description of himself to Mme. Poradowska as a "broken" and discarded "Punch." (Cf. my p. 68–69.)

12. Baines argues that Conrad habitually wrote about struggles between fathers and daughters because he felt compelled to examine his own conflict "between loyalty to his father's memory and the desire to create his own life" (Baines, 155). This is likely enough, although one should be interested to understand what provoked Conrad imaginatively to feminate himself in these fictional situations.

13. Unlike Nina, of course, Conrad was not actually half-caste. But Bobrowski so often insisted upon the distinction between the Korzeniowski and Nałęcz strains that Conrad doubtless *felt* half-caste—as Dickens had been compelled by his experience to regard himself as an orphan, or Joyce to think of himself as a political exile. Too, Conrad implies in his re-

the pieties of either culture. Because she inherits no exploitable science of existence she conducts her life, as must have Conrad, "shivering and helpless as if on the edge of some deep and unknown abyss" (XI.42). Involved with but not herself a part of two contradictory systems of ethic, she is unable to receive either as authoritative. Indeed, she comes quickly to believe that *all* traditions of assumption are more or less attractive artifices by which a people organizes collective excuse for its reprehensible practices. In this respect, the moral life seems to Nina merely aesthetic: [14]

> Her young mind having been unskilfully permitted to glance at better things, and then thrown back again into the hopeless quagmire of barbarism, full of strong and uncontrolled passions, had lost the power to discriminate. It

markable "Punch" letter that he often shared Nina's impression of social stigma. (Cf. my p. 68–69.)

14. By way of confirming Nina's supposition that no civilization legitimately distinguishes one experience of life from another, *Almayer's Folly* consistently repudiates the authority of both the Malayan and European systems of civility. Thus, the novel is at some pain to represent both the Dutch envoys and the governors of Sambir as dissemblers and libertines; as untrustworthy because unethical men who are driven in essentially similar ways by absurd superstitions and prejudices. In this regard Babalatchi and Mrs. Almayer's hilarious imaginations of probity are not for Conrad altogether comic; for it is his assumption here, as it more memorably shall become an assumption of *Heart of Darkness*, that the patterns of both "civilized" and "savage" behavior usually are grotesquely incommensurate with the settings of life or with the covert (and normally sordid) realities of human motivation. Obviously, as *Heart of Darkness* makes clear, Conrad's attitude of wariness toward the pieties of civilized community were conditioned particularly by his experience in the Congo.

Conrad openly articulates his assumption in *A Personal Record*. "The ethical view of the universe," he writes, "involves us at last in so many cruel and absurd contradictions . . . that I have come to suspect that the aim of creation cannot be ethical at all. I would fondly believe that its object is purely spectacular . . ." (VI.92).

> seemed to Nina that there was no change and no dif-
> ference. . . . Nina saw only the same manifestations of
> love and hate and of sordid greed chasing the uncertain
> dollar in all its multifarious and vanishing shapes.
> (XI.42–43)

This being so, Nina rapidly educates herself to prefer the
barbarous imagination of life to the European—not because, like her mother, she believes that it is correct but
because it seems to her more sincerely felt and therefore
more conducive to authenticity:

> After all these years, the savage and uncompromising sin-
> cerity of purpose shown by her Malay kinsmen seemed at
> last preferable to the sleek hypocrisy, to the polite dis-
> guises, to the virtuous pretences of such white people as
> she had had the misfortune to come in contact with. After
> all it was her life; it was going to be her life, and so think-
> ing she fell more and more under the influence of her
> mother. (XI.43)

As an adolescent, then, Nina takes a considered
stand for fervency of expression and feeling as against the
manipulativeness and dull circumspection which seem to
her to characterize the life of European routine. But like
Conrad, who had insisted at a similar age upon the primacy
of "strong and uncontrolled passions," Nina discovers that
it is more difficult to shape one's existence in fact than in
desire. Thus, fully as repulsed by the outer world as Almayer—or as Conrad in Marseilles—Nina feels overwhelmed in Sambir with weariness and torpor: "she might
have been deaf, dumb, without any feeling as far as any
expression of feeling went" (XI.40–41). All of this changes,
though, with the spectacular appearance (one almost had
said annunciation) of Dain Maroola; and in her unfeigned

response to Dain's promise of legitimacy and ardor Nina establishes both alternative to her father [15] and hope for her creator.

From the outset Dain presents himself not merely as a man but as the very principle of uncomplicated potency: a "gorgeous and bold being" (XI.55), he is to be received, Nina is told, not as a trader (in search, after all, of "the uncertain dollar") but as "a great Rajah . . . a Son of Heaven" (XI.51). If one may judge by the effect that this bejeweled prodigy has upon her daughter, Mrs. Almayer has not exaggerated by much either Dain's origin or his power:

> Every time he spoke to her, every time he looked into her eyes, Nina, although averting her face, felt as if this bold-looking being who spoke burning words into her willing ear was the embodiment of her fate, the creature of her dreams— . . . the ideal Malay chief of her mother's tradition. (XI.64)

Conrad's banal language notwithstanding, Nina discovers in Dain none of the insipid communion of sentimental romance but precisely that economy of achieved unconsciousness for which her father had longed. For in her passion for the Son of Heaven Nina is said to discover an absolute escape from the inhibiting boundaries of individual identity:

> She recognized with a thrill of delicious fear the mysterious consciousness of her identity with that being. Listening to his words, it seemed to her she was born only then to a knowledge of a new existence, that her life was com-

15. One might add that she establishes alternative as well to the almost equally unattractive "visions" by which Babalatchi, Lakamba, Abdulla, and her mother shape their existences.

> plete only when near him, and she abandoned herself to a
> feeling of dreamy happiness. . . . (XI.64)

"The dreamy happiness" to which "she *abandoned* herself"—Conrad earlier has applied the identical phrase to describe Almayer—obviously has less to do with the sheerly physical excitation of "love and passion" (XI.64) than with the "entrancing" (XI.16) experience of self-suppression. "The new principle of her life" (XI.103), Nina's in some respect selfless ecstasy proposes itself as a substitute for personality "sweeter to her than life itself" (XI.69)—as a vision, indeed, "that would justify the life she had to endure" (XI.151):

> With the coming of Dain she found the road to freedom by
> obeying the voice of the new-born impulses. . . . She un-
> derstood now the reason and the aim of life; and in the tri-
> umphant unveiling of that mystery she threw away disdain-
> fully her past with its sad thoughts, its bitter feelings and
> its faint affections, now withered and dead in contact with
> her fierce passion. (XI.152)

The agent of Nina's "fierce passion" is reported to experience a similar release from self:

> At the feet of Nina, [Dain] forgot the world, felt himself
> carried away helpless by a great wave of supreme emotion,
> by a rush of joy, pride, and desire; understood once more
> with overpowering certitude that there was no life possible
> without that being he held clasped in his arms. . . .
> (XI.68–69)

But about *this* involvement with ecstasy *Almayer's Folly* is more ambiguous. For even as it secures him in his potency and naturalness, Dain's passion for Nina appears in the novel to threaten his very existence as a bold and free entity. Thus, his frenzies of pleasure are said to render him "helpless," (XI.166) "bereft of his senses," (XI.171) and "like one dead" (XI.128). This implicit evocation of Almayer's moribundity of course is deliberate: it has seemed to Conrad, that is, that Dain's sexual rapture is akin to Almayer's narcotism. Certainly the mechanism of Dain's delight suggests that of the opium-eater: ". . . He remained motionless, without daring to open his eyes, afraid to lose the sensation of intoxicating delight he had tasted for the first time" (XI.72). And his hallucinations suggest those characteristic of narcosis:

> To those two nothing existed then outside the gunwales of the narrow and fragile [canoe]. It was their world, filled with their intense and all-absorbing love. They took no heed of thickening mist, or of the breeze dying away before sunrise; they forgot the existence of the great forests surrounding them, of all the tropical nature. . . . Earth, river, and sky were wrapped up in a deep sleep from which it seemed there would be no waking. (XI.69)

All of this should be acceptable, perhaps, could one be certain of the perfect mutuality of Nina and Dain's interests. What harm, after all, if a man live "bereft of his senses" so long as his stupefaction extend to him a reasonable measure of dignity and pleasure? The novel does not permit us, though, to trust to the permanent integrity of at least these partners' communion. As Mrs. Almayer puts the matter, "there will be other women" for Dain; and Nina "could not live" (XI.153) were that to become so. Too, Nina shall not always be for Dain so unassertive and malleable an object. For she schemes already to mould and drive the man, in fact to usurp his autonomy. It must be said, indeed, that she feels a certain contempt for her lover:

Her mother was right.[16] The man was her slave. As she glanced down at his kneeling form she felt a great pitying tenderness for that man she was used to call—even in her thoughts—the master of life. . . . Did he not say himself that she was the light of his life? She would be his light and his wisdom; she would be his greatness and his strength; yet hidden from the eyes of all men she would be, above all, his only and lasting weakness. (XI.172)

The novel invites us to question even the purity of her love for Dain: "A faint smile seemed to be playing about her firm lips. Who can tell in the fitful light of a camp fire? It might have been a smile of triumph, or of conscious power, or of tender pity, or, perhaps, of love" (XI.172). Suspicious as it is about the quality and consequences of Nina's passion, the novel goes so far as to characterize her sexuality itself as a species of murderous instrument:

She drew back her head and fastened her eyes on his in one of those long looks that are a woman's most terrible weapon; a look that is . . . more dangerous than the thrust of a dagger, because it also whips the soul out of the body, but leaves the body alive and helpless . . . ; a look that enwraps the whole body, and that penetrates into the innermost recesses of the being, bringing terrible defeat in the delirious uplifting of accomplished conquest. (XI.171)

We cannot feel confident, then, about the final yield of Nina and Dain's temporarily self-justifying "vision." Like every other fantasy construction examined in *Almayer's Folly* its authority is likely to be impermanent because it does not take into account the irreconcilable divergence

16. Cf. XI.152–53.

of individual purposes and needs; nor, it might be added, does it provide protection against the brooding animosity of the unarrogated outer world.[17]

And yet, even though exterior circumstances shall be ungentle with them, and even though in *Almayer's Folly* "no two human beings understand each other" (XI.179), Conrad permits his lovers to depart from the novel in a condition of strength and repose. It would appear that for the moment at least "it was their world" (XI.69), because for the moment they successfully have compacted together to engage their experience not from the debilitating vantage point of individual identity—a strategy of existence which has failed each of the novel's people and, to this point in his life, certainly Conrad himself—but from the provisionally sanctioning perspective of secured impersonality. Situated, that is, in sensation alone, Nina and Dain have managed at least for a time to release themselves from conscious subjection to the ravening despotisms of self and world. Their achievement seems to Conrad deeply problematical; but, precarious as it is, it images the great longing of his own life. In his first novel, written from so urgent a condition of need, he could not bring himself altogether to deny its possibility.

17. The novel does not explicitly suggest that Nina's conception of Dain—or Dain's conception of himself—shall be undermined by the unsympathetic conditions of modern history. But it is a major thrust of *Almayer's Folly* to describe the irreversible erosion of that range of heroic possibility traditionally extended to the Malayan warrior class; and Mrs. Almayer makes a point of remarking that, given the new balance of power in the East, Dain cannot conceivably achieve all that he must in order to preserve his own and his wife's "vision" (Cf. XI.153).

Roussel is much more sanguine than I or, as I think, than Conrad himself about the permanence of what Roussel calls Nina and Dain's "miraculous continuity" (Cf. Roussel, 40–42).

Five

This is not to say, of course, that in sum *Almayer's Folly* is a happy book, or that by temporarily empowering Nina and Dain Conrad discovered a mechanism by which to domesticate his own situation of pain. For *Almayer's Folly* is shocking exactly because it so radically confirms that situation. In its geometry of anger, confusion, and unsatisfied need, its extreme description of life as "a mournful round of tearful and endless iteration" (XI.89), *Almayer's Folly* precisely does no more than to detail its author's misery, not cure it. What else is one to say about the fact that Almayer, Mrs. Almayer, Babalatchi, Lakamba, Taminah, Jim-Eng—each of the novel's people—feels brutally pressed and depleted by his existence, that each wishes for nothing from his life so much as for some structure of relief? What else is one to say about the novel's assumption that the principal motivation of all human behavior is to secure escape from experience, as if (as is doubtless so) Conrad had come to believe about the self what he had been made to believe about the universe: that personality, like the outer world, aggresses against peace and pleasure and must be circumvented if one is to survive or to "justify the life [one must] endure" (XI.151)?

Perhaps, though, *Almayer's Folly* did locate for its author one source of relief and renewal; for the novel does establish one distinction at least between its characters' and Conrad's own stratagems of survival. I speak of the fact that at a critical moment in his career the novel's most nearly certified man, Dain Maroola, is found to be markedly less courageous, perhaps even less potent, than his creator.

The moment to which I refer occurs as Dain awaits Nina in Bulangi's clearing. Uncertain and afraid, he tries to restore his character strength by imaginatively reconstructing the "splendour" and "joy" which Nina earlier had seemed to extend to him:

> Crouching in his shady hiding-place, he closed his eyes, trying to evoke the gracious and charming image of the white figure that for him was the beginning and the end of life. With eyes shut tight, his teeth hard set, he tried in a great effort of passionate will to keep his hold on that vision of supreme delight. In vain! (XI.166)

Dain's incipient hysteria is not to be quieted by this great discharge of will: his intense effort is "in vain." "Startled," "weary," "aimless" (XI.166) in his impotent fear, Dain imagines, foolishly, that he may escape in a physical way from the intimidating demands of his existence:

> A man could hide there, thought Dain, as he approached a place where the creepers had been torn and hacked into an archway that might have been the beginning of a path. As he bent down to look through he heard angry grunting, and a sounder of wild pig crashed away in the undergrowth. An acrid smell of damp earth and of decaying leaves took him by the throat, and he drew back with a scared face, as if he had been touched by the breath of Death itself. The very air seemed dead in there—heavy and stagnating, poisoned with the corruption of countless ages. (XI.167)

Dain is a brave man, the most brave in the novel. But in this momentary weakness, in this desperate urge to exempt himself from himself by "hiding" from the sun like an insipid little pig, the Son of Heaven testifies to the general instinct of the novel's imagined people to accept escape under any terms from the crippling data of consciousness. However disheartened Conrad himself may have been made to feel by the pressures of his own character and experience, he at least had ceased by 1895 to share in *this* "corruption of countless ages." No longer attracted to the brutal "forgetting" of Almayer or, as here, to the piggish self-concealment of Dain Maroola, he had determined not to retreat from but linguistically to engage the full measure of his own experience and fears. In this sense the act itself of writing *Almayer's Folly* is to be thought of as Conrad's personal effort of passionate will—as Conrad's own effort to crawl out from the dank "undergrowth" of "his shady hiding place," that in the full light of the sun he might make for himself the more manly "vision . . . of a coherent, justifiable personality." [18]

As I earlier have suggested, Conrad understood full well that each "vision of supreme delight" which he might in this way produce must cease its sanctioning function as soon as his precious pen scratched The End: [19] like Dain's, his imaginative labor in an absolute sense always should be "in vain." The issue for Conrad, though, was not at this time permanence of identity but rather the construction of an "accumulated verisimilitude." [20] If *Almayer's Folly* gave Conrad nothing else which he could put to personal use, it at least extended to him the foundation of that "verisimilitude" which he should "accumulate" during the next five years by writing *An Outcast of the Islands, The Nigger of the "Narcissus," Heart of Darkness,* and *Lord Jim:* it permitted him to define from his own point of view in what respect he was unique from most other men and in what

18. VI. Preface, xxi; cf. my p. 86–87.   19. Cf. my p. 81–82.
20. VI.15; cf. my p. x, 72–73, 85–86.

respect he had become unique from former versions of himself.

This is to say, then, that the fictional history of Sambir had extended to its creator an incipient, if odd, vocabulary of personality—no mean gift to a man who had grown up believing that he had neither the right nor the power to live as a self. *Almayer's Folly* may seem to us a grim, indeed a frightening, book. But to its author, who by writing it had avoided its people's fate, it no doubt seemed the very stuff of heaven.

Chapter Three

My dear fellow, don't—don't you see that the ba—bare
fac—the fact of your existence is off—offensive.
(XIV.367)

Magic Circles
An Outcast of the Islands

The act of writing *Almayer's Folly* extended to Conrad a
measure of hope—and produced the first important friendship of his adult life.[1] But in 1895 he remained in a
dangerously general condition of anxiety. If he had crawled
out of his "shady hiding place," if (at the age of thirty-
eight) he had even created for himself a rudimentary in-
timation of character and will, he had neither lightened the
burden of his history nor dramatically relieved his appalling
isolation. Conrad began his second novel, then, in a mood
encumbered by weariness and suffering. "As I obviously
cannot die," he wrote to his "aunt," "I must concern myself with living, which is very tiresome" (*Poradowska*, 77).[2]
Certainly *An Outcast of the Islands* suffers from Conrad's
"empty head, discouragement, and eternal doubt" (*Poradowska*, 89).[3] The narrative often is contorted and its chief

1. I refer to Conrad's friendship with Edward Garnett. Cf. XVI. *Author's
Note*, vii–viii; Garnett, Edward, ed., *Letters from Joseph Conrad, 1895–1924*
(Indianapolis: Bobbs-Merrill, 1928), Introduction, p. 2f; Baines, 140f.

2. Cf. my p. 83.   3. Cf. my p. 84–85.

characters, filled with their author's tedium, fail to engage one's sympathy, interest, or loyalty. Worse, the novel's systematic antipathy toward existence is never legitimized, if one may say such a thing, by the visionary ethicality which shapes, for example, *Heart of Darkness* or *Under Western Eyes*.

And yet for those readers who are interested in the mind of its author *An Outcast* is likely to make a major effect. For one comes to think of the novel's limitations as the very embodiment of the frightful patterns which governed Conrad's thought in 1895. One comes to understand, that is, that *An Outcast* delineates so few emotions, colors, and textures because by 1895 Conrad's personality had suffered too much damage to perceive with fully human variety or grace. One understands that *An Outcast* permits its characters such scant happiness because Conrad's own life had become too bleak to permit him to imagine the range or the rewards of other men's lives. One understands that *An Outcast* is so uneasily ironic in its tone because Conrad had not received from his experience those certitudes and comforts which permit other authors to establish more settled narrative stances.

In this respect the imperfections of the novel themselves invite attention: if nothing else, they offer access into the habitual attitudes and assumptions of Conrad's mind. Indeed, one feels haunted by *An Outcast* exactly *because* of its imposing failures of structure and spirit: if the novel fails to discover full relation with the world which it describes, it does define more completely than can his biography or correspondence the alarming severity of Conrad's affective distress. This is a way of saying, I suppose, that one feels moved by *An Outcast* out of proportion to its achievement because the novel defines the full range of Conrad's valor. For the disorders which distort the fiction surely should have destroyed the rationality of any less genuinely courageous—or determinedly sane— a man.

One

At one point in *An Outcast* Conrad remarks that all men need to experience life from the vantage point of secured identity. "Mankind," he writes, is a slave to "that desire of singularity . . . without being aware of its presence within his breast" (XIV.202). Peter Willems feels this urge with such incontinent force that he subverts his entire sense of reality to its peremptory demands. A confidential clerk of sorts, he parleys the prestige which accrues to his position into a sweeping endorsement of himself:

> Being of a modest and diffident nature, his successes amazed, almost frightened him, and ended—as he got over the succeeding shocks of surprise—by making him ferociously conceited. He believed in his genius and in his knowledge of the world. (XIV.6)

Unable to "analyze the state of his mind" (XIV.5), "slightly dizzy . . . with the intoxication of his own glory" (XIV.7), Willems celebrates in an apparently endless paean to himself "his own ways, . . . his own abilities, . . . those fate-compelling abilities of his which led him toward that lucrative position which he now filled" (XIV.6). "Drunk with the sound of his own voice celebrating his own prosperity" (XIV.8), he permits himself to suppose that the universe exists solely to provide forum for himself:

> There is always some one thing which the ignorant man knows, and that thing is the only thing worth knowing; it fills the ignorant man's universe. Willems knew all about himself. . . . The road to greatness lay plainly before his eyes, straight and shining, without any obstacle that he could see. (XIV.6; 11)

Willems enjoys such an ecstatic pleasure with himself that in a final access of mindless vainglory he treats his evening snookers as a metaphor for existence itself: "How glorious! How good was life for those that were on the winning side! He had won the game of life; also the game of billiards" (XIV.7).

But Willems' emotion of "rounded and completed" (XIV.4) pleasure is centered exclusively about the tenuous support of other men's good opinion. Indeed, Willems equates "with the very nature of things" the frightened "submission of his wife, the smile of his child, the awe-struck respect" (XIV.3) of his in-laws and co-workers. Should this external ratification of himself collapse, so must his sense of perfect continuity with the universe.

And so, in time, it does. When Willems is exposed as an embezzler and discharged from his exalted position, he is shocked to discover that he has lost not merely his eminence but his whole power to order experience. Scorned by his wife and relatives, hounded by the commercial populace of Macassar, he feels irrevocably separated from his place in the scheme of existence: "Men, women and children slept in there. Human beings. Would he ever sleep, and where? He felt as if he were the outcast of all mankind . . ." (XIV.30).

In this fierce and precipitate expulsion from the agreeable conviction of his own primacy, Willems understandably experiences difficulty in interpreting or even in perceiving previously innocuous inflections of reality: [4] "A thin rope's end lay across his path and he saw it distinctly, yet stumbled heavily across it as if it had been a bar of iron" (XIV.22). His own home seems suddenly imposing and peculiar:

> He found himself in the garden before his house. . . . He looked at it with a vague surprise to find it there. His past was so utterly gone from him that the dwelling which belonged to it appeared to him incongruous standing there intact, neat, and cheerful in the sunshine of the hot afternoon. (XIV.23)

Unable to believe in the "singularity"—and thus, perhaps, in the fact itself—of his personality, Willems finds it impossible to behave as a contained, self-directed entity. He beats his betrayer, but is unaware that he has done so. He makes his way to a jetty, but is unconscious of the act, its motive, or the mode of his movement (XIV.29–30). No longer convinced that he *has* an identity, stripped of his senses of power and place, he cannot perform even the most mundane, the elemental, biological process: "He found himself in the street at last, but could not find air enough to fill his lungs. He walked toward his home, gasping" (XIV.22).

"Stunned" by his calamity "as if somebody had fired a gun close to his ear," filled with "dumb amazement at the mystery" (XIV.27) of his sudden inconsequence, poor Willems "shivered, seeing himself alone in the presence of unknown and terrible dangers" (XIV.31):

4. Cf. J. Hillis Miller's valuable discussion of what he calls the process of "demystification" in Conrad's fiction (J. Hillis Miller, *Poets of Reality* [Cambridge: Belknap Press, 1966], pp. 19–24.)

He felt a terror at this hate that had lived stealthily so near him for years. . . . Bewildered [he asked,] . . . "Is this a madhouse?" . . . It seemed to him that the world was bigger, the night more vast and more black. . . . (XIV.27; 28; 30)

Repudiated by the world, he prepares, as once had his creator, to repudiate himself: "The end of the jetty; and here in one step more the end of life; the end of everything. Better so. What else could he do?" (XIV.30).

Two

This catalogue of collapse is distressing enough merely in its sense of the pain which an unexceptional man may be made to feel in the ordinary course of his life. More troubling is the supposition which controls the description—Conrad's apparent belief that one's power to perceive is dependent less upon the absolute qualities of the exterior world than upon the nature of one's attitude toward existence. Thus, Willems' ability to apprehend shapes and to structure the commonplace manifestations of urban life is not permitted in the novel to survive the destruction of his habitual moral posture. Because "his past was so utterly gone from him" (XIV.23), Willems cannot sustain his hold upon the physical world. Shocked in the patterns of his intelligence, he cannot take air into his lungs, stand composedly before his home, or even lift his foot over a rope.

An Outcast proceeds here as if it believed that everything external to oneself exhibits no discrete modality of its own; as if it believed that those portions of the universe which exist apart from one's own consciousness exhibit themselves in meaning and form only at the behest of one's consciousness.[5] The novel is guided in this judgment, I think, by the chronic disturbance in Conrad's own sensory capacity. For Conrad conducts the scenes which I describe with baffling calm, as if he supposed that he has raised no startling issue but merely has remarked a commonplace. Of *course* my hero could not breathe, he seems to say; nor could he walk, or make connection with things: as we all know, there *are* no fixed or autonomous "things," only shifting and treacherous inflections of vagueness.[6] Nothing more clearly could define the extremity of Conrad's psychic dislocation than this unconscious summary of his personal disaffection from reality.

Three

Willems believes, in any event, that he has learned the worst about himself in Macassar—and that has been enough to drive him to distraction. But when he is shipped to Sambir by the more vigorous Lingard he is made to confront the full measure of his sterility. For amidst the frantic tumult and purposefulness of the Malayan jungle Willems discovers that his "singularity" has to do with no other dis-

5. It will be recalled that, in considering the implications of suicide, Willems remarks to himself: ". . . The end of life; the end of everything" (XIV.30). Willems supposes here as he does throughout the novel that his own power to apprehend confers meaning upon the otherwise incoherent and insubstantial universe.

6. I should emphasize that Conrad does not repudiate in *An Outcast* that striking imagination of the natural world's brutality which informs *Almayer's Folly*. He adds, rather, a new dimension to his already alarming characterization of the universe. The world which he describes is now said to be hideously violent not only in its murderousness but as well—or particularly—in its incoherence and somehow systematic physical vagueness.

tinction than his extraordinary "superfluity" and "useless-
ness" (XIV.65):

> Round him everything stirred, moved, swept by in a rush;
> the earth under his feet and the heavens above his head.
> The very savages around him strove, struggled, fought,
> worked—if only to prolong a miserable existence; but they
> lived, they lived! And it was only himself that seemed to
> be left outside the scheme of creation. . . . (XIV.65)

In fact, as shall be seen, everyone of consequence in
Sambir believes himself to be similarly isolated. Willems,
though, does not know this; and in any case he wishes to
still his pain, not to share it. But no strategy of recovery
presents itself to him—nor really, as I shall suggest, to the
imagination which controls the novel. Willems suffers but
he cannot act. Because he *has* no effective personality he
cannot marshal impulses of character powerful enough to
quell his "bitter and savage rage." Nor can he consult for
the purposes of "refuge from . . . his thoughts" (XIV.65)
the grotesque landscape in which he must conduct his existence. For if the jungle terrain proposes itself to him as
the very standard of authenticity and vitality, it as well unnerves and repulses him by its awful caricature of his own
fetid depression. "Malodorous" and "gloomy" (XIV.65),
full of "dampness" and "decay" (XIV.67), the mephitic Pantai plays charade with Willems' state of mind, annihilates in
the exhausted creature the very longings it provokes.

Four

After weeks of "tormenting anger" (XIV.65) Willems
does manage to evolve for himself a source of temporary
energy and hope. Deprived of every rational stratagem of

existence, he commits himself at last to a mad sort of communion with the terrain which simultaneously has stirred and repelled him: in macabre parody of Wordsworthian exchange, he makes a fervent acceptance of the poisonous Pantai, joins himself in passion and trust with the "tall and graceful" (XIV.68) witch-woman—Aïssa—who seems to him to incarnate the jungle's mysterious "blooming of the dead" (XIV.70).

It is a desperate gesture, involving as it does a deliberate repudiation of every convention by which Willems previously has shaped his life. For a time, though, it works. "Free," "strong," "expectant," Aïssa gentles Willems' distress and excites him to a quickened sense of being. "A breath of wind," she charges him with unexpected "surprise and curiosity and desire":

> [She] touched his brain and heart together. [She] seemed to him to be something loud and stirring like a shout, silent and penetrating like an inspiration. (XIV.69)

"The very spirit of that land" (XIV.70), "the animated and brilliant flower of all that exuberant life" (XIV.76), Aïssa magically reconciles Willems with the world, reinvolves him in a sweeping sexual flourish with the opportunities and occasions of human existence:

> How changed everything seemed! The river was broader, the sky was higher. How fast the canoe flew under the strokes of his paddle! Since when had he acquired the strength of two men or more? (XIV.72)

In her primordial hands—or in some such organ—Willems "seemed able . . . to see through the forbidding gloom" (XIV.70). Joined with the universe at last, he enjoys a sweet and full release from his oppressive instinction of impotence: "In that atmosphere of Nature's workshop Willems felt soothed and lulled into forgetfulness of his past, into indifference as to his future" (XIV.74).

Five

Nothing in the novel has prepared for such a development: as I suggest in my prefatory remarks, *An Outcast* does not often certify the possibility of either "inspiration" or "desire." Nor does it here. *An Outcast* is quick to end Willems' affair and to disassociate itself from the motives which brought it into being.

The novel's principal objection to Willems' liaison is persuasive enough. His passion is illegitimate, the narrative argues, because Willems does not respond so much to Aïssa as to the uses to which he expects he can put her. "I have no people of my own," he tells her. "You are everybody to me" (XIV.143). "He wanted her for himself, far from everybody, in some safe and dumb solitude" (XIV.152). "While she was near there was nothing in the whole world—for that idle man—but her look and her smile" (XIV.76). You are everybody; safe and dumb; nothing in the world. Willems feels aroused by Aïssa only because he regards her as a kind of caulk. He thinks of his mistress, it would appear, not as a woman to cherish but as a bulwark against experience.

Willems' calculus is more ambitious yet. For his passion, as the narrative makes clear, has at its core the desire to evade consciousness itself. Aïssa so enlivens Willems, that is, because he mistakenly assumes that she can extend to him a release from personality, a respite from those bur-

dens of "singularity" which in his nonsexual experience
have proved too difficult to endure. Thus, Aïssa seems to
Willems to embody not only the world but his "own self,"
"his very individuality" [7] (XIV.77). She becomes "his only
thought, his only feeling, . . . all that was himself. . . .
Consciousness . . . had departed under her touch"
(XIV.76–77; 142). In the presence of Aïssa he assumes "an
expression of being taken possession of": [8]

> He experienced a sense of peace, of rest, of happiness,
> and of soothing delight. . . . [His] will, all his sensations,
> his personality—all this seemed to be lost in the abomina-
> ble desire, in *the priceless promise* of that woman.
> (XIV.141; 128–29; my emphasis)

"The priceless promise": Willems feels excited by Aissa
primarily because she extirpates him; he feels passion not
for Aïssa's flesh or, really, for her vitality but for her power
to eradicate his sensibility. What else can explain the intense
pleasure Willems derives from his mistress' dismember-
ment of his consciousness and character?

> She drew the man's soul away from him through his im-
> mobile pupils, and from Willems' features the spark of
> reason vanished under her gaze and was replaced by
> an appearance of physical well-being, an ecstasy of the

7. Willems goes so far as to present, apparently, his entire biological apparatus to Aïssa. At one point in the novel it is said of him: "All his blood,
all his sensation, all his life seemed to rush into her head . . ." (XIV.77).

8. The phrase—Willems' whole sorry syndrome—recalls Conrad's pleased
response to the various usurpations of his own identity function. As I shall
suggest, it is difficult not to regard the sexual situations of *An Outcast* as a
fictional recasting of particularly Conrad's experience with Thaddeus Bobrowski.

senses which had taken possession of his rigid body; an ecstasy which drove out regrets, hesitation and doubt, and proclaimed its terrible work by an appalling aspect of idiotic beatitude. He never stirred a limb, hardly breathed, but stood in stiff immobility, absorbing the delight. . . . (XIV.140)

For a time, we are told, Willems resists this "infamous" and "cowardly" (XIV.142) desire. But after the most tepid of struggles he surrenders to his sad exterminative wish. He yields, it is said, "as a tired swimmer gives up: because the swamped craft is gone from under his feet; because the night is dark and the shore is far—*because death is better than life*" (XIV.81; my emphasis). There can be no mistake. Willems prefers annihilation to life, the "priceless promise" of nullity to the "infamous nightmare" (XIV.146) of individuated existence. Indeed, he is explicit about his preference: "And true life was this:" he thought, "this dreamy immobility . . ." (XIV.146). "He whispered—'I wish I could die like this—now!' . . . He had given himself up. He felt proud of it" (XIV.141; 127).

Six

Willems' impulse to evade the demands of "singularity" should seem to Conrad an acceptable, if unattractive, strategy were he able to believe any longer in its simple efficacy: throughout much of his own life, after all, he had shared his hero's desire to be "taken possession of." No more, though. It is the mark of his developing resolution to survive as a self that in 1895 Conrad could not permit his hero—any more than he could permit himself—a "happiness that is infamous, cowardly" and "debased" [9] (XIV.141–42). *An Outcast* rejects Willems' "inspiration" because Conrad has discovered at last the cost of "that soothing delight" for which he himself once had yearned. The novel subjects Willems to abject physical and moral decline, to death itself, because Conrad has felt it useful, perhaps even necessary, to exorcise in fiction that "infamous" desire of oblivion which so nearly had assumed control over his own life.

It is as a portion of this rite of exorcism that the novel's other characters are made to express such intense contempt toward Willems. " 'He is not a human being at all,' " Lingard remarks. " 'He is . . . I don't know' " (XIV.271; Conrad's ellipsis). " 'Disgusting exhibition,' " Almayer calls him. " '[He is] as estimable as a heap of garbage' " (XIV.91). " 'Pig! Pig! Pig!' " (XIV.94) shrieks the sweetly vicious Nina. Willems is despicable, as each of these scandalized characters tries to suggest, because he refuses to participate in his author's burgeoning faith in asserted personality. He so shocks and appalls his fellows because he is afraid to join in their compact—in their author's compact—against the condition of being human; because he submits without decency or dignity to a fear which they all share, but which they at least *desire* to withstand:

> He was in the grip of a horrible fear; of a fear whose cold hand robs its victim of all will and of all power; of all wish to escape, to resist, or to move. . . . It was not death that

9. It will be recalled that a year earlier Conrad had allowed Nina a release from experience similar to that which he here denies to Willems. It is possible to suggest that Conrad wrote *An Outcast* at least in part to correct the concessions which had shaped *Almayer's Folly*—which had shaped, indeed, the previous two decades of his life.

frightened him; it was the horror of bewildered life where he could understand nothing and nobody round him; where he could guide, control, comprehend nothing and no one—not even himself.[10] (XIV.148–49)

Everyone in the novel shares this "horror"; even Lingard feels bewildered and frightened by what he calls the "unprovoked malevolence" (XIV.235–36) of the universe. But no one else in *An Outcast* enters, like Willems, into wilful complicity with the "sinister meaning" (XIV.150) of existence. No one else in the novel *elects*, like Willems, to become divested "of all will and of all power." Aïssa, Lingard, Babalatchi, Almayer, even the wearisome Joanna at least attempt, like Conrad himself in 1895, to contend by force of personal authenticity against the world's "monstrous and depraved" (XIV.150) suppression of the individual human will. To do anything less, it seems to them, is to surrender not merely one's honor and worth but one's very actuality: "Gone. All gone. All that had been a man within [Willems] was gone, and there remained only the trouble of his heart—that heart which had become a contemptible thing" (XIV.77).

That the novel's people undertake to resist their "horror of bewildered life," and that they contemn the one figure in their community who does not, is a testament to Conrad's increasing determination to withstand his own "unreasoning fear" (XIV.149) of existence. Could the long-

10. Albert Guerard has remarked that *"An Outcast of the Islands* is chiefly interesting for its situational prefiguration of *Lord Jim"* (Albert Guerard, *Conrad the Novelist* [Cambridge: Harvard University Press, 1958], p. 81). (Cf., too, Najder, 23.) Certainly *An Outcast* does anticipate certain of the devices and assumptions of *Lord Jim*. Here, though, the novel reads as a virtual draft version of *Heart of Darkness*. (Cf. in this regard XIV.269; 270; 274.) It might be remarked as well that Joanna Willems presents herself as an early version of The Intended.

suffering Bobrowski have read *An Outcast* he doubtless should have been pleased to confer at last upon his "neurasthenic" nephew his full acceptance and esteem.

Seven

In fact, though, the call for such an endorsement of Conrad's state of mind is overly hasty. For if in *An Outcast* Conrad no longer questions the necessity to declare one's "singularity," he continues to experience radical doubt about one's power to do so.

I have said that, with the exception of Willems, everyone in Sambir attempts to organize a defense against their shared "horror of bewildered life." This is true enough. Captain Tom Lingard, for example, trusts absolutely to the power of his publicly established character. " 'You know me,' " he declares. " 'I am Lingard.' " From "the great and inaccessible height" extended by "the strong consciousness of his own personality," he conducts his life with untroubled confidence. " 'I regret nothing,' " he asserts. " 'Nothing that I have done' " (XIV.273). Aïssa is equally resourceful. "The great catastrophe of her life" (XIV.75) notwithstanding, she sustains herself in "an intoxication of hope for great things born in the proud and tender consciousness of her influence" (XIV.333). The less prepossessing Babalatchi invests everything in his intelligence. "Full of care and wisdom and far-reaching plans" (XIV.215), he lives "undismayed . . . by the sudden ruin and destruction of all that he deemed indispensable to a happy and glorious existence" [11] (XIV.52). Even the pre-

11. Or so he supposes. I shall return to the matter of Babalatchi's self-deception.

posterous Joanna manages to support a "confused conviction" (XIV.302) of personal sovereignty by conceiving of
herself in the sacred role of wife.

Each of these ways of dealing with the world's "unprovoked malevolence" is more admirable than Willems'
cowardly withdrawal. In the end, though, none is more effective. Aïssa eventually sees "with rage and pain the edifice of her love, her own work, crumble slowly to pieces
. . ." (XIV.152–53). " 'I do not understand [Willems]!—' "
she cries. " 'Him!—My life!' " (XIV.249). "Appalled, surprised and angry with the anger of unexpected humiliation" (XIV.153), she leaves the novel a "doubled-up crone"
(XIV.366). Babalatchi is made to feel equally conscious of
impotence and error. " 'There are things I regret . . .' " he
moans. " 'I have been wrong! I have! Haï! Haï!' "
(XIV.232). Drawn, "tired," he ultimately stands on the edge
of his sordid clearing "angry, powerless, empty-handed,
with a cry of bitter discontent ready on his lips . . ."
(XIV.215). Joanna, who can comprehend nothing actual, finally "lost her head altogether" (XIV.358). She departs from
the novel in a condition of abject hysteria, "sending shriek
after shriek in an access of insane terror" (XIV.359). Even
Lingard's manly "edifice" is not dramatically more durable.
"Perfectly done up" (XIV.191), "tired as a dog" (XIV.196),
he too comes to feel "uneasy wonder at the failure of his
judgment" (XIV.223):

> He felt a great emptiness in his heart. . . . Speech, action,
> anger, forgiveness, all appeared to him alike useless and
> vain . . . not worth the effort of hand or brain that was
> needed to give them effect. (XIV.272)

At the last "there remained nothing"—nothing to *this*
superbly vigorous creature—"but the sense of some im-

mense infamy—of something vague, disgusting and terrible, which seemed to surround him . . . like a band of assassins in the darkness of vast and unsafe places" (XIV.265).

It would appear, then, that even the putatively more admirable characters of *An Outcast* come ultimately to share Willems' "disgusting" reaction against the universe. Each person in the novel finally is made to feel, like Willems, powerless to "guide, control, comprehend" anything. Each discovers and feels crippled by "the tremendous fact of our isolation, of the . . . indestructible loneliness that surrounds, envelopes, clothes every human soul from the cradle to the grave . . ." (XIV.250). Each concludes his career as a personality by learning, like Willems, to detest "himself, everybody he had ever known; the earth, the sky, the very air he drew into his oppressed chest . . ." (XIV.156). "Bewitched within the invisible sweep of a magic circle" (XIV.157), each in the end receives the world as had Willems—as a vast and horrifying threat to very life and limb. "Death everywhere!" they all shriek. "Death everywhere—wherever one looks" (XIV.342).

Eight

The novel is so severe with its people's systems of assertion and defense because Conrad considers them all chimerical and decadent. Almayer, for example, can sustain his stratagem of support only by gaming with fortune in the frankest possible way: " 'I must trust to luck now!' " (XIV.315) he blithely exclaims. Aïssa is able to invest so much in the preternaturally vapid Willems only because she "made up for herself . . . a story of a man great amongst his own people . . . ; of a being strong, dangerous, alive, and human, ready to be enslaved" (XIV.75). Even the mighty Lingard engages the world "like a child listening to a fairy tale" (XIV.269). Each of the novel's alternatives to Willems similarly confuses his own "fears and his desires" (XIV.304) with objective manifestations of reality; each constructs his "singularity" upon the curious presumption that the universe must cooperate with one's own presented needs.

This naive readiness to expect sustenance from the outer world seems to Conrad to proceed less from an instinct of peace or of ease with the conditions of existence than from an anxiety about them almost as extreme as Willems' own. Conrad argues, that is, that his characters invent "a story" because they cannot bear facts, that they "trust to luck" because they cannot abide what is provided. He makes each of his characters share in Willems' anguish because, in however subtle a way, each seems to him to have imitated Willems' retreat from legitimate experience. "Trusting the future" (XIV.383) rather than his own "will" and "power," existing "blindly, hopefully" (XIV.333) rather than rationally or courageously, each participates in Willems' extraordinarily intense fear of individuated personality.

Joined together, then, in "a magic circle" of failed authenticity, the novel's otherwise disparate protagonists shape only one arc. Like a pig in a poke or a bug in a bed, they all butt and roll about the closed curve of their "idiotic beatitude." Immobilized, full of "unreasoning fear," the grim little populace of Sambir conspires to a man against the genuine experience of character.

Nine

An Outcast is as contemptuous toward the nature of society in Sambir as it is toward that of the self. Indeed, the novel insists that its characters are incapable of social interaction—unless their attitude of universal belligerence may be taken to imply a community of sorts. In this Almayer makes example for his profane brethren. Himself the merest envelope of wish and want, he treats everyone else in the novel as so many particles of personal problem or use:

> It would not do to fool about with Lingard. But I must risk it. It's the only way I can see. I must tell [Joanna]. She has some little sense. I wish they were a thousand miles off already. A hundred thousand miles. I do. And if it fails. And she blabs out then to Lingard? She seemed a fool. No; probably they will get away. And if they did, would Lingard believe me? Yes. I never lied to him. He would believe. I don't know. . . . Perhaps he won't. . . ." I must do it. Must!" he argued aloud to himself. (XIV.298; Conrad's ellipses)

Almayer's manic manipulativeness is merely characteristic of the people of Sambir. Because the expectations of the novel's characters are so fanciful, the boundaries of their needs inevitably overlap in another variety of "magic circle"—here a frightful circumference of simultaneous dependency and antagonism. Aïssa tries to usurp Willems; Willems impinges upon his mistress, his wife, his friend; Babalatchi flexes at everyone; Lingard supposes that he owns the very river.[12] The possibility of mutual identity or

12. Cf. XIV.43; 45; 202.

of shared purposefulness is "buried" in *An Outcast* "under the dust, ashes, and corruption of personal thoughts, of base fears, of selfish desires" (XIV.298). If the notion of personality is foreign to the novel, so too—necessarily—is the idea of society.

Ten

This, then, is the diseased core of *An Outcast of the Islands*. Conrad had wanted in 1895 to establish a community of triumphantly capable personalities.[13] He had tried to conceive of "the joy, the triumphant delight of sunshine and of life" (XIV.360). But he rather had been compelled to reproduce again his own squat world of uncertain forms and hesitant, transitory souls, his own bleak universe of blood-bat women and loutish pig-men. The victim still of his viciously circular experience, Conrad could not help but shape in *An Outcast* a "magic circle" of shocking abuse: the outer world, he instinctively declares, taxes and tortures one; one's own consciousness taunts and torments one with visions of impotence and "horror"; other men prey upon one, or disappoint one, or are cold to one.

The entire sensation of life in *An Outcast* amounts, really, to a single impression of anguish. For at one or another level of perception, each character in the novel comes to believe, with Almayer, that "the world's a swindle! A swindle!" (XIV.367). Each character in the novel receives the universe, with Willems, as an assembly of "so many enormous hands . . . watching for the opportunity to take him, to enlace him, to strangle him, to hold him till

13. Cf. my p. 77–78; 82–83, 84.

he died . . ." (XIV.331). Each character in the novel is bounded, indeed, by the imposing implications of the narrative's closing exchange. " 'What have I done to be treated so?' " Almayer asks. In unconscious summary of the novel's "sinister meaning" the wandering naturalist brokenly murmurs, " 'My dear fellow, don't—don't you see that the ba—bare fac—the fact of your existence is off—offensive' " (XIV.367).

On several occasions I have suggested that the act of writing fiction permitted Conrad to salvage—or perhaps even to create—his personality. How sparse, though, at least in 1895, was that induced apparatus of character. *An Outcast of the Islands* does not produce a single person whom it can admire or even fully authenticate. It does not believe, evidently, in either the power or the possibility of community. It does not certify the reality of the physical world. It does not consider, in a word, that human experience is endurable. Conrad's only unambiguous commitment in the novel is to the stark, magically circular fact of our own—of his own—elementary offensiveness.

As he concluded this most anxious and ugly performance Conrad obviously could not derive comfort from much. Perhaps, though, he could feel a certain excitement about the *potential* authority of his beckoning profession. For if he were caught still in "the invisible sweep" of his own troubled history, in the "bewildered horror" of his own largely empty experience, he at least by writing his two novels had avoided the "magic circle" of suicide, or of lunacy, or of motiveless seafaring. He had yet to contend satisfactorily with "the ba—bare fac—the fact" of his existence. It should be thought triumph enough, though, that in these terrible months of his life he had managed somehow to sustain it.

Chapter Four

. . . Those men who knew how to exist, beyond the pale
of life and within sight of eternity.

(XXIII.25)

Beyond the Pale of Life
The Nigger of the "Narcissus"

However promising the potential uses of authorship may
have seemed to Conrad, his precarious mental balance deteriorated markedly during the months after he completed
An Outcast of the Islands. His letters to Edward Garnett
suggest, in fact, that Conrad suffered something on the
order of a full-scale collapse during the spring and summer
of 1896. In May, for example, he wrote: "I have been rather
ill. Lots of pain, fever, etc. etc. The left hand is useless still"
(Garnett, 53–54). Nine days later he more accurately defined his symptoms:

> I have long fits of depression, that in a lunatic asylum
> would be called madness. I do not know what it is. It
> springs from nothing. It is ghastly. It lasts an hour or a day;
> and when it departs it leaves a fear. (Garnett, 56)

A week later he confessed, "I doubt the sincerity of my
own impressions. . . . I suspect that I am getting through a
severe mental illness" (Garnett, 58). By early August he
evidently was in the throes of a serious mental disturbance:

> I have been living in a little hell of my own; in a place of torment so subtle and so cruel and so unavoidable that the prospect of theological damnation in the hereafter has no more terrors for me. . . . I am paralyzed by doubt and have just sense enough to feel the agony but am powerless to invent a way out of it. (Garnett, 63–64)

In this threatened situation—familiar enough to him by now—Conrad perhaps should have thought to write another novel: the act of authorship, as I have tried to suggest, had sustained him before. But Conrad attempted twice in 1896 to begin a new novel, and twice found himself unable to work.[1] In August, indeed, it seemed to him that he might never write again:

> It seems to me that I have forgotten how to think—worse! how to write. It is as if something in my head had given way to let in a cold grey mist. I knock about blindly in it till I am positively, physically sick—and then I give up saying—tomorrow! And tomorrow comes—and brings only the renewed and futile agony. I ask myself whether I am breaking up mentally. I am afraid of it. (Garnett, 64)

It would seem that Conrad had lost his ability to write for precisely the same reason that earlier he had been *forced* to write. Like Almayer and Willems, he had lost his power of affect, his fragile capacity—and appetite—for personality:

1. Conrad ceased work on *The Sisters* in March 1896 after completing some 10,000 words in draft. (Cf. Baines, 167f; Garnett, 46.) He abandoned *The Rescuer* in August 1896, but returned to the novel intermittently for some twenty years before publishing the book in 1919 as *The Rescue*. (Cf. Baines, 174f; Garnett, 57–59; 63; 64.) During the months in question Conrad did complete three short tales: "The Idiots" (May 1896), "An Outpost of Progress" (July 1896), and "The Lagoon" (August 1896). He began *The Nigger of the "Narcissus"* during the summer of 1896, and completed the work in January 1897.

I feel nothing clearly. And I am frightened when I remember that I have to drag it all out of myself. Other
writers have some starting point. Something to catch hold
of. . . . They lean on dialect—or on tradition—or on history—or on the prejudice or fad of the hour; they trade
upon some tie or some conviction of their time—or upon
the absence of these things—which they can abuse or
praise. But at any rate they know something to begin with—
while I don't. I have had some impressions, some sensations—in my time:—impressions and sensations of common things. And it's all faded—my very being seems faded
and thin like the ghost of a blonde and sentimental
woman, haunting romantic ruins pervaded by rats. I am ex-
ceedingly miserable. (Garnett, 59)

Nothing from the world but vague "impressions and sensations"—and even these had become "a cold grey mist"
which caused him to feel "positively, physically sick."
Conrad had become unable to write because, evidently, he
scarcely felt able to exist. His extraordinary achievement
notwithstanding, he had been unable yet to define for himself a normative relation with existence: [2]

2. It often has been suggested that Conrad's imaginative sterility in 1896
had to do with one or another variety of sexual disturbance. Thomas
Moser, for example, argues that throughout his career Conrad could not
respond imaginatively to the theme of sexuality. Moser believes that
Conrad experienced such extreme difficulty with The Sisters and The Rescuer because both works explicitly engaged his sexual sensibility; The
Nigger of the "Narcissus", Moser asserts, did not, and therefore was com-
paratively easy for Conrad to write (Thomas Moser, Joseph Conrad:
Achievement and Decline [Cambridge: Harvard University Press, 1957],
pp. 50–130). Bernard Meyer believes that Conrad's inability to complete
the works in question ought to be treated as a symptom of Conrad's terror
before the demands of his suddenly expansive sexual life. (Conrad had
married on 24 March 1896.) He suggests that Conrad so enjoyed writing The
Nigger because the novel offered him a species of flight from his burdensome roles as husband and potential father (Meyer, p. 118f).
      Perhaps one ought to attribute Conrad's inability to complete The
Sisters and The Rescuer to the inroads exacted upon the man's creative in-

> Everything seems so abominable [sic] stupid. You see *the belief* is not in me—and without the belief—the brazen thick headed, thick skinned immovable belief nothing good can be done . . .
>
> I doubt everything. The only certitude left to me is that I cannot work for the present.
>
> I hope you never felt as I feel now and I trust that you will never know what I experience at this very moment. The darkness and the bitterness of it is beyond expression. (Garnett, 65; Conrad's emphasis)

His own life had become so difficult that Conrad renounced even his fabled civility: "I must be a perfect fiend to live with—," he told Garnett, "But I don't care who suffers. I have enough of my own trouble" (Garnett, 65–6). A week later he added: "I always told you I was a kind of inspired humbug. Now you know it" (Garnett, 66).

And yet, no matter how seriously threatened,[3] Conrad did not absolutely collapse during these months of torment and terror. If he suffered much misery, he managed to function. And in late August or early September [4]

---

telligence by one or another localized sexual dysfunction. But it seems to me that his inability to write—and, one might add, his putative sexual discomfort as well—should be regarded as a manifestation of the more general dysfunction which I discuss above. I do not doubt, this is to say, that the novels which Conrad felt impelled to abandon in 1896 were particularly uncongenial to him in their theme. But his manic depressive state of mind during these months should have made virtually any theme uncongenial—as it had made his existence itself. It seems to me, then, that Conrad experienced interruption in his ability to write fiction because he felt less and less able in 1896 to separate himself from what then was really his single theme, the uncongeniality of human life.

3. As if not sufficiently taxed during these months, Conrad lost what little money he possessed in an unwise speculation. (Cf. Garnett, 63; Baines, 176.)

4. Conrad wrote the first pages of *The Nigger* in June 1896. He worked

he found in the explicitly autobiographical material of *The Nigger of the "Narcissus"* the "starting point" for which he had yearned. As *The Nigger* expanded from short story to short novel, Conrad's letters to Garnett became increasingly relaxed, even chipper. "I am letting myself go with the *Nigger*," he wrote in November. "He grows and grows. I do not think it's wholly bad though" (Garnett, 74). By the end of the month he felt able to speak of the book as "my Beloved Nigger" (Garnett, 79). In December he informed his friend, "I have turned to with a will" (Garnett, 80)—as if he had referred to his life as much as to his novel. When the influential editor W. E. Henley agreed to serialize *The Nigger* in *The New Review,* Conrad announced his full recovery: "Now I have conquered Henley I ain't 'fraid of the divvle himself" [5] (Garnett, 81). "I think [*The Nigger*] will do!" he declared in January 1897. "It will do!—Mind I only think—not sure. But if I didn't think so I would jump overboard" (Garnett, 83).

Once again, then, Conrad had sustained himself by his developing commitment to authorship. If his first fictional community had failed to provide him with a "whole new set" of usable personalities, his new novel, for reasons which I shall suggest, apparently extended to him at least

---

with concentration on the novel after abandoning *The Rescuer* on 14 August. (Cf. Baines, 177n; LL,I.164.)

5. He later told Garnett, "To tell you the truth, now Henley has *accepted* me I don't care much whether I appear or not in the *N.R.*" (Garnett, 93; my emphasis). In October 1898, he wrote to Henley that his acceptance of *The Nigger* had given him "an intimate, full, complete and pure satisfaction." "I ask myself sometimes," he added, "whether you know exactly what you have given, to whom, how much" (Baines, 219). As I have remarked earlier, Conrad habitually treated other men's—and women's—responses to his fiction as either a certification or rejection of his personality.

the foundation of "a coherent, justifiable personality." No wonder that, when he completed *The Nigger,* he wrote to Garnett: "I have been in bed for two days. A cheap price for finishing that story" (Garnett, 85).

One

Early in *The Nigger of the "Narcissus"* Conrad evokes the memory of a generation of men who seem to him to have managed instinctively the demands of human life. He argues that unlike Almayer or Willems, unlike himself, indeed, the merchant sailors of "past years" (XXIII.126) did not conceive of existence as a forum for individualized experience. They understood, rather, that the universe accommodates insentient animality more freely than it does the modern attitude of "whining" and "sentimental" singularity. "Turbulent," "unruly," "innocent," (XXIII.25) the lost generation of "real men" (XXIII.126) "lived," Conrad tells us, "inarticulate." They were "strong and mute; they were effaced, bowed and enduring, like stone caryatides that hold up in the night the lighted halls of a resplendent and glorious edifice." Like "children" they "knew how to exist beyond the pale of life and within sight of eternity." And this appears to Conrad to have been their justification and reward as much as their condition. Because these "effaced" creatures were able "to exist beyond the pale of life," they seem to him to have achieved release from it—from that bleak "pale" of "doubts," "hopes," and "fear," that close circumference of "dark menace," which appears to Conrad to comprise the entire experience of "their successors" (XXIII.25).

Singleton exists in *The Nigger* as "a lonely relic" of this "devoured and forgotten" (XXIII.24) generation. "Profound and unconscious" (XXIII.131)—the relationship here is causal—Singleton is said to possess "a sharper vision" than his shipmates, "a clearer knowledge" (XXIII.129) than they of the world and of one's place in it. His great authority among the men and within the novel has to do with the totality of his self-effacement. Compared variously to a cannibal chieftain, a cat, a sage, a patriarch, Father Time (XXIII.6; 7; 23; 61; 24), and often to a child (XXIII.6; 24; 25), Singleton is not reportable as a distinct individual. Indeed, he appears not to possess or even to comprehend the modern quality of personality:

> He stood, still strong, as ever unthinking; a ready man with a vast empty past and with no future, with his childlike impulses and his man's passions already dead within his tattooed breast. . . . [He was] meditative and unthinking, reposeful and hopeless, with a face grim and blank—a sixty-year-old child of the mysterious sea. The thoughts of all his lifetime could have been expressed in six words. . . . Singleton lived untouched by human emotions. Taciturn and unsmiling, he breathed amongst us—in that alone resembling the rest of the crowd. (XXIII.24–25; 26; 41)

Like his forebears, Singleton lives as an entity merely. His humanity does not seem to him a moral problem, for he has, apparently, no awareness of his own existence as opposed to that of others. It does not occur to him that one may establish oneself as a discrete consciousness; nor does it strike him that one even vaguely may define certain properties or qualities as one's own. Literally "beyond the pale of life," he conceives of himself not as an organized sensibility but as a machine of sorts: "Through half a century [he] had measured his strength against the favours and the rages of the sea. He had never given a thought to his mortal self" (XXIII.98–99).

This complete effacement of self-regard permits Sin-

gleton a considerable freedom from the pains which crip-
ple each of Conrad's previous characters. Because he invests nothing in "his mortal self" Singleton is oblivious to
the shocks and burdens felt by others. Protected from disappointment or fury by the simplicity of his expectations,
he meets the terrors which afflict more ordinary men with a
presumably impregnable attitude of "hard unconcern, the
chilling air of resignation" (XXIII.130). Singleton in fact
seems to have produced an absolute defense against
Conrad's imagined universe.[6] "With a vast empty past and
with no future, with his . . . passions already dead within
his tattooed breast," he apparently cannot *feel* at all. "Profound and unconscious," he "measured his strength"
against the sea's—a mode of behavior which presents few
opportunities of joy, perhaps, but which permits one an
uncomplicated impression of coherence and justification.[7]
"Monumental, indistinct," (XXIII.129)—the two qualities
seem to Conrad correlative—Singleton stands in *The Nigger* as an apotheosis of authority. "Impassive and big,"
(XXIII.129) he proposes himself to his crew and to his author as an alluring alternative to "mortal self."

Two

The conditions of marine service are so primitively
exacting that they seem to Conrad automatically to produce among all sailors a somewhat similar release from
personality. A compound of "loneliness," "struggle," and

6. As I shall suggest, Singleton's "defense" ultimately is seen to be
porous.

7. I have remarked previously that Conrad once had felt personally susceptible to this simple economy. (Cf. my p. 39.)

"the more trying endurance of small privations and wearisome duties" (XXIII.15), "the austere servitude of the sea" (XXIII.11) does not appear to Conrad to afford men the *luxury* of self-knowledge:

> On men reprieved by its disdainful mercy, the immortal sea confers in its justice the full privilege of desired unrest. Through the perfect wisdom of its grace they are not permitted to meditate at ease upon the complicated and acrid savour of existence. They must without pause justify their life to the eternal pity that commands toil to be hard and unceasing, from sunrise to sunset, from sunset to sunrise. . . . (XXIII.90)

What is wanted in this situation of endless self-sustenance and vindication is simple physical and moral fortitude. Sailors "justify their life," as Conrad believes, by displaying "courage," "endurance," "unexpressed faith," and "the unspoken loyalty that knits together a ship's company" (XXIII.11). It is this fact, indeed, which redeems "the austere servitude of the sea." Sailors seem to Conrad to feel at ease with the terms of their life because the demands placed upon them are so forthright. Unlike Almayer or Willems, the men of the *Narcissus* understand exactly what is required of them; they never are compelled to ask, " 'Where's the sense of all this?' " [8] More important, they are not compelled to conceive of themselves individually. Members of "a ship's company," they have their identity in their function—a function which obviously is communal. "Knit together," they "justify their life" together; they sail their ship as a crew, legitimize themselves as a crew, inevitably conceive of themselves as a crew.

This process of coalesced personality begins from

8. XIV.367. Cf. my p. 140.

the moment the otherwise discriminable men join their ship. *The Nigger's* opening scene presents the crew of the *Narcissus* not as a collection of disparate individuals but as "the forecastle," "the crowd," "the dark group of mustered men," "men in couples or threes" [9] (XXIII.22; 41; 16; 29). The process is confirmed with the issuance of the first command: "The men [were] knitted together aft into a ready group by the first sharp order of an officer coming to take charge of the deck . . ." (XXIII.51). As the voyage proceeds the men spontaneously "knit themselves" into a single, conglomerate entity. Their emotions become as communal as their labor; their gestures seem composite; they express their shared responses to things by the intermingled motion of their separate limbs. The individual men seem, in fact, to comprise a single human body:

> We swung here and there in a body. . . . The wisps of hair and the tangled beards were grey with the salt of the sea. The faces were earthy, and the dark patches under the eyes extended to the ears, smudged into the hollows of sunken cheeks. The lips were livid and thin. . . . The men listened in scattered groups; they leaned on the fife rail, gazing on the deck; they held their chins in their hands thoughtfully, or, with crossed arms and one knee slightly bent, hung their heads in an attitude of upright meditation. . . . They blinked, hesitated clumsily, as if blinded by the strange quality of the hazy light. . . . (XXIII.71; 74; 159; 170)

They become so nearly incorporated with one another that Conrad repeatedly finds it possible—or necessary—to de-

9. Indeed, the men are said to feel acutely uncomfortable when, during the ship's muster, they are forced to acknowledge their individual presences. They each are quick to rejoin "the dark group of mustered men"—to include themselves again, this is to say, in the comfortable anonymity extended by the crew's corporate personality. Cf. XXIII.15–17.

scribe the entire crew as virtually a single character. "The forecastle [10] . . . was going to sleep," he writes:

> The double row of berths yawned black. . . . A leg hung over the edge very white and lifeless. An arm stuck straight out with a dark palm turned up, and thick fingers half closed. Two light snores, that did not synchronise, quarrelled in funny dialogue. (XXIII.22)

At times he even more directly emphasizes the shared identity of the crew: "Elbows dug ribs, faces brightened, lips murmured . . . and all the heads turning *like one* watched with sardonic grins . . ." (XXIII.52; my emphasis).[11]

Seen from Conrad's point of view, the men of the *Narcissus*, like the venerable Singleton, may be thought to derive great benefit from the eradication of their individuality. "Big children" with "simple minds," they live "dreamy-eyed." "Silent, and smiling placidly" (XXIII.6), "industrious and dumb" (XXIII.8), "fiery, menacing, and friendly at the same time" (XXIII.11), they live in an uncomplicated atmosphere of rowdy good will. Unconscious partners with one another, they have it in their power, Conrad believes, to remove themselves from the pain of

10. Conrad uses the word "forecastle" in *The Nigger* to convey a meaning interchangeable, really, with "community" or "society"—as, for example, Jane Austen uses "Highbury" in *Emma,* or George Eliot uses "Middlemarch" in *Middlemarch.* In fact, Conrad often refers specifically to the *Narcissus* as a "minute world." (Cf. XXIII.31; 29; 103.) It may be taken as an indication of how circumscribed Conrad's personal "pale" was in 1896–97 that he felt it necessary to make of a ship's hold *his* metaphor for the social world.

11. Conrad repeatedly suggests in this way the absoluteness of the crew's experience and expression of community. Cf. XXIII.5; 61; 71; 74; 77; 82; 85–86; 88; 92–97; 109; 122; 126; 128; 133; 135; 159; 160; 168; 170–72.

ordinary human existence—from that "frontier of infamy and filth, . . . that border of dirt and hunger, or misery and dissipation, that comes down on all sides to the water's edge . . ." (XXIII.6).

Three

But the crew's happiness and authority depend upon the absoluteness of each of its members' commitment to the sheltering principles of unconsciousness, hard work, and shared identity. Unlike Singleton, who belongs, after all, to another generation, the men of the Narcissus must depend upon one another for their justification and "grace." Most of the men, nearly all, spontaneously submit to the protective ethos of the sea. Donkin and Wait, though, do not. Their refusal to be autonomic, industrious, and undiverse has a devastating effect upon the crew's solidarity and, therefore, upon its well-being. And by the novel's end Donkin and Wait's oddly similar motivations, the very modes of their behavior, come to serve as Conrad's metaphor for "the complicated and acrid savour" of individualized existence—as Conrad's metaphor, indeed, for himself.

Donkin undermines the crew's exuberant harmony from the moment he enters the "clean white forecastle." "A startling visitor from a world of nightmares," he declares his loathsome particularity in his "repulsive and smiling" (XXIII.10) visage, his "incredibly delapidated figure" (XXIII.16):

This clean white forecastle was his refuge; the place where he could be lazy; where he could wallow, and lie and

eat—and curse the food he ate; where he could display his
talents for shirking work, for cheating, for cadging; where
he could find surely some one to wheedle and some one
to bully—and where he would be paid for doing all this.
They all knew him. Is there a spot on earth where such a
man is unknown . . . ? (XXIII.10)

In one encompassing gesture of "ignoble . . . disdain and
hate" (XXIII.11) Donkin announces his disruptive and
deadly genius. " '. . . I can look after my rights!' " he
shrieks. " 'I will show 'em!' " (XXIII.9). It is his only note,
and a terrible one. For, repeated often enough, it erodes
the men's perfect compatibility and thus endangers their
delicate "grace." Donkin's perverse unwillingness to cooperate with the crew's sense of community and purpose, his
strident insistence that every man regard himself as an in-
jured bundle of properties and privileges, inexorably taints
the crew, threatens to make of the men of the *Narcissus* a
contentious crowd of grasping individualists. A genius of
rage and calumny, an excrescence against rational vitality,
Donkin manipulates the men's sensibility, teaches them to
suspect one another, their officers, and the sanction of the
sea. "Fascinating," a "consummate artist" (XXIII.100) full of
"picturesque and filthy loquacity," he infects the men with
his own "poisoned source" (XXIII.101).

Precisely why Donkin should wish to contaminate
his shipmates with this diseased sense of victimization is
not discoverable. Perhaps he merely yearns for fellowship:
if he could believe that everyone on board the *Narcissus*
raged and suffered as much as he, perhaps he might feel
less personally humiliated by the conditions of his life.
Conrad suggests, though, that Donkin is not even so social
as this. He seems to Conrad, rather, simply cantankerous,
an incarnation of loathsomeness as foul and metronomic as

the sound of his squat little name. "A sick vulture" [12] (XXIII.128), Donkin luxuriates in suspicion and hatred (XXIII.38). A "cur," a "blackguard" (XXIII.136), he apparently regards anarchy and violence as self-justifying principles.[13] In fact he seems to Conrad psychopathic. For he has but one urge—the unholy need to defile others' pleasure:

> On all sides invisible men slept, breathing calmly. He seemed to draw courage and fury from the peace around him. Venomous and thin-faced, he glared from the ample misfit of borrowed clothes as if looking for something he could smash. His heart leaped wildly in his narrow chest. They slept! He wanted to wring necks, gouge eyes, spit on faces. (XXIII.132)

Crippled by his grotesque consciousness of assault and loss, Donkin chafes at the quietude and plenty which surround him:

> Donkin [was] . . . like a blind man feeling in his darkness the fatal antagonism of all the surrounding existences, that to him shall for ever remain irrealisable, unseen and enviable. He had a desire to assert his importance, to break, to crush; to be even with everybody for everything; to tear the veil, unmask, expose, leave no refuge—a perfidious desire of truthfulness! (XXIII.149–50)

12. Conrad repeatedly compares Donkin with beasts, particularly with beasts which prey upon dead flesh. Cf. especially XXIII.22; 110; 136.

13. Donkin is "so hot on making trouble," he tells Wait, " 'Cos it's a bloomin' shayme. We are put upon . . . bad food, bad pay . . . I want us to kick up a bloomin' row; a blamed 'owling row that would make 'em remember! Knocking people about . . .brain us . . . indeed! Ain't we men?" (XXIII.112; Conrad's ellipses). He earlier tells Wait that he is "proud" of being "a jail-prop" (XXIII.111).

Donkin is so absolute in his diabolic repudiation of vigorous existence that with marvelous efficiency he carries his destructive compulsion against even himself:

> Donkin sat down heavily; he blew with force through quivering nostrils, he ground and snapped his teeth, and, with the chin pressed hard against the breast, he seemed busy gnawing his way through it, as if to get at the heart within. . . . (XXIII.132; Conrad's ellipsis)

James Wait is not a psychopath—but he establishes himself in *The Nigger* as an even more consumptive creature than Donkin.[14] Set apart from the crew by his ill health,[15] Wait is unable to join in the other men's protective corporateness. At times, indeed, it is difficult to detect him at all. "Tall and powerless," "like an apparition," he behaves throughout the novel "as if distrustful of his own solidity" (XXIII.22; 139; 140). Knowable only as a "sonorous voice" (XXIII.17)—the same shall be said of Kurtz in *Heart of Darkness*—Wait disorganizes the routines of the *Narcissus* in part by his peculiar insubstantiality.

It is Wait's individualism, though, his uncompromising presentation of himself as a separate and singular being, that most threatens the fragile sanctity of the crew. Imperious by nature, Wait makes of his failed health an occasion for radical self-dramatization:

14. Wait presumably suffers, in fact, from tuberculosis—from literal consumption. Meyer suggests that Conrad attempts to "re-order" his reaction to the deaths of his mother and father by recreating in *The Nigger* the disease which killed them. (Meyer, 120–21).

15. Wait is isolated, too, of course, by the fact of his blackness. As Conrad remarks in his Note to the American edition of *The Nigger* (1914), "A Negro in a British forecastle is a lonely being. He has no chums" (XXIII. *Author's Note*, ix).

> That idea of a stalking death [was] thrust at them many
> times a day like a boast and like a menace by this obnox-
> ious nigger. He seemed to take a pride in that death . . . ;
> he was overbearing about it, as if no one else in the world
> had ever been intimate with such a companion; he
> paraded it unceasingly before us. . . . On the slightest
> provocation, he shook before our eyes the bones of his
> bothersome and infamous skeleton. He was for ever trot-
> ting him out. (XXIII.36)

Jimmy's idea of himself as a main force on board the *Narcissus,* as a principle of existence as imperial as the
weather, the captaincy, even the obligation itself to sail the
ship, has the effect of forcing the crew to enter into conscious relationship with the desiccating concept of individualism. On each occasion that they are compelled to acknowledge Jimmy (or, for that matter, Donkin) as a unique
quality, the men are forced to complicate their own ideology of composite identity: if Wait is knowable as a "both-
ersome and infamous" personality, so is each one of them.
Thus, Jimmy seems to the crew "sick," "obnoxious," "infamous," "a mortal enemy," "hateful," "an unfair burden"
(XXIII. 35; 36; 69; 70; 153; 160).

And rightly so. For Wait's obtrusive sense of self ultimately erodes every principle of "grace" conferred upon
the crew by "the immortal sea." Initially he disturbs the
men's comfortable compatibility with the physical universe:

> He seemed to hasten the retreat of departing light by his
> very presence; the setting sun dipped sharply, as though
> fleeing before our nigger; a black mist emanated from
> him; a subtle and dismal influence; a something cold and
> gloomy that floated out and settled on all the faces like a
> mourning veil. (XXIII.34)

In time he disrupts the ship's boisterous routine of life, threatens the crew's sustaining principle of shared experience:

> [He] interfered daily with our occupations, with our leisure, with our amusements. We had no songs and no music within that fo'c'sle as though it had been a church. We ate our meals in silence and dread. . . . (XXIII.36–37)

In the end he undermines the ship's entire ethical structure. By refusing in his "fastidious appetite" to submit to the common menu—to the crew's common personality, as one might say—he virtually compels the susceptible Belfast to steal the officers' Sunday pie. It is a momentous action both in itself and in its consequences. The cook—any ship's domestic center—becomes "overwhelmed with grief"; the men's own privileges are threatened; the mate and captain are made to feel "mistrustful" of the crew. "Such stealing in a merchant ship," the narrator reports, ". . . is a bad symptom":

> It may end in God knows what trouble. The *Narcissus* was still a peaceful ship, but mutual confidence was shaken. . . . We were on doubtful terms with our officers; [16] the cook had given us up for lost; we had overheard the boatswain's opinion that "we were a crowd of softies." We suspected Jimmy, one another, and even our very selves. We did not know what to do. . . . It was a weird servitude. (XXIII.38; 43)

16. At Jimmy's behest the men go so far as to question an officer's order: ". . . The starboard watch came as near as possible to refusing duty, when ordered one morning to wash out their forecastle. It appears Jimmy objected to a wet floor. . . . Only Mr. Baker's delicate tact prevented an all-fired row . . ." (XXIII.46).

Never before have the men of the *Narcissus* had to consider the meaning—the existence, indeed—of their own or "one another's" "very selves." Never before have they had to imagine "what to do": the exacting demands of seafaring and the co-optative "etiquette of the forecastle" (XXIII.41) previously have performed that crucial function for them. The men feel so impotent and uncertain because they have been compelled by the uncooperative Donkin and Wait to engage that "weird servitude" which Conrad believes is implied by the fact itself of individual personality.[17] They feel so disorganized and helpless because they have been forced by the "sick vulture" and "this obnoxious nigger" into "the pale" of ordinary human life. The terms of the novel's drama, then, have been set. Will the men become "a crowd of softies"? Will they succumb to their "whining" and "sentimental" singularity, the "dark menace" of diversified experience? Or will they repudiate Donkin and Wait, those debilitating avatars of the singular self? Will they renounce "the complicated and acrid savour" of individualized existence and become again "strong and mute," safely "effaced," joined once more with the "glorious and resplendent" authenticity of "the immortal sea"?

Four

The terrible Cape hurricane temporarily obscures the novel's "weird" issue. For the storm is so fierce, its

17. It will be recalled that Conrad once described his own character as a burdensome fetter: "One must drag the ball and chain of one's selfhood to the end," he wrote to Mme. Poradowska (*Poradowska,* 72; cf. my p. 67n; 82). I shall return to the question of Conrad's personal investment in the values and action of *The Nigger.*

demands so peremptory, that the men literally do not have time for metaphysical speculation ("They could not spare a moment or a thought from the great mental occupation of wishing to live.") (XXIII.82). Regardless, then, of the discomfort and danger it causes, the hurricane acts upon the crew as a blessing of sorts. The perfect expression of their profession's uncomplicated terms, the storm compels the men once again to measure their strength against the elemental "rages of the sea." Their newly acquired "mortal self" can be of no meaning or use in this basic struggle: the men must either withstand the storm or perish; they must either perform together as an absolute unit or drown "like vermin . . . in a confused mass" (XXIII.58).

Carried in this irresistible and merciful way "beyond the pale" of individualized experience, the crew of the *Narcissus* is reduced by the hurricane's insuperable "grace" to a condition of completed self-effacement: "In all that crowd of cold and hungry men, waiting wearily for a violent death, not a word was heard; they were mute, and in sombre thoughtfulness listened to the horrible imprecations of the gale" (XXIII.61). Clustered once more, the men cling to one another, warm one another, save one another (XXIII.60–63). Connected again in attitude and purpose, they seem, as earlier, to merge in *physical* identity: "They breathed heavily. Their lips twitched, and at every sickening heave of the overturned ship they opened them wide as if to shout. . . . A pair of shoulders would writhe a little. Teeth chattered" (XXIII.61). As if to confirm their recovered coalescence, the sea breaches the forecastle door and carries off the men's "chests, pillows, blankets, clothing" (XXIII.58)—the sad artifacts of their burgeoning particularity. "Apathetic and enduring" (XXIII.82), the men cling in "limp clusters" (XXIII.92) to the ship's ropes and spars.

However bruised, they have legitimized themselves anew—as indicated by the expressive fact that they have forgotten the very existence of Donkin and Wait: "We took no notice of [Donkin]; we hardly gave a thought to Jimmy. . . . There was no leisure for idle probing of hearts. Sails blew adrift. Things broke loose" (XXIII.53).

Five

But this imposed rehabilitation is as momentary as it is accidental. The instant an unnamed sailor asks for the missing Wait the crew's redeeming stupefaction is shattered: "Suddenly some one cried:—'Where's Jimmy?' and we were appalled once more" (XXIII.63).

The men's apprehension is well-founded, for the party which ultimately rescues Jimmy is made to rediscover all the confusion and pain which the hurricane seemingly had exorcised:

> The agony of [Wait's] fear wrung our hearts so terribly that we longed to abandon him, . . . to get out of his hearing, back on the poop where we could wait passively for death in incomparable repose. (XXIII.67)

Wait's hysterical fear demoralizes the men because it re-awakens their awareness of both their situation and their essential separateness.[18] In rescuing Jimmy, that is, the men are forced to engage again Jimmy's odious self-asser-

18. It is as a symptom of this anxiety that the narrator feels it necessary to identify so precisely the crewmen who rescue Jimmy. (XXIII.64–66). Although he has named other characters throughout his description of the gale, he has not before felt obliged to particularize as he does here: the individual men earlier have seemed to him, as I have remarked, discriminable members of one corporate entity.

tiveness, his disconcerting power to declare the "agony" of his own—and his shipmates'—metaphysical condition:

> Jimmy kept up a distracting row; he screamed piercingly, without drawing breath, like a tortured woman; he banged with hands and feet. . . . We could picture him crouching on the edge of the upper berth, letting out with both fists at the wood, in the dark, and with his mouth wide open for that unceasing cry. (XXIII.67)

Wait's battering and screeching, his "letting out with both fists" at the universe, necessarily reminds the men how artificial their own quietude has been—even though the sheer din he raises makes them long for their spurious passivity and "repose." Once again, then, Jimmy's rescuers must make a choice, this time a direct and deliberate one: either "abandon him," as they "longed" to do, or "preserve" him, together with his detestable tendency to promote sentience and singularity.

The men's instinctive decision to save Wait establishes an early juncture in *The Nigger*. For the first time Jimmy's shipmates assume conscious responsibility for their "mortal enemy" (XXIII.70); for the first time they declare their preference for Jimmy's plaintive and solitary sensibility. For the first time, therefore, it may be understood that during the course of the voyage the men of the *Narcissus* involve themselves so fully in "the complicated and acrid savour of existence" because at one or another level of desire they *want* to. The men cannot "be done with it, . . . get away, and lay down to rest somewhere" because, in electing to risk their own lives for Jimmy's, they have confessed that they conceived an irresistible appeal in Wait—which is to say, in the "vexation, the strain, the fatigue" (XXIII.69) of individuated personality.

Conrad emphasizes the importance of the party's

decision by making of Wait's rescue an obtrusively metaphoric drama of parturition. He describes Jimmy's deliverance, that is, as a literal delivery, makes of the men's momentous sponsorship of Wait a symbolic paternity. Thus, the novel locates the rescue in what might appear to be a vaginal canal (". . . That place deep as a well and swaying like a tree . . .") (XXIII.67). The overturned bulkhead is said to be protected by a fearsome layer of sharp tacks and nails which strongly suggest pubic hair (XXIII.67–68). The bulkhead itself evokes the sense of an undilated uterus: "We got to the bulkhead at last. Those were stout planks . . . They were the stoutest planks ever put into a ship's bulkhead . . ." (XXIII.68). Jimmy himself seems unmistakably an anxious (and possibly breeched) foetus:

> We could hear the object of our exasperated solicitude darting to and fro under the planks. He had cracked his voice at last, and could only squeak miserably. His back or else his head rubbed the planks . . . in a puzzling manner. (XXIII.68)

The men finally make [19]—or perceive—a species of opening for Wait: ". . . [Archie] struck time after time in the join of the planks. They cracked. Suddenly the crowbar went halfway in through a splintered oblong hole . . ." (XXIII.69). Jimmy tips at last, and births as he has lived:

> That infamous nigger rushed at the hole, put his lips to it, and whispered "Help" in an almost extinct voice; he

19. Archie performs a brutal episiotomy on the bulkhead with "a crowbar" and "a small hatchet" for scalpels (XXIII.68–69). If Meyer is correct in his hypothesis that The Nigger extended to Conrad "a flight" from Jessie Conrad and "the oppressive embrace of physical intimacy" (Meyer, 123), Archie's savage assault upon the Narcissus's metaphoric labia invites alarming interpretation.

pressed his head to it, trying madly to get through that opening one inch wide and three inches long. . . . Suddenly Jimmy's head and shoulders appeared. He stuck half-way. . . . He was only a cold black skin loosely stuffed with soft cotton wool; his arms and legs swung jointless and pliable; his head rolled about; the lower lip hung down, enormous and heavy. (XXIII.69; 70; 71)

Both parent and physician, the five-man team triumphantly delivers its chosen burden:

Belfast plunged in head and shoulders and groped viciously. "I've got 'im! Got 'im," he shouted. . . . We tugged at [Jimmy's] ears, we panted over him; and all at once he came away in our hands as though somebody had let go his legs. With the same movement, without a pause, we swung him up. (XXIII.70)

The men no longer possess clothing and bedding. But in place of those minor artifacts they symbolically have fathered the principle itself of human singularity—"that pitiful, that limp, that hateful burden" (XXIII.72). Overturned in a gale, the crew of the *Narcissus* has entered "the pale of life" with a vengeance.

Six

The officers' imprecations [20] cannot any longer hold or help the men. Nor, really, can the men's own residual decency: if they prevent Donkin from committing actual murder (XXIII.123), they cannot prevent themselves from committing assault upon their profession's great gift of

20. Cf. XXIII.76; 84–85; 92–93.

grace. For the men no longer consider either their corporateness or their calling self-justifying. They have come to
believe with Donkin and Wait that they are entitled to individual recognition and reward. Indeed, whatever they pur-
port to think of Donkin, they accept his contention that the
sacred life they lead ought to be defined by the sordid ma-
teriality of the shore:

> We began at last to think it was rather awful. . . . [We] lis-
> tened to the fascinating Donkin. His care for our rights, his
> disinterested concern for our dignity, were not discour-
> aged by the invariable contumely of our words, by the dis-
> dain of our looks. . . . He told us we were good men—a
> "bloomin' condemned lot of good men." Who thanked
> us? Who took any notice of our wrongs? Didn't we lead a
> "dorg's loife for two poun' ten a month?" Did we think
> that miserable pay enough to compensate us for the loss
> of our clothes? (XXIII.100)

"Rights"; "dignity"; compensation. The men of the *Narcissus* have exchanged their serene stupefaction for the
unresolvable and "unaccountable ill-will" (XXIII.103) which
Conrad believes is the very condition of individuated consciousness:

> We were indubitably good men; our deserts were great
> and our pay small. . . . We were oppressed by the injus-
> tice of the world, surprised to perceive how long we had
> lived under its burden without realising our unfortunate
> state, annoyed by the uneasy suspicion of our undiscern-
> ing stupidity. . . . On deck the men exchanged bitter
> words, suggested by a silly exasperation against something
> unjust and irremediable that would not be denied. . . .
> (XXIII.101; 102; 103)

The symptoms of the men's sad alteration are immediate and comical. They "dreamed enthusiastically," on the

one hand, "of the time when every lonely ship would travel over a serene sea, manned by a wealthy and well-fed crew of satisfied skippers" (XXIII.103). They expect, on the other, that they may save Wait from death as earlier they had saved him from entrapment—by dint of will and intensity of effort. They are twin impulses, proceeding as they do from "their vague and burning desire" to impose the force of their own "mortal self" upon the restrictive and humiliating structures of the universe. But the men do not know that this is what they want. Indeed, when pressed by their captain to define their demands they find themselves quite unable to respond:

> They wanted great things. And suddenly all the simple words they knew seemed to be lost for ever in the immensity of their vague and buring desire. They knew what they wanted, but they could not find anything worth saying. (XXIII.134)

Only Donkin, the men's tutor, can infer the nature of their shared fear: " 'Are we bloomin' masheens?' inquired Donkin in a piercing tone . . ." (XXIII.121).

The men's moral and linguistic confusion reduces them in the end to a gaggle of chattering beasts: ". . . The men became gesticulating shadows that growled, hissed, laughed excitedly." Their language, which earlier had been joyful, even sweet, sounds now a foul admixture of "growls and screeches," "exclamation and . . . curse," "menacing mutters." The men can communicate only in a "burst of squabbling uproar," "confused shouts," "a stormy chaos of speech" (XXIII.121; 122; 128). They continue to act in unison, but their corporateness has become as perverted as their "facile emotion" (XXIII.122). "A dark mass," a "black cluster of human forms" (XXIII.122; 123), they seem to their captain not men at all (XXIII.121). To their narrator they seem "like animals going into lairs" (XXIII.130). " 'They're gone silly,' " [21] Mr. Baker remarks.

The men have been afflicted with more than mere silliness, though. The narrator thinks that "the fit emblem of their aspirations" is death itself [22] (XXIII.122). If he exaggerates (the men do not actually kill anyone, after all) it is true that their senseless agitation provokes Donkin into a murderous attack (XXIII.123). Worse, perhaps, their "row" so excites the helmsman that he abandons the helm—that he, in effect, renounces on behalf of the crew the ship, the ethos of seafaring, and the instinct itself of survival. Left to herself, the Narcissus turns, wallows, nearly flounders: "It was as if an invisible hand had given the ship an angry shake to recall the men who peopled her deck to the sense of reality, vigilance, and duty" (XXIII.124).

Wait radically exacerbates the crew's "silly" reaction against "the sense of reality." In his steadfast refusal to acknowledge his moribundity, his wilfully "untruthful attitude in the face of the inevitable truth" (XXIII.138), he seems to the men "a manifestation grand and incomprehensible" (XXIII.138), a rallying point for their own "exasperation" with the universe. Shorn of their faith in earlier models, they make Jimmy's mechanism of resistance their own. However "droll" (XXIII.138), his self-asser-

21. A year after completing The Nigger, Conrad described to R. B. Cunninghame Graham his impression of human nature—an impression which had informed this and the concluding scenes of the novel. "Not that I think humankind intrinsically bad," he wrote to Cunninghame Graham. "It is only silly and cowardly. Now You know that in cowardice is every evil . . ." (Watts, 68; Conrad's emphasis). (Cf. XXIII.103 and 130; XXIII.130 quoted above.)

22. The narrator later likens the forecastle—previously described as the very cathedral of the men's faith, authenticity, and vigorousness—to "a crypt" (XXIII.129).

tiveness seems to them redemptive and heroic; they admire and try to appropriate his apparently triumphant singularity: "He was unique, and as fascinating as only something inhuman could be. . . . He influenced the moral tone of our world." It need not be said that Wait's influence fails to stand the men in good stead:

> He was demoralising. Through him we were becoming highly humanised, tender, complex, excessively decadent; we understood the subtlety of his fear, sympathised with all his repulsions, shrinkings, evasions, delusions—as though we had been over-civilised, and rotten, and without any knowledge of the meaning of life. . . . We were inexpressibly vile and very much pleased with ourselves. (XXIII.139)

The preference which the crew implicitly had declared by its rescue of Wait has become, then, programmatic. The men actively have renounced their "knowledge of the meaning of life." "Effaced" no more, they long to exchange their unconsciousness and perfect commonalty—"the realm of safety and peace" (XXIII.138) for Jimmy's "superb impudence" (XXIII.141). As might "a crowd of ambitious lubbers" (XXIII.139), they invest all their hopes and needs, their whole idea of existence, in "the developing anxiety not to see Wait die" [23] (XXIII.138). "Lubberly fools" (XXIII.142), the men of the *Narcissus* barter their received authenticity for the "inexpressibly vile" appeal of a "moral trick" (XXIII.139). They have preferred Donkin and Wait to Singleton, "the pale of life" to "the true peace of God" (XXIII.31).

23. In a sense never fully defined in the novel, Wait affects the course of nature in much the same way in which he affects the emotions of the crew. (Cf. XXIII.130; 142–43.) Perhaps, then, the men ought not to be too much condemned for their apostasy.

Seven

The men have so much invested in their "trick" of defying reality that Wait's death seems to them an explicitly moral calamity: [24]

> Jimmy's death, after all, came as a tremendous surprise. We did not know till then how much faith we had put in his delusions. . . . His death, like the death of an old belief, shook the foundations of our society. A common bond was gone; the strong, effective and respectable bond of a sentimental lie. (XXIII.155)

Wait's "going" not only invalidates the men's systematic revision of reality but as well erodes what little sense of community remains to them:

> In going he took away with himself the gloomy and solemn shadow in which our folly had posed, with humane satisfaction, as a tender arbiter of fate. And now we saw it was no such thing. It was just common foolishness; a silly and ineffectual meddling with issues of majestic import [25]. . . . We were profoundly scandalised with each other. Men spoke unkindly to their best chums. Others refused to speak at all. (XXIII.156)

24. It is Donkin, oddly, who explodes the myth of Wait's "unquenchable life" (XXIII.140). In his perfidious truthfulness he perceives that Jimmy is not a "manifestation grand and incomprehensible" but a nonentity, a fraud. " 'Yer nobody!' " he sneers. " 'Yer nobody. Yer no one at all! . . . Yer bloomin' useless fraud. . . . Ye're a thing—a bloody thing. Yah—you corpse!' " (XXIII.150–52). His perception is unpleasant and his use of it is characteristically cruel. But by effectively killing Wait Donkin does manage to return the men to "the sense of reality." In a sense, therefore (albeit a peculiar sense), he, and not Allistoun or Baker or Singleton, must be regarded as the savior of the ship and the crew.

25. Cf. my p. 166n.

As the *Narcissus* enters the English Channel, then, her crew's original justification and "grace" have disintegrated. Obstinately self-conscious, deliberately individual, the men have chosen absolutely to reject the "safety and peace" extended by the sea. Filled already with "mental disquiet" (XXIII.156), they must now confront the "mad jumble" (XXIII.164) of the "soulless" and "sordid earth" (XXIII.165).

The very image of "the pale of life"—of the crew's chosen way of being—the shore appears in *The Nigger* as a hideous embodiment of ugliness and malignant unreality.[26] "One unbroken line of gloom" (XXIII.162), the land encloses the *Narcissus* and saps her fragile vitality:

> The *Narcissus* came gently into her berth; the shadows of soulless walls fell upon her, the dust of all the continents leaped upon her deck, and a swarm of strange men, clambering up her sides, took possession of her in the name of the sordid earth. She had ceased to live. (XXIII.165)

The men have disavowed their legitimizing corporateness; but as they depart the ship they find themselves co-opted into a new coalition, this one "precious and disgusting" (XXIII.165). For, stripped as they are of the special sanction available to a sailing ship at sea, the men cannot help but join "the mysterious and unholy" combine of "the busy earth" (XXIII.170):

> A low cloud hung before [the *Narcissus*]—a great opalescent and tremulous cloud, that seemed to rise from the

26. In spite of his marvelous and moving animosity against London, Conrad describes his adopted country as the most desirable of nations. (XXIII.162–63). The distinction which he accords to the city is ambiguous, though, for he suggests that all life as it is lived on shore is "unholy"—indeed, unbearable.

> steaming brows of millions of men. Long drifts of smoky
> vapours soiled it with livid trails; it throbbed to the beat of
> millions of hearts, and from it came an immense and la-
> mentable murmur—the murmur of millions of lips praying,
> cursing, sighing, jeering—the undying murmur of folly,
> regret, and hope exhaled by the crowds of the anxious
> earth. (XXIII.163–64)

"Scattered by the dissolving contact of the land"
(XXIII.167), the men inevitably include themselves in this
uninviting federation—the "deafened and distracted"
(XXIII.170) community of those already overcome by "the
complicated and acrid savour" of individuated existence.

And yet, there is much remaining to the crew which
the novel encourages us to admire, perhaps even to envy.
For if the men have not been able to make themselves altogether saintly, if they have refused an impersonal and
often joyless way of life which Conrad should have
cherished for himself, they do still retain a careless insensibility which fascinates and deeply attracts their author.
However "discomposed" (XXIII.170), they continue in their
"irresolute and noisy" (XXIII.171) gregariousness, their easy
responsiveness to life's stimuli. Their pleasures seem to
Conrad facile, their hopes and ideas illusory. But at least
they *have* appetites; and they have them readily—even
chemically:

> They were bound for the Black Horse, where men, in fur
> caps with brutal faces and in shirt sleeves, dispense out of
> varnished barrels the illusions of strength, mirth, happi-
> ness; the illusion of splendour and poetry of life, to the
> paid-off crews of southern-going ships. (XXIII.171)

"Reckless and joyous," "mad" (XXIII.172) perhaps, they
leave the novel at once diminished and raised, at once fail-

ures of the human spirit and guarantors of it. The men of the *Narcissus* do not become what they might have been. But no matter how disorganized or scarred, embattled or deluded, they apparently manage to live in close familiarity with happiness.

Eight

One cannot say as much for *The Nigger*'s narrator.[27] Although he has been at great pain in his account of the voyage to attach himself to the emotions and affections of the crew, the narrator apparently discovers little in common between himself and his shipmates. Brilliantly conscious, instinctively metaphysical in his intelligence, he seems detached from the men's "irresolute and noisy" mode of life both by the disposition and the power of his mind. The men pack pipes, pick teeth, tie knots, tell tales. The narrator thinks, inquires, describes. They enact, he examines. They perform, he explains. As if disconcerted by their odd comrade's probing, essentially unparticipative presence, the uncomplicated seamen scarcely acknowledge the narrator's existence. No one speaks to him. No one calls him by name. No officer gives him a parting word. Only Craik in *The Nigger*'s last pages explicitly addresses the estranged and lonely creature—and that when no one else will have anything to do with his own unbal-

27. Nor, curiously, can one say as much for Singleton. Alone among the men Singleton has been impervious to the corrupting appeal of Donkin and Wait. But *he* is disabled by a more simple and harsh inflection of "the sense of reality." Unable to accommodate the fact of his age (XXIII.97–99), Singleton is said to feel, if not quite yet to have become, "broken at last" (XXIII.99). He leaves the novel "uncertain" and unsteady, apparently without resource for recovery (XXIII.168–69).

anced grief. It confirms and completes one's impression of the narrator as a solitary and socially damaged man that he is unable to endure even this simple wish for sympathy. So embarrassed is he by the single recorded appeal to his humanity that he "disengages" himself from it for fear, as he puts it, that Craik will end by fighting with him or that, of all things, the "bulky policemen" on the corner disapprove of their conversation (XXIII.171).

Once they have been paid off the men are able to make unmistakably clear their already evident discomfort with the narrator: freed of the arbitrary (and for *this* reason celebrated?) intimacy of the forecastle, the crew goes off in a "reckless and joyous" body, excluding from its company only Donkin, the half-maddened Craik, the cabin boy Charley—and the narrator.[28] The narrator signals his understanding of his implicit ostracism by shifting for the first time in the novel from the inclusive to the exclusive voice:

> Outside, on Tower Hill, *they* blinked, hesitated clumsily. . . . "To the Black Horse! To the Black Horse!" cried some. "Let *us* have a drink together before *we* part." *They* crossed the road, clinging to one another. Only Charley and Belfast wandered off alone. As *I* came up I saw a red-faced, blowsy woman . . . fall on Charley's neck. It was his mother. (XXIII.170; my emphases)

Only Belfast [29] and Charley walked alone, indeed! And Charley at least keeps company with his mother, however disreputable she may be. No, only the narrator and Belfast are quite alone at the novel's end, and, as I have remarked,

28. Singleton previously has disassociated himself from the crew: "Someone opened a door for him, and the patriarchal seaman passed through unsteadily, without as much as a glance at any of us" (XXIII.169).

29. Craik is nicknamed "Belfast."

the narrator wants nothing to do with Belfast's proffered friendship: " 'So long!' I said, and went on *my* way." (XXIII.171; my emphasis)

The narrator's "way" seems a sad and sterile one. He describes the future course of his existence by discriminating himself absolutely from the men whom he always before has envied and the mode of being which he always before has cherished:

> But at the corner I stopped to take my last look at the crew of the *Narcissus*. . . . From afar I saw them discoursing, with jovial eyes and clumsy gestures, while the sea of life thundered into their ears ceaseless and unheeded. . . . I never met one of them again. But at times the spring-flood of memory sets with force up the dark River of the Nine Bends. Then on the waters of the forlorn stream drifts a ship—a shadowy ship manned by a crew of Shades. They pass and make a sign, in a shadowy hail. Haven't we, together and upon the immortal sea, wrung out a meaning from our sinful lives? Good-bye, brothers! You were a good crowd. As good a crowd as ever fisted with wild cries the beating canvas of a heavy foresail; or tossing aloft, invisible in the night, gave back yell for yell to a westerly gale. (XXIII.171; 173)

Presumably the narrator turns that corner to leave not only *The Nigger* and the *Narcissus* but the life of the sea as well. Certainly he does everything but say that he will not sail again ("[I] went on *my* way"; "I never met one of them again"; "Good-by, brothers!"). Much as he has loved the sea and the habits of life it recommends, the narrator evidently has been taught by his shipmates' harsh disdain that their "joyous" way of being cannot contain him as it can "the ignorant hearts that know nothing of life" (XXIII.31). If he wishes like the men of the *Narcissus* not to "heed" life but simply and deeply to respond to it—like his shipmates to make "merry in the storm" (XXIII.172)—he finds that he cannot now and perhaps never could. For the narrator's eyes are not so jovial as his fellows', nor his gestures so careless; he has more terrible gales than they to resist; he has other meanings to wring from a separate sense of sin.

This is not to say that *The Nigger* extends to its chief character an easy, emptily formal maturation. It is true that, as he confronts the fact of his incompatibility with the crew, the narrator is able to say, " 'So be it! Let the earth and the sea each have its own' " (XXIII.172). But in consigning himself to the "soulless," "lifeless" earth the narrator has not achieved precisely a renewal of himself. Like that other isolated soul, James Wait, he rather has been forced in the course of the voyage to adjust to an inexorable passing from a preferred mode of being; he has been compelled, in fact, consciously to enter into a state of existence which he has been careful to characterize as exanimate and unreal. For all the other creatures in the novel who accept the life of the "earth" before that of the sea have seemed to the narrator egregious and repulsive—"a toff in a black coat and high hat"; "sallow-faced men"; "a pasty-faced clerk" stark and dull like "a caged bird" [30] (XXIII.165; 164; 167). Genuine "Shades," these; and it is with their company that the narrator has aligned himself. It must be said, indeed, that in connecting himself with the lifelessness of the shore he directly associates himself with the dreadful Donkin:

30. By way of expressing his contempt for their vacuousness, the narrator goes so far as to describe landspeople with the neuter personal pronoun: "A toff in a black coat and high hat scrambled with agility . . . *It* was [the second mate's] brother . . . A lady appeared suddenly . . . *It* was the Master's wife" (XXIII.165; my emphases). Later he adds, ". . . I saw a red-faced, blowsy woman. . . . It was [Charley's] mother" (XXIII.170).

Singleton has no doubt taken with him the long record of his faithful work into the peaceful depths of an hospitable sea. And Donkin, who never did a decent day's work in his life, no doubt earns his living by discoursing with filthy eloquence upon the right of labour to live. So be it! Let the earth and the sea each have its own. (XXIII.172)

The narrator, then, cannot leave *The Nigger* with the fresh hope of Paul Morel, or the inflated self-esteem of Stephen Dedalus, or even the mad impersonality of Hans Castorp. He leaves the novel—and the sea—as presumably he came to it, full of pain and without help for his suddenly confronted needs. Perhaps narrating *The Nigger*, returning in imagination to earlier days of deluded peace, has made more full for the narrator an experience which does not appear to have been at any time before either happy or wholly expressed. One hopes so, because if "the regions of memory that know nothing of time" (XXIII.149) can do so much as this, perhaps one need not be troubled by one's necessary association of the narrator with Conrad himself. For as we read *The Nigger* are we not invited to speculate how many times in his sea-going life Conrad must have taken to ship to flee from his own tormented idea of himself? And are we not meant to wonder on how many filthy quays of how many sordid ports Conrad himself must have stood while less complicated men rushed off to drink, chattering in English, without care or farewell for their alien mate?

Nine

It would appear, in any event, that by making imaginative demand upon his sadly unfulfilling career at sea the

narrator learns tentatively to escape its manifold restric-
tions and untruths; that by confronting his artificially sustained sense of himself he learns to accept, if not yet to admire or fully to enjoy, his actual identity. I think that
Conrad devises so complicated a role for his narrator because he had himself undergone a similar experience in
writing *Almayer's Folly, An Outcast of the Islands,* and, in
particular, *The Nigger* itself. I believe, that is, that Conrad
wrote *The Nigger* primarily to explore and to reinforce that
developing process of reconciliation with his own
character—or, as I have put it earlier, that continuing *cre-*
ation of his character—which he had begun in 1889. If
Conrad did discover in literature so much authority over
his past, if the claims of fiction extended for him so richly
to those of experience, *The Nigger* must be read not simply
as an adventure of the sea or as a testimonial to a beloved
way of life but as an extraordinary experiment in autobiography. No doubt this is what Conrad meant to imply when
he remarked of the novel:

> It is the book by which, not as a novelist perhaps, but as
> an artist striving for the utmost sincerity of expression, I
> am willing to stand or fall. . . . After writing the last words
> of that book, in the revulsion of feeling before the ac-
> complished task,[31] I understood that I had done with the
> sea, and that henceforth I had to be a writer. (XXIII. To My
> Readers in America)

No wonder, then, Conrad was so excited by his third
novel—and so confident and quick about its composition.
The Nigger did not propose itself to him as an escape from
the reality of his experience; far from it. It seemed to him,

31. Cf. my p. 81–82.

rather, directly to engage his history at last, to address itself outright to that opportunity for self-elaboration which originally had made authorship seem to him an inviting and necessary act.

But for Conrad no more than for his narrator does *The Nigger* extend a comfortable accommodation with existence. For if by composing the novel Conrad resolved to regard himself as a writer, he did not learn to suppose that writing is an acceptable occupation for a man. It seems to me, indeed, that much of *The Nigger*'s peculiarly intense animosity against Donkin and Wait has to do with Conrad's anger against himself—with Conrad's frightened concern about the procedures and assumptions which had come to govern his own linguistic enterprise. Certainly he makes it one of the points of the novel to suggest that sophisticated uses of language are linked inextricably with violent, nihilistic, and cowardly human impulses.[32] James Wait, for example, is said first to captivate the crew with his voice, which is deep, resonant, as richly modulated—or crafted— as any writer's more consciously stylized prose. Wait plays with such authority upon the resources of language that he seems at times to compel the crew by the force more of his rhetoric than of his personality or action:

32. By contrast, the novel's chief ethical agent achieves his authority at least in part because he rejects language as an instrument of his existence. Singleton rarely speaks in *The Nigger* because he is able to imagine for the larger portion of his life that he is perfectly suited to the demands of his experience. When forced to speak he does so reluctantly—and exclusively to satisfy others' needs. His language invariably is automatic, unarbitrated, apparently compelled from primal qualities for the service of mankind (e.g., "The wisdom of half a century spent in listening to the thunder of the waves had spoken unconsciously through his old lips." [XXIII.24]). It is the final mark of his primacy in the novel that Singleton cannot sign his name, that he has not felt even this, the most primitive, urge to write (XXIII.167–68).

He enunciated distinctly, with soft precision. The deep, rolling tones of his voice filled the deck without effort. He was naturally scornful, unaffectedly condescending, as if from his height of six feet three he had surveyed all the vastness of human folly and made up his mind not to be too hard on it. . . . [His] words, spoken sonorously, with an even intonation, were heard all over the ship, and [his demands were] put in a manner that made refusal impossible. (XXIII.18–19)

Similarly, Donkin's authority with the crew is said to be based less upon the persuasiveness of his ideas than upon the power of his rhetoric. The men do not believe at heart in Donkin's unreasonable arguments and theories. But they are unequipped to resist his uses of language, which, however unconscious, are brilliantly manipulative. Donkin is an instinctive phrasemaker, a speaker of such mesmerizing resourcefulness that in his exasperation the narrator calls him a "consummate artist" (XXIII.100).

It is a stunning description, connecting as it does Donkin's devices and temperament with Conrad's own. The association, always implied, is secured by the novel's equation of Donkin's desire "to tear the veil" with "a perfidious desire of truthfulness" (XXIII.50); for Conrad is at much labor in his celebrated Preface to *The Nigger* to suggest that, like Donkin, "The artist . . . *seeks the truth* and makes his appeal" [33] (XXIII.*Preface*, xi; my emphasis). The inclination and power to disclose the truth perhaps should seem to most men unambiguously desirable. But not to Conrad, because he fears—correctly, I think—that

33. In a letter to one of his readers, Conrad defined his pleasure with *The Nigger* in a way which emphasizes the association which I remark: "Candidly, I think [*The Nigger*] has certain qualities of art that make it a thing apart. I tried *to get through the veil* of details at the essence of life" (LL,I.200; my emphasis).

"the truth" to which *he* is in response is sociopathic and perhaps cannot be borne by men. Conrad in some respects feels appalled by his second career, that is, because he fears to leave men "no refuge"; because he fears that by defining the scarified patterns of his intelligence he must make his readers' lives as disordered, painful, and self-destructive as his own. No doubt it is for this reason that Conrad expresses in the novel's last paragraphs such relieved pleasure that the crew of the *Narcissus* retains its "veil," that the men remain able to maintain against even the realities which the voyage has exposed "the illusions of strength, mirth, happiness; the illusion of splendour and poetry of life. . . ." Of all things in *The Nigger* Conrad most dislikes "the truth," even the novel's own truth, because he does not wish other men to be provoked, like Donkin, Wait, the narrator—or himself—into a condition of futile reaction against either their own character or the inalterable circumstances of existence.

As I have implied, Conrad goes so far in *The Nigger* as to connect his own temperament as an artist with the misanthropic psychologies of Donkin and Wait. He seems often to suspect, that is, that he writes much as Donkin orates: merely "to assert his importance" in the face of his estrangement from "all the surrounding existences, that to him shall remain for ever irrealisable, unseen, and enviable." [34] Worse, he appears in his careful association of himself with Donkin to suggest that he shares something of that "sick vulture's" psychotic compulsion simply "to break, to crush; to be even with everybody for everything. . . ." He appears to fear, in a word, that he writes—and shatters other men's more comfortable imagina-

34. Cf. my p. 68–69.

tions [35]—because he feels, like Donkin, a diseased need to punish the society at large for his own ineradicable experience of isolation, poverty, and self-doubt. And if, perhaps, he does not consider himself so absolutely rapacious as Donkin, Conrad unquestionably thinks himself like him— and like Wait—in the solipsism engendered by his new profession. For authorship, as Conrad confessed in *A Personal Record,* is "a task which mainly consists in laying one's soul more or less bare to the world" (VI. *Preface,* xix). At the very least he indicates in *The Nigger* that he feels anxious about this fact. The novel repeatedly takes the crew to task, after all, for its inveterate interest in individual identity; yet, as a writer Conrad concerns *him*self with nothing but his own "soul"—and requires his readers to do the same with theirs. In this he likely thinks himself akin above all to Wait, to that "Negro in a British forecastle" who so disturbs and threatens his small society by refusing to acknowledge any other substance in the universe but his own thirsting sensibility.[36]

All of this is as nothing, though, when compared with Conrad's greater reservation about his craft, his increasing understanding that, unlike sailors, novelists do not achieve "reckless and joyous" life of their own; they

35. It is significant in this regard that Conrad borrows Donkin's most "perfidious" phrase in his own most perfidious letter. Conrad's fascinating and terrible metaphor of the "knitting-machine" has its origin, I think, in Donkin's "piercing" question, " 'Are we bloomin' masheens?' " (XXIII.121; cf. my p. 165). Conrad's letter is reprinted in Watts, pp. 56–57; cf. my p. 188–89.

36. Or perhaps, at a less complicated level, Conrad merely fears that, like Donkin and Wait, writers are malingerers; that one commits by writing fiction a wilful evasion of "a decent day's work" (XXIII.172). It may have been to counter this interesting anxiety that in his letters Conrad complains so vociferously to his friends that he is working hard—that, indeed, no other task could be more difficult for him than to write books.

rather document or imagine others'. Already separated by his history and disposition from the seamen's "irresolute and noisy" authenticity, Conrad at times in *The Nigger* appears to consider that by becoming a writer he has committed his existence to a virtually institutional rejection of his former shipmates' redeeming simplicity and genuineness.[37] Certainly he felt some such emotion as he wrote the novel, for he confessed on several occasions during the period in question that he thought himself only peripherally human. To Edward Sanderson, for example, he wrote:

> I am getting more sophisticated from day to day. And more uncertain! . . . I would blaze like a bonfire and shall consume myself to give the feeble glimmer of a penny dip,—if even so much.[38] (LL.,I.,196)

To Garnett he remarked:

> Events crowd and push and nothing happens. You know what I mean. The opportunities do not last long enough. Unless in a boy's book of adventures. Mine were never finished. They fizzled out before I had a chance to do more than another man would. (Garnett, 80)

And to R. B. Cunninghame Graham—the very model of authentic personality—he admitted: "When I think of you I feel as tho' I had lived all my life in a dark hole without ever seeing or knowing anything" (Watts, 64).

37. It might be remarked, for example, that as *The Nigger*'s author Conrad narrates a narrator's narration, and thus exists at a double remove from the seamen's primal naturalness.

38. Some months earlier Conrad had written to Edward Noble, ". . . I shall be used up in a short and miserable splutter of dim flame" (LL,I.176).

Ten

And yet, if Conrad imagined that in becoming an author he had become a frightful combination of Wait, Donkin, and the narrator, of invalid, agitator, and wraith, he did discover by writing *The Nigger* that torment and impending dissolution may be made to yield to determined resistance. His strategy in this regard was related to the narrator's. Like his imagined man, Conrad managed his unsatisfactory experience in 1896–1897 by writing literature about it; he furnished his otherwise empty life by shaping a drama around it. No matter how deeply unsettled he may have felt by the implications of authorship—unsettled in ways which he should remain unable to resolve until he wrote *Lord Jim* in 1900—, Conrad seized with splendid courage upon what hope he was able to derive from his new profession. Thus, he remarked to Charles Zagórski:

> Only literature remains to me as a means of existence. You understand, my dear friend, that if I have undertaken this thing, it is with the firm resolution to make a name—and I have no doubt that I shall be successful in this connection. I know what I can do. (LL.,I.,185)

To make a name. For Conrad that normally metaphoric phrase operated in a literal way: he had still to design and sustain a character, and to convince others by the mere effectiveness of his language that the artifice was real. No wonder, then, that he released *The Nigger* with some trepidation—for how much he had at stake in his novel's complicated textures:

> I shall buy chickens, make them sacred, watch the auspices of the sky, the flight of crows—the agitations of plan-

ets. Never was ambitious scoundrel of republican Rome more anxious about the signs of the future. And if I knew of a temple anywhere—of an undesecrated temple, within the land—I would go scattering flowers, offering sacrifices, and prostrate on marble floors at the foot of lofty columns, beseech the gods. . . . I do not ask myself how much I have succeeded. I only dare to hope that [*The Nigger*] is not a shameful failure, that perhaps, here and there, may be found a few men and women who will see what I have tried for. It would be triumph enough for me. (Garnett, 82; LL.,I.,200)

The astonishing decade of creative genius which *The Nigger* introduces suggests the delighted and powerful use to which the "ambitious scoundrel" put his evolving theory of self-generation; perhaps his future "triumph" even confirms the novel's assertion that imaginatively to engage one's "sinful life" may be to "wring out a meaning" from it. It is for this reason appropriate, in any event, that *The Nigger* does not dramatically conclude, that the narrator, ready to commence a second but undefined life, simply terminates his narrative on a busy London corner. So, too, must the narrator's narrator detach *himself* from the novel. Conrad leaves *The Nigger* knowing only (at the age of thirty-nine) that "the artist descends within himself"; that in the as-yet undefined second half of his own life he must carry his "justification in every line"; that, before all else, he must be "sincere" (XXIII.*Preface*, xii; xi; xiii). Unlike most other autobiographies, then, *The Nigger of the "Narcissus"* is open to further history, is anticipative of ongoing struggle and continuing pain. How curious and admirable one must find it that a writer so fundamentally discomforted by the act of writing should have invested so much in its processes—or that a man who believed himself so radically estranged from the "pale" of human experience should have opened himself so unequivocally to it.

Chapter Five

I am not able to say one cheering word. It seems to me I
am disintegrating slowly. Cold shadows stand around. . . .
I am too wretched, and its [*sic*] worse than the plague.
(Watts, 111)

Regression
1897-1899

If by writing *The Nigger of the "Narcissus"* Conrad had
made his personality more "coherent," he had still to secure his created character and to "justify" it to himself. In
some respects *The Nigger* seemed itself to discharge this
crucial function. The book's reviews were generous.[1] William Blackwood made an offer for all of his future work
which was "so flattering," as Conrad put it, "that for a
whole day I walked about with my nose in the air"
(LL,I.,206). More important, the novel excited the regard of
certain readers whose attention Conrad long had wished to
attract. "The clearest gain so far from *The Nigger*," he exul-
ted, "was the other day a letter from [Sir Arthur Quiller-
Couch]":

> The excellent man,—may his star ever be propitious,—
> writes enthusiastically a message short but packed full of
> sweetness. . . . In this way I am paid for the life and the
> writing that went up to the making of the book. . . . In a

1. Cf. LL,I.219.

sense it is enough. When writing one thinks of half a dozen (at least I do) men or so,—and if these are satisfied and take the trouble to say it in so many words, then no writer deserves a more splendid recompense. (LL,I.,219)

"On the other hand," as Conrad went on to remark, "there is the problem of the daily bread which cannot be solved by praise, public or private" (LL,I.,219). "I enjoy a good reputation," he acknowledged, "but no popularity" (LL,I.,217). Conrad's financial "problem," always acute, became drastically intensified in April 1897, when Jessie, whom Conrad had married in March 1896, discovered that she had become pregnant. Conrad wrote:

> Something always turns up to give a turn to the screw. . . . Every added happiness is another terror added to life [2]. . . . That I shall someday attain material success there is no reason to doubt. But that requires time and meanwhile??? (LL,I.,218–19; 217)

"Meanwhile???," indeed. Under the pressure of his "terror" Conrad tried desperately to complete new work. But more than any other novelist who has ever lived, perhaps, Conrad could not write merely to earn money: given the self-generative nature of *his* enterprise, he could not well hope to perform under merely economic impulsion.

And so, in fact, he could not. Compelled to work impersonally, Conrad found himself scarcely able to work at all.[3] "Horribly irritable and muddle-headed" (Garnett, 98),

2. Meyer offers an interesting account of Conrad's anxiety at the prospect of becoming a father (Meyer, 125–32). The analysis is marred, though, by Meyer's peculiar attitude of contempt toward Conrad's rather justifiably intense fear. I shall return to the point.

3. Meyer suggests that Conrad in fact *elected* to experience difficulty with "The Return" because "he unconsciously identified himself with his preg-

he wrote to his publisher in July 1897, ". . . I am worried almost to death by a short story ["The Return"] I have been trying to write for the last three months. . . . I can't shake it off—but I am doing my best to murder it . . ." (Blackburn, 8). The following day he remarked to Sanderson:

> I've been ten weeks trying to write a story of about 20 pages of print. I haven't finished it yet! and what I've written seems to me too contemptible for words. . . . This state of affairs spells Ruin,—and I can't help it,—I can't. (LL,I.,206–7)

". . . That story has been a heavy trial to me while I was writing it," he told Garnett. "It has made me ill: I hated while I wrote. . . . It is bad—and in sober truth I can't bear the sight of it any more" (Garnett, 109;129). In August he added, ". . . I have a physical horror of that story. I simply won't look at it any more. It has embittered five months of my life. I hate it" (Garnett, 106).

In his by now automatic way, Conrad went so far as to treat the inevitable deficiencies of "The Return" as hard evidence of his personal illegitimacy. "I've egregiously failed" (Garnett, 107), he told Garnett:

> How horribly tired of me you must be. . . . I am too obtuse. . . . But my feelings are fine enough for me to be horrified at the thought of all the time you are wasting upon my unworthy person. . . . There is not a single redeeming line in ["The Return"]!! I can't look at it. . . . I should not have written that thing. It's criminal. (Garnett, 108)

---

nant wife" and wished to imitate her physiological distress (Meyer, 127–28). I think the view far-fetched. Meyer is closer to the truth, perhaps, when he remarks that "the subject of the story—the breakup of a marriage—was too close to [Conrad's] own discomfort as a married man to permit him to compose with ease and detachment" (Meyer, 125).

The story's impotence struck him as the sign of his own ir-
redeemable vapidity:

> I am unreal even when I try for reality, so when I don't try I
> must be exasperating. I feel like a man who can't move, in
> a dream. To move is vital—it's salvation—and I can't! . . .
> It's like being in a cataleptic trance . . . I feel—and I can't
> understand. I am stirred—and I can't grasp my own emo-
> tion . . . I don't think I will ever write anything more. That
> shall wear off. . . . (Garnett, 108–10)

"That" did wear off. But it was not the "infernal Return" (Garnett, 104) alone which dissatisfied and exhausted
Conrad during this long period of his hysterical retrogres-
sion. As if in unconscious testimony to his inability to
"move"—or, more mundanely, to his abject need of income [4]—he returned in the autumn of 1897 to *The Rescue*,[5]
the novel he had abandoned more than a year before. He
did not expect much from the resurrected project: "All my
ambition," he declared, "is to make it good enough for a
magazine—readable in a word" (Garnett, 120). As he ought
by now to have understood, though, he could not write at
the behest of so limited, for him, indeed, so *self-destructive*, an impulse. *The Rescue* festered and dragged; and
each day of delay further menaced Conrad's precarious
sense of "coherence":

> I can't get on with the *Rescue*. In all these days I haven't
> written a line, but there hadn't been a day when I did not
> wish myself dead. It is too ghastly. I positively don't know
> what to do. Am I out to the end of my tether? . . . I can't,

4. Pressed by the impending birth of his child, Conrad hoped to sell *The
Rescue* to Blackwood for serialization in *Maga*. Cf. Baines, 194 and 194n.

5. Conrad apparently changed the title of the novel from *The Rescuer* to
The Rescue in August 1897. (Cf. Baines, 194n.)

somehow, swing out—so to speak . . . I struggle without pleasure like a man certain of defeat. (Garnett, 112–13; 115; 120)

Conrad's "tether" ran out in December 1897. ". . . On [3 December]," he wrote, "I went over the rise of forty to travel downwards—and a little more lonely than before" (Garnett, 121). ". . . My health is not good," he confessed to Mme. Zagórska. *"Les nerfs, les nerfs!* Uncertainty torments me" (LL,I.,217). He spoke more explicitly of his confusion and pain to Edward Sanderson:

> [My] nerves are stretched like fiddle strings. . . . You know where you're driving to. A great thing,—in fact everything! But I don't,—I don't. (LL,I.,218)

"I've been strangely seedy—," he told Cunninghame Graham:

> Nothing very tangible, but for nearly a week I have thought not at all and eaten very little—and didn't see the use of doing anything. . . . It is a very sad and fiendish—well, indisposition, and too real for words. (Watts, 49)

He summarized his "indisposition" in a later note to Sanderson:

> Sometimes I think I am following an *ignis fatuus* that shall inevitably lead me to destruction: sometimes I try not to think at all. And all the time I am trying to write. Here you have the essence of my existence unveiled. (LL,I.,219)

On 20 December Conrad proclaimed the collapse of his painfully won affectual capacity. He informed Cunninghame Graham that the world once again seemed to

him stark and sterile, despotically co-optative of his power
to experience either "aspiration" or "desire." "There is,"
he wrote, "a—let us say—a machine":

> It evolved itself (I am severely scientific) out of a chaos of
> scraps of iron and behold!—it knits. I am horrified at the
> horrible work and stand appalled. I feel it ought to em-
> broider—but it goes on knitting. . . . And the most wither-
> ing thought is that the infamous thing has made itself;
> made itself without thought, without conscience, without
> foresight, without eyes, without heart. It is a tragic ac-
> cident—and it has happened. You can't interfere with it.
> The last drop of bitterness is in the suspicion that you can't
> even smash it. . . . It knits us in and it knits us out. It has
> knitted time space, pain, death, corruption, despair and all
> the illusions—and nothing matters. I'll admit however that
> to look at the remorseless process is sometimes amusing.
> . . . (Watts, 56–57)

Once again, then (the letter's closing irony notwithstanding), the boundaries of Conrad's desperately fragile
personality had closed. Because he had forsaken for eleven
months the intricate demands and data of his self-elabora-
tive stratagem, he had become separated once more from
emotional relationship with the universe and himself. "The
Return" and *The Rescue* could not sustain Conrad as had
Almayer's Folly, An Outcast of the Islands, and *The Nigger
of the "Narcissus"* because they had engaged not his
"thought" or his "conscience" or his "foresight," not his
"eyes" or his "heart," but his purse alone—a luxury, in the
context of Conrad's uses of literature, which he could ill afford.[6] Unalive any longer to "time space, pain, death, cor-

6. Perhaps Conrad meant to suggest as much when, in a letter written on
24 October 1897, he remarked, "I've been a *martyr* to various [domestic]
worries . . ." (Garnett, 101; my emphasis).

ruption, despair''—unalive, that is to say, to emotive life—
he paid in the last weeks of 1897 a severe price for the year
of his impersonal, indeed, *insincere*, attitude toward authorship. Thus, as happier men celebrated the birth of
Christ, Conrad awaited the delivery of his child at a full
pitch of despair:

> The attitude of cold unconcern is the only reasonable one.
> Of course reason is hateful—but why? Because it demon-
> strates (to those who have the courage) that we, living, are
> out of life—utterly out of it. . . . Life knows us not and we
> do not know life—we don't know even our own thoughts.
> Half the words we use have no meaning whatever and of
> the other half each man understands each word after the
> fashion of his own folly and conceit. Faith is a myth and
> beliefs shift like mists on the shore; thoughts vanish;
> words, once pronounced, die; and the memory of yester-
> day is as shadowy as the hope of to-morrow—only the

During these months Conrad looked to his friends for the support
and sanction which earlier he had derived from his fiction. Thus, he
thanked Sanderson for his "fidelity which is for me one of the few real
things in this world." He told Galsworthy, "You have no idea how your interest in me *keeps me up.*" To Hugh Clifford he wrote, "Our meeting—
your visit here—mark an epoch in my life. . . . I feel distinctly the richer
for your friendship" (LL,I.284; 278; 281; Conrad's emphasis). To Garnett
he remarked, "All of you stand by me so nobly that I must still exist" (Garnett, 172). (Cf., too, Watts, 45–46; LL,I.238; 252; 256; 276; 285; Blackwood,
23–24; 46; 80; 83; 103.) Conrad was particularly effusive in this regard in
his correspondence with Garnett, whom he described as "a living factor in
my individual and artistic existence" (Garnett, 164). (Cf. Garnett, 60; 100;
101; 103; 106; 114; 127; 116; 121; 159; 161; 168; 171.)

A crucial portion of Conrad's attitude toward friendship in these
unhappy months was his intense fear that he did not deserve his inti-
mates' sustaining affection, and that in time he inevitably must lose it. He
wrote to Cunninghame Graham, for example: "I can not help thinking
with alarm of the day when you shall find me out or rather find out that
there is nothing there." Later he added, "You'll have to forgive me many
things if you continue to know me on the basis of sincerity and friendship" (Watts, 47; 68).

string of my platitudes seems to have no end. As our peas-
ants say: "Pray, brother, forgive me for the love of God."
And we don't know what forgiveness is, nor what is love,
nor where God is. Assez. (Watts, 65)

"Out of life" again, "utterly out of it," Conrad entered the
new year in a grim and powerless state of mind.

One

The birth of his son dramatically exacerbated
Conrad's anxiety and despair. "The child is born to a dismal heritage," he moaned (LL,I.,227). "Borys is very fat and
unruly . . ." he told Cunninghame Graham. "Poor little
devil; if he had a decent father he would come to something perhaps" [7] (Watts, 133).

Under this new burden of necessity—another belly
to feed, another role to fulfill—Conrad's attitude toward
his work suffered further corrosion. He wrote to Garnett,
"I go into harness again to pull out of the mire, out of the
slough of despond that damned and bloody romance [*The*

7. Meyer treats Conrad's dejection as a species of neurotic jealousy; he
suggests, this is to say, that Conrad "reacted to the advent of . . . Borys as
if he were a usurper threatening [his] position of 'only child' . . ."
(Meyer, 148). I should think that Conrad felt anxious, rather, about his capacity to satisfy his paternal responsibilities. A man who has said of himself that "there is nothing there" (cf. my p. 190n) could not well feel
pleased about having sired a child; certainly the letters from which I quote
above suggest this view. One is hesitant, too, to accept Meyer's view that
Conrad "responded to the new circumstances of his life by seeking to escape" (Meyer, 148). As I shall suggest, Conrad tried desperately to return
to work after the birth of his son. It is to the point, too, that in spite of his
own severely straitened circumstances Conrad felt it possible to assume financial responsibility for his wife's two orphaned nieces within months of
Borys's birth. (Cf. Blackwood, *Introduction*, xxi.)

Rescue]." To Mme. Zagórska he complained, "The day before yesterday I returned to my work; it could not be otherwise. And it is thus, with poignant grief in my heart, that I write novels to amuse the English." ". . . The work itself," he confessed, "is only like throwing words into a bottomless hole" (LL,I.,227; 235; 227). Even authorship, then, had become for Conrad an inflection of the "machine," a manifestation of "a universe made of drops of fire and clots of mud" (Watts, 65). For it seemed to him that he wrote now not to inspirit or to shape his existence but solely to shelter it—and to shelter his family:

> Upon [my work] depends the daily bread of the house (literally—from day to day); not to mention (I dare hardly think of it) the future of my child, of those nearest and dearest to me, between whom and the bleakest want there is only my pen—as long as life lasts. . . . Sometimes it takes all my resolution and power of self control to refrain from butting my head against the wall. I want to howl and foam at the mouth but I daren't do it for fear of waking that baby and alarming my wife. It's no joking matter. (LL,I.,280; Garnett, 135)

In February 1898, Conrad surrendered outright the motivational basis of his work—and so forfeited the "coherent, justifiable" personality which he had struggled so splendidly to create. "I've gone and done it," he told Garnett:

> I write for the press!!!!!! I've sent to the *Outlook* an inconceivably silly thing about A. Daudet. "Words! words! words!" . . . Damn! I've lost the last shred of belief in myself. (Garnett, 130)

". . . I've taken to writing for the press," he informed Sanderson. "More words,—another hole" (LL,I.,227).

This capitulation to the "false pretences" (LL,I.,240) which had come to govern his existence wrested from Conrad his last reserve of comfort and resolve. Exanimate and exhausted, he described himself in March 1898 as nothing more than an ineffectual assembly of dysfunctions:

> I doze for hours still half conscious that there is that story I am unable to write. Then I wake up, try again—and at last go to bed completely done-up. So the days pass and nothing is done. At night I sleep. In the morning I get up with the horror of that powerlessness I must face through a day of vain efforts. (Garnett, 135)

Because his power to write—his power, that is to say, to style and to certify himself—had become so critical to his fragile sense of affect, Conrad rapidly lost whatever capacity to experience emotion he had managed to engender for himself. By the spring of 1898 he again had come to regard himself as a broken Punch doll [8]—as an unorganized, helpless, and radically repulsive jumble of tissues and organs:

> I seem to have lost all *sense* of style and yet I am haunted, mercilessly haunted by the *necessity* of style. And that thing I can't write weaves itself into all I see, into all I speak, into all I think, into the lines of every book I try to read. You know how bad it is when one *feels* one's liver, or lungs. Well I feel my brain. I am distinctly conscious of the contents of my head. (Garnett, 135; Conrad's emphases)

He told Cunninghame Graham:

> An extreme weariness oppresses me. It seems as though I had seen and felt everything since the beginning of the world. I *suspect* my brain to be yeast and my backbone to be cotton. And I *know* that the quality of my work is of the kind to confirm my suspicions. I would yell for help to

8. Cf. my p. 68–69.

anybody—man or devil if I could persuade myself that anybody would care—and, caring, could help. (Watts, 78;
Conrad's emphases)

"What shall I say?" he wrote in May. "Things aren't well
with me dear friend. I grow a little helpless now . . . I am
horribly sick of life." Later he added, "It's like a curse. I
can't *imagine* anything" [9] (Garnett, 137; 138. Conrad's emphasis).

By August Conrad openly characterized his "indisposition" as a mental illness: "I feel suicidal. . . . I am
afraid there's something wrong with my thinking apparatus. I am utterly out of touch with my work—and I can't get
in touch. All is darkness" (Garnett, 141). To Cunninghame
Graham he wrote, "I am really in a deplorable state, men-
tally. I feel utterly wretched. I haven't the courage to tackle
my work." He went on: "I am making desperate efforts to
write something. Why the devil did I ever begin? Que ton-
teria! . . . I wish you would come to shoot me" (Watts,
102; 103–4). He closed the month in a state of abject despair:

> I see how ill, mentally, I have been these last four months.
> . . . This horror . . . has destroyed already the little belief
> in myself I used to have. I am appalled at the absurdity of
> my situation. . . . Most appalled to feel that all the doors
> behind me are shut and that I must remain where I have
> come blundering in the dark. (Garnett, 142)

Two

Understandably enough, Conrad identified his afflic-
tion with his inability to complete *The Rescue:* it seemed to

9. By late May Conrad's closest friends had become deeply concerned
about his state of mind. (Cf. Watts, 212–13.)

him, that is, that if he could but conclude his novel he might reorganize his character and reclaim his hold upon the world. He wrote to this effect to Garnett: "My story"—here, surely, he has meant to write, My *self*—"is there in a fluid—in an evading shape. I can't get hold of it. It is all there—to bursting, yet I can't get hold of it no more than you can grasp a handful of water." In a later note he added: ". . . This *Rescue* makes me miserable—frightens me—and I shall not abandon it—even temporarily. I must get on with it, and it will destroy my reputation" (Garnett, 135; 139).

At less courageous moments, though, Conrad thought to discharge his suffering merely by evading it—as if he might relieve his despondency by returning to the outgrown strategies of his adolescence. His letters from 1898 confess an increasingly unresisted infatuation with insensibility; like Almayer or Willems or the paid-off crew of the *Narcissus* Conrad at times permitted himself to experience the full winsome appeal of systematic nullity. He told Garnett, for example: "I would like to make a bargeman of my son: strong, knowing his business and thinking of nothing. That is *the* life my dear fellow. Thinking of nothing! O! bliss" (Garnett, 136; Conrad's emphasis). To Cunninghame Graham he wrote, "If only one could get rid of consciousness" (Watts, 70). He went on to remark: "I would pray to a god . . . for a little forgetfulness. Say half an hour. Oh bliss. I would give him my soul for it and he would be cheated" [10] (Watts, 101).

On several occasions during this year of his degeneration Conrad even made effort to return to sea—to return, as he may have imagined, to his old experience of imposed incognizance. He wrote to Cunninghame Graham:

10. Cf., too, Watts, 53–54.

I lay awake thinking that I would give ever so much (the most flattering criticism) for being at sea, the soul of some patient faithful ship. . . . I am almost frantic with the longing to get away. Absurd! [11] (Watts, 72; 93)

"Absurd" indeed—as Conrad came quickly to understand. "It would be giving up everything," he acknowledged, "to begin life for the third time and I am not young enough for that." Too, he added, "The fact is from novel writing to skippering il y a trop de tirage. This confounded literature has ruined me entirely" (Watts, 100; 105).

Three

It need hardly be said that it was not *literature* which had "ruined" Conrad so much as the perversely impersonal uses to which he had put literature in 1897–1898. Certainly, in any event, it was literature which restored him. For in December 1898, Conrad returned at last to his proper enterprise. By writing *Heart of Darkness*—by abandoning the sterile unparticularity of *The Rescue* and returning in imagination to "experience pushed a little (and only very little) beyond the actual facts of the case" (XVI. Author's Note, xi)—Conrad discovered anew the gestatory and certifying authority of autobiographical fiction.[12]

11. Cf., too, Watts, 91; 92; 100; 102; 105; 114; LL,I.251; Garnett, 135. Baines discusses Conrad's sluggish search for a command (Baines, 213–14).

In *this* behavior, it might be said, Conrad obviously displays the escapist impulse to which Meyer assigns so much of his conduct from 1897 to 1898. (Cf. Meyer, 131; my p. 191n.)

12. Both Baines and Meyer argue that Conrad's intimacy with Ford Madox Ford was crucial to the recovery of his stability and, therefore, of his

If by writing *Heart of Darkness* Conrad did not immediately or permanently reconstruct his sense of absolute "coherence" (he continued to suffer from his "indisposition" throughout 1899 and much of 1900) he at least managed to check his regressive decline. More important, in recovering his self-descriptive disposition Conrad permitted himself, in ways which I shall examine, not only to define the sources of his misery but ultimately—by writing *Lord Jim*—to contain them. In this respect Conrad's final commitment in 1898–1899 to the literature of "sincerity" [13] did not simply preserve or "justify" his character. It rather established it.

---

power to write. Baines describes the friendship with Ford as "the most important event in Conrad's literary career" (Baines, 214–15). Meyer suggests that "Conrad transferred upon Hueffer attitudes, feelings, and desires which at an earlier time had been directed toward persons who had occupied the position of substitute parents." "There can be no question," Meyer asserts, "that the advent of Hueffer marked the beginning of a period of rich productivity during which . . . [Conrad earned] his position of eminence in English literature" (Meyer, 139; 150). Both reactions to the relationship are excessive, I think. No doubt Conrad's friendship with Ford was intense and valuable to him. It does seem to me, though, that the processes which I describe above were decisive to Conrad's recovery of himself. That which exerted "a quasi-catalytic effect upon Conrad's creative energy" (Meyer, 151), I think, was not his intimacy with Ford (or, for that matter, his intimacy with Garnett, or Crane, or Cunninghame Graham) but the successful renewal of his superbly audacious investment in the resources of autobiography. One might add that *Heart of Darkness* and *Lord Jim*, that each of the works from Conrad's "period of rich productivity," are perfectly continuous as imaginative acts with *Almayer's Folly*, *An Outcast of the Islands*, and, in particular, *The Nigger of the "Narcissus."* Conrad wrote his first three novels, of course, before he met Ford or responded to his "quasi-catalytic effect."

13. Cf. my p. 183; 190.

Chapter Six

Now I understand that strange sense of insecurity in my
past. I always suspected that I might be no good. And here
is proof positive, I am shirking it, I am no good.

(XVII.107)

The Horror
Heart of Darkness

Heart of Darkness is about the crisis of Conrad's sea experience and Marlow's desperate pursuit of the power to feel.
But before anything else *Heart of Darkness* is, I think, a
sequel to *The Nigger of the "Narcissus"*: for in *Heart of
Darkness* Conrad again describes his certainty that he is insufficiently individual, his terrible persuasion that he is not
deeply alive—that, indeed, no human being can be boldly
and freely alive. *Heart of Darkness*, then, is before anything
else about death—the death of many men, the death of
ethical behavior, the death of goodness and civility, the
death, crucially, of our authority as selves.

One

I was glad to get out.

Although Marlow associates his first excitement with
the Congo with that of his culture, he is quick to separate

his own purposes and passions there from those of the European community. His resistance is in part to the "rot" and "humbug" (XVI.59) by which Europe expresses its excessive commercial and religious interest in Africa; but it is chiefly directed against the inability of Europeans to appreciate what a singular occasion for experience Africa extends, what an extraordinary opportunity for adventure and life. Thus Marlow is careful to imply that *he* was attracted to the Congo primarily because he had been repulsed by the vapidity of modern Europe. He establishes his authority in this regard by reminding his friends that even before leaving for the Congo he had been unable to accede to the lifeless modalities of the modern culture:

> I had then, as you remember, just returned to London after a lot of Indian Ocean, Pacific, China Seas—a regular dose of the East—six years or so, and I was loafing about, hindering you fellows in your work and invading your homes, just as though I had got a heavenly mission to civilize you. It was very fine for a time, but after a bit I did get tired of resting. (XVI.51–52)

It is an odd speech—odd even for Marlow to have made, who is the most odd of Conrad's men. For although he obviously means to ridicule the modes of unbeing suggested by his friends' way of life, he is no less harsh with his own. If his friends' lives have seemed to him to be marked by empty "work" and arid "homes," he has felt his own to be conspicuous for its indirection and dreadful listlessness. "A lot of"; "a regular dose of"; "I did get tired": Marlow seems to have conceived of his own experience as nothing but an aimless "game" (XVI.52), an objectless wandering from port to port.

Marlow tells us it was exactly to make his life more

energetic and meaningful that he decided to go to Africa. And if, as he confesses, his decision to seek a command in the Congo first presented itself as an irrational whim (XVI.52–53), the fancy rapidly accumulated authority with him, so much so that it inspired "a fresh departure" in his personality (XVI.53) and made him feel that he "must get there by hook or by crook . . . the notion drove me" (XVI.53).

Marlow does not at once understand what that "notion" was, or why it "drove" him. He first connects it with his childhood longing for openness and mystery (XVI.52), then with his desire to recover something of the splendid masculinity of imperial Rome, or with his hope of arrogating to himself "all that mysterious life of the wilderness that stirs in the forests, in the jungles, in the hearts of wild men" (XVI.50). He feels more coherent about his impulse, though, once he has been officially appointed to his Congo captaincy. For then, as he tells us, when he understood that he was actually to make the break of a pioneer from his past, he was able—or compelled—to separate himself from his habitual assumptions of character and to respond to Europe with the less interested regard of an alien or exile.

And what a Europe Marlow sees! Against the anticipated life of the African wilderness he discovers a stunning emptiness about the commercial culture, a grim disposition to craziness and nonentity which appalls his spirit and encourages his resolve to be different. Particularly does he find Brussels to be an unactual, ugly, and ridiculous place: in his famous phrase the city suggests to him "a whited sepulchre," marked as it is by the dark shadows, harsh angles, and "dead silence" of the grave (XVI.55). And if he receives the city as a necropolis, he responds to its inhabitants as cadavers. Marlow meets no one in Brussels who does not strike him by his gravity, listlessness, and seeming loss of affect: "The slim one got up and walked straight at me—still knitting with downcast eyes—and only just as I began to think of getting out of her way, as you would for a somnambulist, stood still and looked up" (XVI.55). In the Company offices Marlow seems to see not people but disembodied organs: "A door opened, a white-haired secretarial head, but wearing a compassionate expression, appeared, and a skinny forefinger beckoned me into the sanctuary" (XVI.56). Thoroughly unsettled, Marlow even sees a ghost! "From behind that structure came out an impression of pale plumpness in a frock coat" (XVI.56). Not only are the Belgians apparitional: as disturbing to Marlow is their loose hold on reality and their deterioration of person. Secretaries sit crazily with abstract looks and sleeping cats; his own "excellent aunt" sips tea and speaks nonsense; a weird disheveled clerk gulps vermouth and says peculiar things; an unkempt doctor raves like a loony about crania and calipers.

In the very extremity of his brilliantly felt aversion to European life Marlow discovers the source of his "notion" and the great purpose of his adventure. For once he was able to detach himself from his habitual relation with Europe, Marlow tells us, he was able to understand with shocking rapidity and completeness that Europe had nothing to offer him, that in fact the paucity of his own experience had been conditioned by that of the commercial civilization. Marlow tells us, indeed, that his otherwise inexplicable notion to go to Africa was really prompted by his horror of nullity: the impulse "drove" him because he feels an instinct for passionate life—an instinct which modern Europe does not seem to him to share.

His decision to adventure after authenticity is not an easy one to make: everyone in Brussels finds a way to warn Marlow that Europeans die in Africa, or go crazy, or become horribly ill. But his impression of exanimacy has been so overwhelming, his sense of habit so assaulted, that no vision of death or hell can interfere with his—shall one call it religious?—determination "somehow to throw a kind of light on everything about me—and into my thoughts" (XVI.51). No wonder, then, that as he bids his aunt farewell and takes his leave of Belgium Marlow feels that he is not assuming a command but beginning a destiny, that he is not starting a new job but forming, against the grain of his past, against, as he believes, the idea of civilization, a second and truer self: "The best way I can explain it to you is by saying that, for a second or two, I felt as though, instead of going to the centre of a continent, I were about to set off for the centre of the earth" (XVI.60). Marlow has been warned that he shall discover a nightmare in the Congo; but he has already felt modern Europe to be an oppressing and dangerous dream. He is prepared, he thinks, to make the first of his decisions for life.

Two

. . . a weary pilgrimage amongst hints for nightmares.

Marlow has been prepared by his first contacts with the Company to anticipate the hypocrisy of its propaganda and the inefficiency of its devices. But nothing he can have guessed prepares him for the lunatic unreality of Belgium in the Congo. Ships land custom agents in "God-forsaken wilderness" (XVI.60). Soldiers play at forts and guns. The famous gunboat insanely shells an apparently unpeopled forest (XVI.62). The Company blows up a harmless cliff (XVI.64). Someone digs a huge hole, "the purpose of which I found it impossible to divine" (XVI.65). The imperial enterprise is not only foolish but impossibly improvident: boilers and railway cars lie rotting in the sun; great piles of nails rust in stacks; drainage pipes are imported, then dumped into ravines (XVI.63–65).

Marlow had known, though, that the commercial culture is incompetent and ridiculous. What he had not known—or had not permitted himself to imagine—is that imperial Europe also is dangerous and cruel, that it is committed on a vast scale to the ownership and murder of helpless men. Marlow's intellectual objection to his civilization achieves coherence and passion when, in what he calls "the grove of death" (XVI.70), he confronts the "pain, abandonment, and despair" (XVI.66) which are the sources of imperial power and the perfect image of its lawless soul. It is one of Marlow's worst moments in *Heart of Darkness* when he is compelled to understand that the great adventure of life to which he has attached himself is really in the business of death; that he has fled one "gloomy circle" of Hell to join himself to another:

> Black shapes crouched, lay, sat between the trees leaning against the trunks, clinging to the earth, half coming out, half effaced within the dim light, in all the attitudes of pain, abandonment, and despair. . . . The work was going on. The work! And this was the place where some of the helpers had withdrawn to die. (XVI.66)

The further into Central Africa Marlow travels, the more asinine he feels his programme of life to be. For he discovers that if the imperial culture has contaminated the continent it exploits, if the Company has cast the taint of

Europe over even the Congo, Africa itself is not the charmed country of his imagining. Certainly the Congo *is* splendidly unsepulchral in its atmosphere: like its people it has "bone, muscle, a wild vitality, an intense energy of movement" (XVI.61). But it is marked in its fierce and natural reality not so much by freedom and life as by a deadly rapaciousness. Her very rivers seem to Marlow "streams of death in life, whose banks were rotting into mud, whose waters thickened into slime, invaded the contorted mangroves, that seemed to writhe at us in the extremity of an impotent despair (XVI.62). And against this "sinister backcloth" (XVI.61) of natural corruption and gloom men die like so many fleas. Belgians kill Blacks, Blacks kill Belgians. The jungle gives white men fever, or it drives them mad. One is broiled by day and chilled by night. The sun cooks the countryside and steams the sense out of men; and always there is "a solitude, a solitude, nobody, not a hut" (XVI.70).

Too, those few men in the Congo with whom Marlow *can* associate are the very type from which he has wished to flee. The Company's manager, like the lifeless men of Brussels, strikes Marlow by his odd and terrifying inanimateness:

> His eyes, of the usual blue, were perhaps remarkably cold.
> . . . Otherwise there was only an indefinable, faint expression of his lips, something stealthy—a smile—not a smile—
> I remember it, but I can't explain. . . . He was obeyed, yet he inspired neither love nor fear, nor even respect. He inspired uneasiness. That was it! Uneasiness. Not a definite mistrust—just uneasiness—nothing more. (XVI.73)

As might an icecold cadaver met one fine afternoon. And Marlow's other comrades are only a little less unsettling.

There is a fat mustachioed fool who "with great volubility and many digressions" (XVI.72) becomes hysterical about almost anything. "Sixteen or twenty" (XVI.77) creatures wander fatuously about the Station "with their absurd long staves in their hands, like a lot of faithless pilgrims bewitched inside a rotten fence" (XVI.76). A brickmaker who makes no bricks spies on Marlow and reads other men's letters. A band of boobies wanders in from the forest, full of empty talk and absurd manners (XVI.87). Marlow meets no one in the Congo who is not vapid and gutless, no one who has not succumbed to the "flabby, pretending, weak-eyed devil" of imperial Europe; no one who believes in the "strong, lusty, red-eyed devils" (XVI.65) of passionate life and imperious selfhood.

It is the final inflection of Marlow's second nightmare that his boat itself has been scuttled, that someone has ripped out its bottom and left it stuck, together with Marlow's other dreams, in the muck of the Congo. With nothing useful to do and with no idea left to serve, surrounded by idiots, confounded by nonentity, Marlow paces about his fenced-in compound possessed by the terrible notion that human life is everywhere bleak, that Europe and Africa are indiscriminable in their nullity; that there are forums for Companies in the world, but none for the self.

Three

What I really wanted was rivets, by heaven!

But Marlow has just begun his ascent into consciousness. For it is the first crisis of his Congo experience that he responds to this landscape of nothingness by discovering in it an appeal: that from amidst his fierce boredom and despair he begins to receive the jungle in its awful character of primitive life—and so to feel an urge toward a power of self.

The jungle does its work with Marlow by slow manipulations of his affectual apparatus. Earlier, for instance, when he was making his grim march to the Central Station, Marlow tells us that he was struck by the sounds of the Congo night:

> Perhaps on some quiet night the tremor of far-off drums, sinking, swelling, a tremor vast, faint; a sound weird, appealing, suggestive, and wild—and perhaps with as profound a meaning as the sound of bells in a Christian country. (XVI.71)

That sexual tremor of "sinking" and "swelling" sounds less faint to Marlow after he has arrived at the Station and reached the pitch of his bewilderment and despair. For then, against "the faint sounds" of the Station's men and machines, its vague murmurs of listless stereotypy, the jungle's momentous quiet sounds material and grave: ". . . the silence of the land went home to one's very heart—its mystery, its greatness, the amazing reality of its concealed life" (XVI.80).

Too, the smells of the Congo stir Marlow, and open him to the strange beauties of the jungle night:

> The smell of mud, of primeval mud, by Jove! was in my nostrils, the high stillness of primeval forest was before my eyes; there were shiny patches on the black creek. The moon had spread over everything a thin layer of silver. . . . (XVI.81)

"All this was great, expectant, mute"—but it is also, Marlow tells us, dangerous and terrifying. For although the jungle's cadence of life has sounded to him as "profound" as that of Christian bells, its pressure of assertion seems to him more urgent, more native and naked, the call of a being more brutally pure and demanding than his own. And if he finds himself responding to "the amazing reality" of the Congo, he well understands—fascinating Marlow!—that his attraction is exactly to the sordidness of that reality. Marlow is not delighted by his growing communion with the jungle because he knows himself to be drawn principally to its aspects of violent feeling and insinuated evil, to its unacceptable suggestion of prehistory and sexual release. All that stirring movement in the night, those secret tom-toms of the soul, those heady odors of ceremony and sex, marzipans of mud and blood. . . .

Abominable but attractive, dreaded but desired, that faint call to rank life—the jungle's imperialism—seems to Marlow as frightening as it is compelling. He has wanted to be spirited, invigorated by the life of passionate intensity. But with that sweet stink of the jungle in his nose, its humming quietude in his ears, its blotchy beauty in his eyes, Marlow feels, he tells us, a great instinct of terror and equivocation, a terrible fear for that unloved bundle of little habits and sensations that is himself:

> I wondered whether the stillness of the face of the immensity looking at us two were meant as an appeal or as a menace. What were we who had strayed in here? Could we handle that dumb thing or would it handle us? I felt how big, how confoundedly big, was that thing that couldn't talk, and perhaps was deaf as well. What was in there? (XVI.81)

He has been a known thing, a timid little assembly of moderate feelings that has had to offer, if no passions or possibilities, no surprises either. But now that he has opened himself to the "amazing reality" of being human, Marlow has the great good sense to recognize that the primal "immensity" to which he has made appeal may be as much a "menace" as a boon; that it may not just enrich but altogether subsume his own energy of being and identity of person. As Marlow leans on the wreck of his scuttled ship, the smashed hull of his purposes and personality, he feels a great fear that "that dumb thing" which he has come to find, life, may kill him. In this first crisis of his narrative the true terms of his drama at last become as clear to Marlow as they have been to us. For the first time he understands that what is at issue for him in the middle of darkest Africa is not merely his entertainment and adventure but his survival as a humane and individual soul, his whole identity as a morally organized man.

But like a child who takes to his thumb when the world is hard, Marlow moves to repel this latest and most devastating assault on his habits by reverting to habit. That is to say, he goes to work, as if by reclaiming his steamer he can resist his soul. As he puts it, labor, sheer engaged busyness, may release one from nightmare by recalling one to a simpler reality. Who has not been rescued from dreadful dreams by the dear, bright sun?

> I went back to work the next day, turning, so to speak, my back on that station. In that way only it seemed to me I could keep my hold on the redeeming facts of life. (XVI.75)

Marlow insists that labor purifies one by purifying the demands placed upon one's life: that hard work purges pain because it urges men toward the fundaments of the human existence. He insists, indeed, that even against all the pressures toward nonentity in the world, labor *defines* one, makes one strong in earned selfhood and peace: [1]

> I had expended enough hard work on [the steamboat] to make me love her. No influential friend would have served me better. She had given me a chance to come out a bit—to find out what I could do. . . . I don't like work,— no man does—but I like what is in the work,—the chance to find yourself. Your own reality—for yourself, not for others—what no other man can ever know. They can only see the mere show, and never can tell what it really means. (XVI.85)

Marlow is so convinced of this power of his worker's self to counter the Congo that he dances a jig to his own achievement of character (XVI.86). But his sweet drunken dance gives phrase to only an assumed stability; for the claims of work cannot long repel those of the jungle. Thus, as Marlow steams upriver, steams ever deeper into the heart of the Congo's "prehistoric" life (XVI.95), he feels a movement of soul toward "the overwhelming realities of this strange world of plants and water, and silence" (XVI.93). He still thinks that by working hard he can resist

1. It is for this reason that Marlow has admired the otherwise ludicrous accountant; for he believes that, although the accountant is extravagantly ridiculous, he at least is serene and certain in his character: "Yes; I respected his collars, his vast cuffs, his brushed hair. His appearance was certainly that of a hairdresser's dummy; but in the great demoralization of the land he kept up his appearance. That's backbone. His starched collars and got-up shirt fronts were achievements of character." The accountant is able to keep such firm hold on himself, Marlow believes, primarily because he works at his accounting: "And he was devoted to his books, which were in apple-pie order. . . . Of faultless appearance (and even slightly scented), perched on a high stool, he wrote, he wrote" (XVI.68–69). As with the hairdresser's dummy, Marlow tries to imagine, so with himself. . . .

their "brooding appeal; but the Congo—and his secret responsive self—are far too strong for his naive and presumptuous devices:

> I had to keep guessing at the channel. . . . When you have to attend to things of that sort, to the mere incidents of the surface, the reality—the reality I tell you—fades. The inner truth is hidden—luckily, luckily. *But I felt it all the same:* I felt often its mysterious stillness watching me at my monkey tricks. . . . (XVI.93–94; my emphasis)

It is a classically complicated Marlovian moment. I didn't feel it, I didn't feel it, I did feel it. I don't know what it was that I felt, but I felt it strongly. His own confusion, though, does not disguise from *us* the failure of his labored defence. "But I felt it all the same": once he has had to make that confession, the jungle sweeps about him freely in all its authenticity and appeal, beckons to him madly from "the night of first ages":

> It was unearthly, and the men were—No, they were not inhuman. Well, you know, that was the worst of it—this suspicion of their not being inhuman. It would come slowly to one. They howled and leaped, and spun, and made horrid faces; but what thrilled you was just the thought of their humanity—like yours—the thought of your remote kinship with all this wild and passionate uproar. Ugly. Yes, it was ugly enough; but if you were man enough you would admit to yourself that there was in you just the faintest trace of a response to the terrible frankness of that noise. . . .[2] (XVI.96)

2. I think this one of the novel's most powerfully imagined moments, because we are invited here to join with Conrad in *his* sense of a morally burgeoning Marlow. Like Conrad privy to Marlow's assaulted intelligence, we hear him feel, consider, and learn. (It is as if we are permitted to overhear Marlow saying to himself: I am not like them, not like them . . .

Marlow prides himself that he did not "go ashore for a howl and a dance"; or, rather, he takes pride in the fact that his work kept him from going (XVI.97). But he *wants* to go; he thinks that he may need to go. In making that crucial admission he describes the terms of the issue as clearly for himself as Conrad has described them for us. Work does not work. However busy he keeps himself, Marlow likes the jungle, likes it in and for its awful depravity; no matter what he does, he is "man enough" to understand that he wants to join with its terrible but exciting life.[3] For it is safe to work, but "wild and passionate" to howl; dull to be a man, but thrilling—and more authentic?—to go crazy with "frank" animal frenzy.

There is still more to be said against Marlow's tired doctrine of wholesome labor—and Marlow himself says it. I speak of Marlow's implicit understanding that activity, oc-

---

not like them. But, Lord help me, they draw me, they thrill me, I am like them. Just a bit like them; but like them, like them. . . .) *Heart of Darkness* produces here, then, a kind of stream-of-consciousness technique which allows us perfect and fascinating access to its chief character's moral imagination.

3. I think that, at some level, Marlow always has understood that his sad doctrine in fact is practically powerless; that the protective edifice of labor is archaic in the primeval context of the Congo. It can be no development of mere chance that on each occasion that Marlow describes the powers of work he cannot help but to submit to the greater power of the reality which he has wished to evade. Thus, after insisting that his work has kept him too busy to be much troubled by the absurdities of the Central Station, he feels compelled to remark, "Still one must look about one sometimes . . ." (XVI.75). And when he does permit himself to "look about" he apprehends everything which he has tried not to apprehend (Cf. XVI.76). Similarly, after dancing his wonderful jig to Labor he beholds with horror that the obdurate actuality of the threatening jungle is unchanged (XVI.86). Too, after he has asserted in such a complicated way that his keeping busy has prevented him from responding to "the inner truth" of the Congo, he acknowledges that he has "felt it all the same"—that, indeed, he has felt it fully and "often" (XVI.93).

cupation, work, are not themselves different from the mere inanimate biology of the story's Belgians. He who has asked for what men live must as well ask at what men work: the questions, after all, are continuous. The accountant has backbone; but is he alive? is he alive in a passionate and interesting way? Marlow fixes boats; but what does it mean to fix boats? Marlow began his narrative by confessing that his own sailor's life was aimless because it served no idea and gave him no feeling of energy or character (XVI. 51–52). Here in the Congo he cannot help but understand that, although his labor is honorable, it is unimportant, the senseless busyness of a simian: "I felt often [the jungle's] mysterious stillness watching me at my monkey tricks. . . ." His boat does need to be repaired; but is a man to engineer his way through life? Is a man to carpenter his way through the Congo? [4]

4. Marlow earlier has made comedy out of other men's aimless devotion to work. But the Belgians in the Congo who have struck him as being so funny and so absurd after all have done nothing very different from what Marlow has attempted to do. Even the fat Belgian who tries to douse a fire with a bottomless bucket does what he thinks to be useful work (XVI.76); no doubt the crew of the preposterous gunboat imagines that even its hilarious enterprise is necessary and valuable. One must regard Marlow's paeans to labor, then, as the moral equivalent of Europe's "humbug" and "rot" about the Congo, or as the correlative of what Marlow has called the "beautiful" but fantastic self-deception of women (XVI.59).

It is of interest that Conrad subjects Marlow's ideology of work to such censure here, given the fact that throughout his writing life he himself expressed rather a similar faith in the redemptive authority of labor. *The Nigger of the "Narcissus,"* it will be recalled, is full of complicated testimony to the value of labor. *Typhoon* (1902) is unambiguous in its endorsement of work. And in a late essay (1918), Conrad celebrates work in language strikingly like that which here he gives to Marlow. He writes: "A man is a worker. If he is not that, he is nothing—like a mere adventurer" (III.190; cf. also XVI.85). Perhaps, then, *Heart of Darkness* has an authority of its own, such that it is able to probe beneath Conrad's own "surface truths."

This, for Marlow and for us, is a crucial question. What does Marlow want: life, "the terrible frankness" of "truth—truth stripped of its cloak of time" (XVI. 96–97)? Or the macabre unbeing of Belgians and boobies, the timid unreality of "a fool," who "with sheer fright and fine sentiments, is always safe" (XVI.97)? He has come to the Congo exactly to probe beneath "the mere incidents of the surface," exactly to discover who he is and what life is like. Now that he is beginning to find out, now that life has shocked him by its "overwhelming realities," its "vengeful aspect" (XVI.93), its suggestion of nightmare, is he to wish life to fade away behind that vulnerable shield of his culture's meaningless industriousness? And now that he is beginning to "find" himself—his own reality—for himself, not for the others—what no other man can ever know—is he, like his poor African fireman, to embrace mere "surface-truth" (XVI.97)? Is he, too, to be "a dog in a parody of breeches and a feather hat, walking on his hindlegs" (XVI.97)? Does Marlow want selfhood and life or, as he once has said, rivets? "What I really wanted was rivets, by heaven! Rivets. To get on with the work—to stop the hole. Rivets I wanted" (XVI.83). Rivets. Does Marlow want to fix holes or to be born? Does he want to be a fool or a man, a dog or a person?

Four

. . . an angel or a fiend.

Marlow, of course, does not know which he wants to be: he needs the rest of the novel to decide. Confused and desperately frightened by the "overwhelming realities" to which with such great courage he has opened himself, Marlow at this critical point in his nightmarish life knows only one thing—that he has become rather interested in the Mr. Kurtz of whom he has heard so much.

To others a goody-goody, agent *par excellence,* political comer, a strange paragon of efficiency and power, Kurtz to Marlow is first a painter. He hears of him from The Accountant, who tells Marlow that he is "a first-class agent" and "a very remarkable person" (XVI.69). Successful *and* interesting—a large order in *Heart of Darkness!* And known, The Accountant insists, a protégé to power: "Oh, he will go far, very far. . . . He will be a somebody in the Administration before long. They, above—the Council in Europe, you know—mean him to be" (XVI.70).

Marlow, though, is interested in other, more authoritative versions of the self than that species of "somebody" implied by The Accountant. Kurtz slips from his mind, filed, no doubt, with the other nonentities of his voyage. Nor is his disinterest relieved by the manager's echo of the bookkeeper's refrain: "Mr. Kurtz was the best agent he had, an exceptional man, of the greatest importance to the Company . . ." (XVI.75). Exceptional, but in ways which Marlow has dismissed: healthy, ill, alive or dead, "Hang Kurtz," Marlow thinks. Let me get on, let me get to real life, true life, deep life.

No, it is finally as an artist, as an interpreter of life, that Kurtz makes his appeal to Marlow. For when things at the Station are at their worst, when Marlow has had to submit to the inane inquisition of a brickmaker,[5] he sees a por-

---

5. The absurd brickmaker ("the manager's spy") tries to discover why Marlow has come to the Congo, and whether he will become a threat to anyone's established position there. Of course it is altogether beyond the brickmaker's powers to imagine Marlow's actual project in the Congo. (Cf. XVI.77f.)

trait in oils on his interrogator's wall, a portrait which compels him by its expression of a mood fully as dark as his own: "Then I noticed a small sketch in oils, on a panel, representing a woman, draped and blind-folded, carrying a lighted torch. . . . It arrested me" (XVI.79).

Kurtz's painting is the first thing about the Congo that *has* arrested Marlow. And after he learns that Kurtz had painted the "sombre" and "sinister" sketch when, like himself, he had been stuck in the Central Station, Marlow feels a quiet affinity with this "prodigy" he had earlier dismissed, with this "emissary of pity, and science, and progress, and devil knows what else." How could he not, when the brickmaker joins them together and condemns them both as men of unwelcome integrity and civility?

> To-day he is chief of the best station, next year he will be assistant-manager, two years more and . . . but I daresay you know what he will be in two years' time. You are of the new gang—the gang of virtue. The same people who sent him specially also recommended you. (XVI.79; Conrad's ellipsis)

It is a specious identity, Marlow knows, but he accepts it nevertheless. To be loathed jointly and with such venom by such a spook as the brickmaker must imply between himself and Kurtz some similarity of soul, some community of character.

Indeed, so intensely does Marlow feel the possible connection between himself and Kurtz that, even though he has no clear sense of the man—"no more than if I had been told an angel or a fiend was in there" (XVI.81)—he lies for him. It is no mean gesture, at least by his reckoning. For Marlow fears that "by letting that young fool believe anything he liked as to my influence in Europe," he again commits himself to "exactly what I hate and detest in

the world—what I want to forget." Postures, imperson-
ations, pretences. All that charlatanry that he has come to
the Congo to escape: and here he is, strange bogus man,
at one stroke repeating it all:

> I became in an instant as much of a pretence as the rest of
> the bewitched pilgrims. This simply because I had a notion
> it somehow would be of help to that Kurtz whom at the
> time I did not see—you understand. He was just a word for
> me. I did not see the man in the name any more than you
> do. (XVI.82)

Maybe not. But he has seen enough to attach himself to
Kurtz as the only man besides himself in whom he can feel
interest. He has seen enough to make him wonder if this
"universal genius" (XVI.83) has not been able to handle
"that dumb thing" which he himself has so mismanaged:
"I was curious to see whether this man, who had come out
equipped with moral ideas of some sort, would climb to
the top after all and how he would set about his work when
there" (XVI.88). The idea of a great man, of a capacious,
secured self, still has some prestige with Marlow—as does,
evidently, the idea of culture, the received authority of
inherited "moral ideas."

Marlow's interest is quickened to passion when he
overhears the manager scheming with his uncle about
Kurtz. For then Marlow learns that, like himself, Kurtz has
responded to the necromantic claims of the jungle; that,
like himself, Kurtz seems to prefer the life of the tribe to
the inanimateness of the city:

> Kurtz had apparently intended to return himself, the Sta-
> tion being by that time bare of goods and stores, but after
> coming three hundred miles, had suddenly decided to go

back, which he started to do in a small dugout with four paddlers, leaving the half-caste to continue down the river with the ivory.

The bush before ivory; passion before profit. At last Marlow has his image of Kurtz—as the prototype, perhaps, of the man whom he himself would like to become:

> They were at a loss for an adequate motive. As to me, I seemed to see Kurtz for the first time. It was a distinct glimpse: the dugout, four paddling savages, and the lone white man turning his back suddenly on the headquarters, on relief, on thoughts of home—perhaps; setting his face towards the depths of the wilderness, towards his empty and desolate station. I did not know the motive. (XVI.90)

He does not "know" it, not for a certainty. But he has come near enough to doing the same thing himself to be able to suppose the motive—and to feel "rather excited at the prospect of meeting Kurtz very soon" (XVI.92).

In fact, Marlow becomes obsessed with meeting Kurtz. It is a conspicuous change in his purposes that, as he steams upriver to relieve the Inner Station, as the Congo's "inner truth" more and more disturbs his already devastated particularity, Marlow feels that he exists *for* Kurtz, that he has come to the Congo not to describe himself for himself but—a continuous achievement?—to listen to Kurtz talk:

> That was exactly what I had been looking forward to—a talk with Kurtz. . . . The man presented himself as a voice. . . . The point was in his being a gifted creature, and that of all his gifts the one that stood out preeminently, that carried with it a sense of real presence, was his ability to talk, his words—the gift of expression, the bewildering,

> the illuminating, the most exalted and the most contempt-
> ible, the pulsating stream of light, or the deceitful flow
> from the heart of an impenetrable darkness.[6] (XVI.113–14)

Like the *Nellie*, then, Marlow has swung full course. He had come to the Congo for experience and self, in the ancient belief that a man is shaped by what he does, that character is formed by what happens to one. But now that he has been pressed by experience, now that he has been so overwhelmed by reality that he cannot morally find his way, he feels a passionate wish for, in effect, literature. Life has been too bold for Marlow; he feels that he wants art. Stirred by a painting, he wants a more particular "gift of expression"—not the bewildering activeness of actuality but the "real presence," however bewildering that may be, of human words.

Language, like experience, provokes a passion of a kind; no doubt words, too, participate in, as they flow from, that genius of reality Marlow fled Europe to discover. But what strikes one here is that Marlow temporarily has yielded himself to that energy which earlier he had thought he loathed: he has allied himself with his culture. In this he has performed a crucial modernist act—at least in that

6. At this point in the narrative Marlow remarks that he now has become interested in Kurtz to the *exclusion* of all his earlier purposes in the Congo: "For me [the boat] crawled towards Kurtz—exclusively. . . . And we crept on, towards Kurtz. . . . Sometimes I would pick out a tree a little way ahead to measure our progress towards Kurtz by . . ." (XVI.95; 98; 100). Marlow thus semantically at least has come to equate Kurtz with primeval, premoral life, with the actual "heart of darkness": "Going up that river was like travelling back to the earliest beginnings of the world. . . . We penetrated deeper and deeper into the heart of darkness (XVI.92; 95)." We steamed into prehistory, toward Kurtz; we made our way into the heart of darkness, toward Kurtz. It is a striking, if somewhat murky economy—one which increasingly will control Marlow's responses to Kurtz, to the Congo, and, ultimately, to himself.

sense which Lionel Trilling defines in his celebrated suggestion that the "intense conviction of the existence of the self apart from culture is, as culture well knows, its noblest and most generous achievement." [7]

Five

You lost your way.

But one does not in Conrad's severe world commit oneself to anything without severe trial. So it is that in his search for Kurtz Marlow is made to confront tests more demanding by far than those he has experienced at the Stations downriver—tests so nightmarish in their quality that he scarcely can find language to recall them. To be sure, *certain* horrors no longer affect him. The droll absurdities of his inane passengers, for instance, do not much disturb him: he has grown accustomed to mere nullity. Nor is he drastically upset by the fact that his antiquated boat is likely at any moment to fail, leaving him to flail like a log in the

7. Lionel Trilling, *Beyond Culture* (New York: Viking, 1965), p. 118. Jerome Thrale less interestingly suggests that *Heart of Darkness* imagines a modern quest for the Grail (Jerome Thrale, "Marlow's Quest," *University of Toronto Quarterly*, XXIV [July, 1955], pp. 351–58; reprinted in R. W. Stallman, ed. *The Art of Joseph Conrad: A Critical Symposium* [Ann Arbor: Michigan State University Press, 1960], pp. 154–61). Guy Owens, Jr. remarks that a parenthetical purpose of *Heart of Darkness* is to rework the Arthurian legend (Owens, "A Note on Heart of Darkness," *Nineteenth Century Fiction*, XII, [September, 1957], pp. 168–69). In other well-known essays, Lillian Feder, Robert O. Evans, William Bysshe Stein, and Seymour L. Gross variously associate Marlow's quest with the voyages of Aeneas and Dante, and with the experience of Bodhisattva. But their engagingly fierce quarrel does not contribute importantly, I fear, to our response to the novel. (The essays in question are reprinted in Stallman, pp. 162–70; 171–78.)

filthy river. Machines work or break for reasons which can be known. One kicks them, one patches them, they get fixed or they're broke: there is nothing mysterious about a steamboat. Nor, however alarming, is there anything deeply mysterious about even the savages' assault. An ambush is frightening but comprehensible, a contingency which one includes within the range of one's understanding and even of one's expectation. One would not oneself wish to spear another man or to make a warhoop, take a scalp; but one knows that such things happen, and certainly one knows how to fight back, why to fight back.

No, the insuperable terrors of Marlow's journey toward Kurtz are pyschological, pressures against his economies of person and place, his structures of vision and balance, reference and perspective:

> The broadening waters flowed through a mob of wooded islands; you lost your way on that river as you would in a desert, and butted all day long against shoals, trying to find the channel, till you thought yourself bewitched and cut off forever from everything you had known once— somewhere—far away—in another existence perhaps. (XVI.93)

Marlow's vocabulary is failing, but no wonder. His assumptions about the world are failing; his systems of compensation, his patterns of configuration, less and less can manage the demands of his experience.

> We were cut off from the comprehension of our surroundings; we glided past like phantoms, wondering and secretly appalled, as sane men would be before an enthusiastic outbreak in a madhouse . . . the earth seemed unearthly. (XVI.96)

You lost your way; you couldn't find the channel; you thought yourself bewitched; the earth seemed unearthly. The language is clumsy, but how does one speak not of metaphors but of facts, of anxiety-dreams come to life, of all those extravagant terrors we all have had? Bowel-training and sights of sex, fathers' strength and mothers' rage, crossing the street, staring at the stars, "the overwhelming realities of his strange world of plants, and water and silence"? That strange world is our world, after all, full of mystery and assault, intimations of neurosis, invitations to psychosis. Marlow cannot articulately describe his fear and dissociation; but we understand what he means.

We understand, too, when Marlow tells us that in this sleep world [8] nothing seems clear, nothing feels right. Trees like meanings are hidden from sight; channels are unnavigable, events unfathomable: "But the snags were thick, the water was treacherous and shallow, the boiler seemed indeed to have a sulky devil in it . . ." (XVI.98). Also, someone leaves him an incomprehensible message in a rude hut. He finds a seaman's book annotated in cipher. ("It was an extravagant mystery" [XVI.99].) The river bank "seemed unnatural, like a state of trance." As in a crazy dream or a narcotic madness, images of life and the world flood upon Marlow and make his organs of sense

8. It is the very point of Marlow's pain, of course, that *this* world exactly is real, and the workaday world illusory. Thus, even though Towson's *Inquiry* gives him a lovely moment of relief, "a delicious sensation of having come upon something unmistakably real" (XVI.99), Marlow always understands that the horrors of the Congo are more actual, if one may produce such a phrase, than the book's gentle universe of charts and tables, or its "talk of chains and purchases." The imagination of science and sailors promotes a more congenial idea of reality than that which Marlow has uncovered; but its truth, he knows, is less authentic than the jungle's.

feel witless and stupid: "Not the faintest sound of any kind could be heard. You looked on amazed, and began to suspect yourself of being deaf—then the night came suddenly, and struck you blind as well" (XVI.101). No ears, no eyes, no world to behold. Do we not all share the terror that the world one day will become like that, that it will die from us, be blown suddenly to silly, suffocating bits? Here, though, that babyish anxiety feels like a fact; caught in a fog more complete, a human terror more realized than anything in, say, *Bleak House*, Marlow feels himself annihilated, the universe strangling and gone:

> The rest of the world was nowhere, as far as our eyes and ears were concerned. Just nowhere. Gone, disappeared; swept off without leaving a whisper or a shadow behind. . . . Were we to let go our hold of the bottom, we would be absolutely in the air—in space. . . . Our eyes were of no more use to us than if we had been buried miles deep in a heap of cotton-wool. It felt like it, too—choking, warm, stifling. (XVI.102; 106–7)

Against such a grotesque nightmare as this, all the rest—the inexplicable cries in the night, the assault of the savages, the tomfoolery of the pilgrims, even the grisly death of the helmsman—seem to Marlow traditional, albeit ghastly, horrors. But these hidden banks, these secret snags; this deadly night, this choking fog! These go to the font of nightmares, to the cradle of terrors. For these bad Congo dreams, not dreams at all, at last confirm Marlow in everything he most has feared. Their terrible images persuade him that men are indeed "very small, very lost" (XVI.95), neither persons nor powers, that men indeed are morally insignificant, and insufficiently alive:

> It occurred to me that my speech or my silence, indeed
> any action of mine, would be a mere futility. What did it
> matter what anyone knew or ignored? What did it matter
> who was manager? One gets sometimes such a flash of in-
> sight. The essentials of this affair lay deep under the sur-
> face, beyond my reach, and beyond my power of med-
> dling. (XVI.100)

The geography of nonentity has struck home; the
spawning-ground of nightmares, the secret stuff of autism,
has become Marlow's landscape of opinion. As he steams
into Kurtz's compound, Marlow thinks that his experience
has become a whole horror, that life can do to him no
more than it has done. We hear no more talk of rivets.

Six

> There are two more instalments in which the
> idea is so wrapped up in secondary notions
> that You—even You!—may miss it. (Watts.116)

As the Fool eases Lear's pain but prepares him for
more, so the Russian harlequin entertains Marlow but organizes his sense of Kurtz, soothes him, but opens him to
truths he has not earlier imagined. The harlequin is dressed
like a clown, gestures like a clown, is droll like a clown. But
he does not amuse Marlow or us, because in explaining so
many of *Heart of Darkness's* mysteries he rehearses for
both the narrator and the reader the story's grim climax of
self-exposure.

He *is* a great explainer of riddles, Kurtz's harlequin:
how appropriate that in Conrad's Congo only a daft clown

knows the whole truth about Kurtz—or about ciphers in Towson, warnings in huts. "His very existence was improbable, inexplicable, and altogether bewildering" (XVI.126). Maybe so, but this bizarre creature knows what Marlow does not: that Kurtz, a gross imperialist, raids for ivory and kills for elephant tusks (XVI.128); that Kurtz, a contaminator, "got the tribe to follow him" (XVI.128), that he made savages "adore" him by presiding "at certain midnight dances ending with unspeakable rites," which were "offered up" to himself (XVI.118). The Russian is a buffoon; but he knows that Kurtz, the great man of Marlow's private culture, impales men's heads on poles (XVI.130–31), mates with savage women, and believes that there is "nothing on earth to prevent him killing whom he jolly well pleased" (XVI.128). The Russian may be unlikely and apparitional, but he knows that Kurtz, in whom Marlow has invested eveything he has left of hope and passion and faith, is a beast, a bare, bad man who—what? eats flesh? sips blood? screws hippos?

And yet, the harlequin insists that Kurtz is not to be condemned, nor even to be judged. For like Marlow, the harlequin believes that Kurtz is a great man, a thinker of mighty and melodious mind, an artist, even a saint of sorts. Just as Marlow has supposed, Kurtz understands life and can interpret experience: "I tell you . . . this man has enlarged my mind. . . . He made me see things. . . . A man like this, with such ideas. . . . Ah! I'll never, never meet such a man again" (XVI.125; 127; 132; 140). The Russian insists, indeed, that Kurtz is a genius of life. It is true that he has behaved in gross and heinous ways. But he is so bold a man that—Kurtz's clown is not articulate—he has passed beyond our normal assumptions about the right or wrong behavior of normal men: "You can't judge Mr. Kurtz as you would an ordinary man. No, no, no" (XVI.128).

Kurtz does not look like a genius of life, though. For when Marlow at last sees him Kurtz looks to be a ghastly "apparition," "an animated image of death carved out of old ivory":

> He looked at least seven feet long. His covering had fallen off, and his body emerged from it pitiful and appalling as if from a winding-sheet. I could see the cage of his ribs all astir, the bones of his arms waving. (XVI.134)

He can't walk, he can't sit up on his stretcher, he can't even hold his hands steady. Marlow thinks he is "as good as buried" (XVI.138). And yet, Kurtz is marked still by a fierce aspect of assertion, by a fine and fiery energy of self. This cadaver whose head "nodded with grotesque jerks" (XVI.134), who looks like "an atrocious phantom" (XVI.133), stirs Marlow still by the "fire" in its eyes; this emaciated stiff whose "hand roamed freely" strikes Marlow still by the vehemence of its urge to consume, by the passion of its will to be: "I saw him open his mouth wide—it gave him a weirdly voracious aspect, as though he had wanted to swallow all the air, all the earth, all the men before him" (XVI.134). And his voice! Four-fifths dead, Kurtz is still all alive in his undulating voice: "The volume of tone he emitted without effort, almost without the trouble of moving his lips, amazed me. A voice! It was grave, profound, vibrating, while the man did not seem capable of a whisper" (XVI.135). His voice, his eyes, his fervid power of self: whatever he has done, whatever he has been, Kurtz seems to Marlow unusual, extraordinary, thrilling. And taken against the mindless manager, the vapid pilgrims, all Marlow's "hints for nightmare" in the Congo, Kurtz seems to his latest disciple a miracle of sanity and life:

> It seemed to me that I had never before breathed an atmosphere so vile, and I turned mentally to Kurtz for relief—positively for relief. "Nevertheless I think Mr. Kurtz is a remarkable man," I said with emphasis . . . it was something to have at least a choice of nightmares. (XVI.138)

It sounds like an endorsement—yet, ambiguous Marlow, who can feel nothing completely, does not know what to make of the great genius of culture and being. He loves Kurtz's genuineness, his fierce quality of identity and life. But he loathes his history; and unlike Kurtz's clown, Marlow is still European enough to suppose that behavior matters, that what one does has at least something to do with who one is: "Everything belonged to him—but that was a trifle. The thing was to know what he belonged to, how many powers of darkness claimed him for their own. That was the reflection that made you feel creepy all over" (XVI.116). The genius has joined in dark ceremonies, slept with dark women. He has given himself to greed, larceny, lust. He has murdered! He has raped, robbed, danced at midnight. As Marlow reminds us, these things matter; indeed, they so much matter that it is a question with Marlow whether Kurtz is quite human, whether in his savage urge to pleasure Kurtz has not become rabid, insensate—a brute. Those shrunken heads, for instance, staked on skinned poles all about his compound:

> They only showed that Mr. Kurtz lacked restraint in the gratification of his various lusts, that there was something missing in him—some small matter which, when the press-

ing need arose, could not be found under his magnificent
eloquence. (XVI.131)

"Some small matter," called, say, soul, or mind, or self;
the humane spark, that smack of something which makes a
monkey a Marlow, a primate a prelate. What, Marlow wonders, if there is nothing to Kurtz but this fine will to feel? if
all of Kurtz's purposefulness and passion—themselves
moral properties—are all that there is to the man? What if
Kurtz is just insane? if "his—let us say—nerves, went wrong
. . ." (XVI.117)? Or what if Kurtz is, let us say, a canker, a
cavern, a cavity? A convenient summary, this: nothing to
Kurtz but whispers of wind; no need to measure Kurtz, to
love or to loathe him, to deal with him, "Because he was
hollow at the core . . ." (XVI.131; Conrad's ellipsis). Marlow can domesticate anything—even Kurtz, the final inflection of the Congo's "overwhelming realities."

Kurtz, though, is not to be domesticated, not by the
manager ("You with your little peddling notions . . ."
[XVI.137]), not by the clown, not by Marlow, not by rescue.
No, Kurtz is something more pure than Marlow has understood him to be—as Marlow himself learns when he looks
to tuck Kurtz in and finds that, wasted as he is, he somehow has dragged his ghostly self back into the ghastly
Congo. He is the appropriate pilgrim to make the discovery: no one else among the unrequired rescuers could
have interpreted rightly Kurtz's final gesture of authenticity. Marlow is frank about his shock and terror, about his
perfect apprehension of *personal* crisis:

> The fact is I was completely unnerved by a sheer blank
> fright, pure abstract terror, unconnected with any distinct
> shape of physical danger. What made this emotion so
> overpowering was—how shall I define it?—the moral

shock I received, as if something altogether monstrous, intolerable to thought and odious to the soul, had been
thrust upon me unexpectedly. (XVI.141)

It is with good cause that Marlow feels so disturbed. For by
this last desperate escape from rescue Kurtz has declared
in an indelible way how passionately a man may love what
his life has been, how madly a man may care for who he is.
By creeping away from the Company's squalid little tub,
Kurtz has shown Marlow that he *is* what Marlow has come
to the Congo to become: a completed self. All this folderol
of Marlow's about painting, writing, and speaking; all this
balderdash about work, inner stuff, restraint! However intolerable to thought or odious to the soul, one's "choice of
nightmares," Marlow at last must understand, is perfectly
simple. One either wants forest or sepulcher, dance or
death. Being or nothingness: Kurtz "unnerves" Marlow by
showing him that, like all other "overwhelming realities,"
the human self is absolute. A choice of nightmares, whispers the great genius of discourse: Company or Congo,
community or self, you or me. Get me back to the high,
sweet pitch—and you, Marlow, begone with your shadows
and shades, your horrible shuffling bones. Unlike you, I
have really fled "the dust-bin of progress . . . all the dead
cats of civilization" (XVI.119). I stink, Marlow. But, unlike
you, I am.

No wonder Marlow feels unnerved. He had not earlier supposed that the extremes of existence could be so
severe as this; nor had he guessed, at least in a conscious
way, that he was so unparticular a self, so unexpressed, so
nearly unactual a creature. It must come as a "moral
shock" to *us*, then, that Marlow responds to this often-
postponed crisis of consciousness, this stern occasion for

choice, not by joining with Kurtz, but by opposing him; not by connecting himself to Kurtz's passionate life, but by tracking him down and recovering him for the way of being Kurtz has rejected so decisively. It shocks us, too, that Marlow can misinterpret so completely his power with Kurtz, that he can overestimate so radically the authority of his hollow principles, the appeal of his exhausted clichés. I won Kurtz's soul, he exults! I inspired, against "the heavy, mute spell of the wilderness," a great act of contrition:

> Soul! If anybody had ever struggled with a soul, I am the man. . . . He struggled with himself, too. I saw it,— I heard it. I saw the inconceivable mystery of a soul that knew no restraint, no faith, and no fear, yet struggling blindly with itself. (XVI.144–45)

Hogwash. It is exactly "inconceivable" that Kurtz's "brutal instincts" should be susceptible to the gentle claims of community, or that his "monstrous passions" should yield to the quaint probities of civility. It is exactly inconceivable that Kurtz should be intimidated by Marlow's silly injunctions:

> "You will be lost," I said—"utterly lost." One gets sometimes such a flash of inspiration, you know. I did say the right thing, though indeed he could not have been more irretrievably lost than he was at this very moment. . . . (XVI.143)

"Lost." It was the right thing to say, all right, but not for the reason Marlow thinks. For Kurtz does not receive his phrase in its original evangelical intention. He understands it, rather, in its less complicated tonality—as if Marlow had meant to say, "If you stay here, you will be misplaced. No one in Europe will see you, hear you, follow you. You will lose power you might have had." Kurtz afraid for his soul? Bah! [9]

Once again Marlow has shied from a fact to accommodate an appearance, fled from a reality to preserve a "surface-truth." Kurtz has not renounced his sordid intemperance; he is conspicuously unrepentant. Marlow tells us himself, after all, that Kurtz gazed at his savage hordes with undiminished passion and love, that he looked upon his superb mistress "with fiery, longing eyes"—and not, as he incredibly adds, with "a mingled expression of wistfulness and hate" (XVI.146). Kurtz "mingles" nothing; he repudiates nothing. He longs in an open and craving, uncomplicated way for the life of extremity. How else can one interpret his terrible imprecation? " 'Oh, but I will wring your heart yet!' he cried at the invisible wilderness" (XVI.148). Kurtz could be no more explicit or extravagant! Yet Marlow cannot consent to his purity. Against what he sees and knows he hysterically tries to persuade himself that Kurtz is not unambiguously extreme; that, like himself, Kurtz is uncertain, indefinite, unformed—as if to say, This great genius is as timid and equivocal as myself, for I am all that a man may be:

> The shade of the original Kurtz frequented the bedside of the hollow sham, whose fate it was to be buried presently in the mould of the primeval earth. But both the diabolic love and the unearthly hate of the mysteries it had penetrated fought for the possession of that soul. . . . (XVI.147)

---

9. It hardly is necessary to add that here and elsewhere *Heart of Darkness* has been disingenuous with us. Time and again the novel manipulates us into sharing with Marlow impossible and foolish opinions, for reasons which I shall examine shortly.

No: this is Marlow's struggle, not Kurtz's. Kurtz *is* possessed; unqualified, a pure diabolic, on his very deathbed he is full of fervor, full of claim, full of self ("My Intended, my station, my career, my ideas . . ." [XVI.147]). Undiminished to the end, autonomous unto death, Kurtz loves his sovereign self, adores his lawless life. His soul rests in peace: it is Marlow's which is at war.

Marlow's famous uncertainty about Kurtz's last moments opens the final campaign of that heated and hidden war. As he has done so often before when opposed by an unwelcome but self-evident truth, Marlow makes the obvious mysterious, the unquestionable irresolvable. "As if transfixed," Marlow one last time imposes his own equivocation upon a reality which he finds "overwhelming":

> One evening coming in with a candle I was startled to hear him say a little tremulously, "I am lying here in the dark waiting for death". . . . Anything approaching the change that came over his features I have never seen before, and hope never to see again. . . . It was as though a veil had been rent. I saw on that ivory face the expression of sombre pride, of ruthless power, of craven terror—of an intense and hopeless despair. Did he live his life again in every detail of desire, temptation, and surrender during that supreme moment of complete knowledge? He cried in a whisper at some image, some vision—he cried out twice, a cry that was no more than a breath—"The horror! The horror!" (XVI.149)

Perhaps Kurtz did relive his life; perhaps he even repented every one of its excesses. Everything in his history, though, suggests that he could not make such a banal contrition; and nothing about the scene Marlow describes suggests that he did. Who else but Marlow, indeed, can have thought this dying declaration so complicated? "I am dying," Kurtz says. An expression of horror—redolent, characteristically, with "pride" and "power"—passes over his face. Filled with "intense and hopeless despair," marked, understandably, by acute "terror," Kurtz whispers that it is horrible to have to die. That is all.[10] A death so assertive and uncompromising is in every way typical of Kurtz's intemperate and intrepid life. His last moments are not complicated—or if they are, they have been made so not by a vast and inexplicably sudden change in Kurtz's character and consciousness, but by the demands of Marlow's own temerity and domesticity, by Marlow's own need to believe that Kurtz is no more vigorous in death than he is himself in life.[11]

10. It is possible to suggest that Kurtz's celebrated phrase may be yet more simple in its reference. For it appears that in one of his more bizarre moments Marlow has attempted a peculiar "joke" upon Kurtz. " 'I am lying here in the dark waiting for death,' " Kurtz tells Marlow. "The light," Marlow remarks, "was within a foot of his eyes. I forced myself to murmur, 'Oh, nonsense!' . . ." Of course Kurtz is unlikely in his desperate condition to take the silly joke. Perhaps, then, he understands Marlow to be shrinking (as he is) from the fact of his moribundity, and abhors as a "horror" Marlow's skittish wish to cheer him up. Oh no, Kurtz: you've no pulse, no heart, 110 degrees of fever, but you'll be all right, old boy. Let us laugh together. This *should* be "a horror"; nor is Marlow's actual jest, if that be what it is, much less sad or grim.

11. Or perhaps our response to this occasion in the narrative has been shaped by our own needs. It is remarkable how completely the criticism of *Heart of Darkness* has been conditioned by Marlow's unreliable experience of Kurtz: among the novel's critics only Lionel Trilling has suggested with sufficient fullness that Marlow may misrepresent the significance of Kurtz's last words. (Cf. Trilling, p. 20.)

As I remarked earlier, *Heart of Darkness* is marked by its wish to manipulate us into errors of assumption. Here the novel has invited us to misinterpret its apparent climax (in fact, as shall be seen, Kurtz's death only introduces the narrative's crisis)—as if the novel wishes us to reproduce Marlow's mistakes, that we may discover with something of Marlow's sense of immediacy similar information about our own limitations of character.

Marlow's distortion is so forced and feeble that even he cannot maintain it long. Just to sit at table with the spectral nonentities of the Company is enough to remind him how uncommon and valuable a man Kurtz had been. The manager is so forbidding in his "meanness"; his wretched little servant is so mindlessly "insolent"; the pilgrims are so imbecile in their stupid rush to stare at a corpse. Seen against such vapidity as this,—the way of the world, after all—Kurtz strikes Marlow again and finally as a "remarkable man" (XVI.150). Particularly so when Marlow at last compares himself to Kurtz, to discover, terribly, that Kurtz's life has been more authentic than his own. For whatever he has done and been, Kurtz has hungered after life: so fiercely and freely has he lived that he has felt it a horror to die. Marlow, though, feels nothing for his life, nothing strong or bold, nothing desperate. As he has told us so often, human life seems to him a barely perceptible dream—so much so that the very idea of existence has no authority with him. It is exactly the point of difference between himself and Kurtz that, because he has lived incompletely, Marlow does not care whether he survives or dies:

> I have wrestled with death. It is the most unexciting contest you can imagine. It takes place in an impalpable grayness, with nothing underfoot, with nothing around, without spectators, without clamour, without glory, without the great desire of victory, without the great fear of defeat, in a sickly atmosphere of tepid skepticism, without much belief in your own right, and still less in that of your adversary. (XVI.150)

It is a famous moment in *Heart of Darkness*, and rightly so. For here Marlow has understood, now and forever, that Kurtz has broadened the range of human life; that, if he has been gross and brutal, Kurtz has extended the experience of the self and increased its power. He has done barbarous things, exerted a criminal will. But he has felt. Against the indifference of the universe and all the insipidity of men, he has forced life to expand to the pressures of the self, to yield to human need energy and excitement, tangibility and form. Against the bleak nonurgency of ordinary life, Kurtz has discovered a locus for feeling—an uncommon achievement in the last days of the nineteenth century.

This is not to say that Kurtz has been happy or that he has "liked" life, that he has thought it gracious or good to be alive. But so much as this is never a question in *Heart of Darkness*. The novel takes it as its first assumption that life is terrible; it does not doubt that only unintelligent men could disagree with Marlow's sense of the world: "Droll thing life is—that mysterious arrangement of merciless logic for a futile purpose. The most you can hope from it is some knowledge of yourself—that comes too late— a crop of inextinguishable regrets." Empty hopes, unfilled needs, wish but not harvest. Marlow does not think that Kurtz has changed all this, that he has made life merciful or congenial to men. He believes it remarkable, rather, that, knowing what he knew, Kurtz could even survive—let alone long to live. And he believes it remarkable that, whatever the price, Kurtz had some knowledge of himself, after all, and he had it in time to act upon it, in time in some measure to gratify the needs of character he discovered. It is more than Marlow had thought a man can do; certainly it is more than Marlow can do himself. For even now, even when, like the clown, he has had his mind "enlarged" by Kurtz, Marlow still has no sense of himself. Less connected than ever to the world, Marlow still cannot say what it means to be a man, what it has meant to Charlie to be Marlow:

> I was within a hair's-breadth of the last opportunity for pronouncement, and I found with humiliation that probably I would have nothing to say. This is the reason why I affirm that Kurtz was a remarkable man. He had something to say. He said it. Since I had peeped over the edge myself, I understand better the meaning of his stare, that could not see the flame of the candle, but was wide enough to embrace the whole universe, piercing enough to penetrate all the hearts that beat in the darkness. He had summed up—he had judged. "The horror!" He was a remarkable man. After all, this was the expression of some sort of belief. . . . (XVI.151)

Kurtz felt pain but he had a belief. He lived a worse life than most men, but his meant something to him.

We hear no nonsense now about repudiation or repentance, for Marlow understands at last that Kurtz regretted nothing about his conduct; that at the end Kurtz abhorred not his own history—of that he was boastfully proud—but the experience itself of being human. Marlow understands at last, that is, that Kurtz's dying declaration was directed against not himself but the whole economy of human borders and bounds, the whole sordid harmony of edges and points beyond which human purposes cease to be possible. That such a prodigious experiment as his should end in that repulsive Company tug! That such genius and might should end in nonentity! *That* is what Kurtz meant to say: that human life is a horror.

It is the mark of Marlow's "enlarged" sophistication that he does not try to interpret Kurtz's terrible distress as an evidence of submission or failure. Marlow is quick to insist, indeed, that in his final expression of revulsion Kurtz described a great victory over the forbidding conditions of life. For in that moment of "sombre pride," as Marlow thinks, Kurtz has grasped "all the wisdom, and all truth, and all sincerity." In that second of "ruthless power" he had thrust himself through all the hazy glows and "misty halos" which conceal from lesser men the complexion and meaning of their lives.[12] Seen in this way, Kurtz's dying declaration presents itself to Marlow as the final inflection of Kurtz's moral ascendancy, as his purest moment of authenticity and grace: ". . . he had made that last stride, he had stepped over the edge, while I had been permitted to draw back my hesitating foot." "Permitted"! Well! Only Kurtz can know the price he paid for stepping over "the threshold of the invisible." But better that pain, Marlow tells us, better any pain, than his own docile repose, his own plaintive separation from selfhood and life:

> I like to think my summing-up would not have been a word of careless contempt. Better his cry—much better. It was an affirmation, a moral victory paid for by innumerable defeats, by abominable terrors, by abominable satisfactions. But it was a victory! That is why I have remained loyal to Kurtz to the last. . . . (XVI.151)

12. The novel's unidentified narrator remarks that Marlow's own experiences are "inconclusive" (XVI.51); that Marlow's moral imagination exists in a sort of "misty halo" or hazy glow: ". . . To him the meaning of an episode was not inside like a kernel but outside, enveloping the tale which brought it out only as a glow brings out a haze, in the likeness of one of those misty halos that sometimes are made visible by the spectral illumination of moonshine" (XVI.48). Marlow exactly detests this inconclusive spectrality of his. He admires Kurtz because he imagines that Kurtz is able to conclude, able to speak—able, as Marlow thinks, authentically and fully to be (as Marlow puts it: "He had something to say. He said it."). The narrator, too, shall learn to admire Kurtz's certitude. Indeed, he shall learn to admire even Marlow's.

Better Kurtz's torment than Marlow's tedium. Better Kurtz's anguish than Marlow's "careless contempt for the evanescence of all things." Better Kurtz's horror of life and death than Marlow's "grayness without form." God knows what Kurtz suffered, but he died a self. Separate and fierce, he pushed against life, made its horrible essences touch for a moment with his own. His last words, as Marlow tells us, bespoke bounds to power, but none to passion, ends to biology, but none to life. Better that, Marlow is the first to say, than dim little Charlie's thin little plaints.

Marlow has returned, then, to his original impression of Kurtz. No longer dismayed by the awful details of his life, he esteems Kurtz as one would a philosopher or prophet—as a seeker of truth, a sainted genius of sincerity. In his extremity Kurtz again and finally presents himself to Marlow as an interpreting "voice," as a holy experimenter in what Conrad earlier had called "the condition of art":

> Art itself may be defined as a single-minded attempt to render the highest kind of justice to the visible universe, by bringing to light the truth, manifold and one, underlying its every aspect. It is an attempt to find in its forms, in its colours, in its light, in its shadows, in the aspects of matter and the facts of life what of each is fundamental, what is enduring and essential—their one illuminating and convincing quality—the very truth of their existence. The artist, then, like the thinker or the scientist, seeks the truth and makes his appeal.[13] (XXIII.vii)

13. If, as I have suggested is the case, Conrad associates himself with Wait, Donkin, and the narrator in The Nigger of the "Narcissus," he connects himself here with Kurtz. It is a resonant economy.

One might add that in August 1908, Conrad wrote to Arthur Symons a letter which at first reading should appear to refute this assumption. "I did not know," Conrad wrote, "that I had 'a heart of darkness' and an

Kurtz, too,—it is the principle of his character—has looked for the truth and made from it his appeal. "He had summed up—he had judged." He is a hero, Marlow tells us; a hero of culture, a hero of life, a hero of the human spirit. An angel, not a fiend.

Seven

> The interview of the man and the girl locks in—as it were—the whole 30,000 words of narrative description into one suggestive view of a whole phase of life. . . . (*Blackwood*, 154)

Marlow leaves the Congo, then, with a programme. More than ever human life seems to him deadly and closed. But his own life has opened drastically, has yielded an example of authenticity and courage more authoritative by far than any other his career has extended—more au-

---

'unlawful' soul. Mr Kurz [sic] had, and I have not treated him with the easy nonchalance of an amateur. . . . The fact is that I am really a much simpler person." In fact, of course, Conrad was anything but "a much simpler person" than Mr. Kurtz. Later in the letter, in fact, Conrad confesses that he may have treated the matter of his own "simpleness" with "easy nonchalance." "And for the other things you say, things splendid and laudatory, particularizing and generalizing your generous appreciation, I will simply say, I don't know. I've never asked myself, or looked into myself or thought of myself. There was no time in these years to turn my head away from the table." The letter's key and controlling phrase, then, is "I did not know." It is the mark of his perfect authenticity as a novelist, this is to say, that Conrad could produce the stunning self-exposures of *Heart of Darkness* without fully tolerating—or, evidently, even fully recognizing—their implications. Perhaps Conrad meant to suggest something of this to Symons when he went on to remark: ". . . I stand outside and feel grateful to you for the recognition of the work, not the man. Once the last page is written the man does not count. He is nowhere" (LL,II.73).

thoritative, certainly, than the puerile fantasizing by which he began his great voyage.[14] Kurtz has "enlarged" Marlow as his profession has not. If he cannot take Kurtz's "last stride," Marlow imagines that at least he can appreciate its edge. If he cannot be so "translucently pure" as Kurtz, he thinks at least to ape Kurtz's approaches to life, to imitate his allegiance to reality and his fidelity to experience. It is a worthy project, one which we expect him to undertake: surely he must respond in *some* way to the extraordinary "enlargement" the Congo has worked upon his habits and assumptions. (Marlow remarks, after all, that this "was the farthest point of navigation and the culminating point of my experience" [XVI.51].)

Respond Marlow does, but with a curious quality of incertitude—as if his fervor were a matter more of fever than of persuasion.[15] It is not that he feels receptive to the ways of being Kurtz and the Congo have exposed, for he tells us that ordinary men repel him by their ignorance and banality:

> I found myself back in the sepulchral city resenting the sight of people hurrying through the streets to filch a little money from each other, to devour their infamous cookery, to gulp their unwholesome beer, to dream their insignificant and silly dreams. They trespassed upon my thoughts. They were intruders whose knowledge of life was to me an irritating pretence, because I felt so sure they could not possibly know the things I knew. (XVI.152)

14. Marlow first determined to go to the Congo because a chance window-shopping expedition recalled to him a childhood longing to explore the "blank spaces on the earth" (XVI.52). The earth's blankest space soon shall seem to him to be himself.

15. Perhaps Marlow's behavior in Brussels in fact is controlled by a kind of illness. As had Conrad himself, Marlow is said to have returned to Europe in severely compromised health (XVI.152).

Trespassers, pretenders, intruders: they are worse than that, as Marlow by now ought to realize. For in their triviality they are terrified by legitimate authenticity—as they acknowledge by their compulsive need to domesticate, or even to arrogate to themselves, Marlow's whole memory of Kurtz's vigorous and particular life. Thus Marlow is positively flooded by weird agents of nonentity who crawl from every nook and cranny of the grave to snatch from him pieces of memory, fragments of assumption—portions of self. A ruddy-cheeked fool wants "certain 'documents,' " and insists that Kurtz was an explorer, no more than a geographer. A "senile" cousin of the deceased plunders letters and memos, and remarks of Kurtz that he was "essentially a great musician." A "furry" journalist walks off with Kurtz's Report (which in a deliberate and dreadful gesture of concession Marlow himself drastically expurgates), and describes Kurtz as an undiscriminating orator, a genius merely of demagogy.

What is called for in this contest for Kurtz's memory and Marlow's spirit is not repressed animadversion but passionate struggle. But what a wearied, private fight Marlow wages! I scorn thee, he whispers. I know more than all of you; I am more passionate, more alive, more actual, than any of you: "I had no particular desire to enlighten them, but I had some difficulty in restraining myself from laughing in their faces, so full of stupid importance" (XVI.152). In this second and more momentous struggle for his moral life Marlow again can imagine only a gray and unexciting contest. "I had no particular desire. . . ." Can he not, like Kurtz, shriek out in one pure energy of integrity, Begone: "You with your little peddling notions—you are interfering with me" (XVI.137)? For Marlow *is* being interfered with. Nonentity is reclaiming him, probing at his memories and passions till, little by little, they wear out and grow dim.

And because his imagination "wanted soothing" (XVI.152) he yields to the process. Because like a mindless Willems he feels it less difficult to die than to live, he is pleased to surrender Kurtz's authenticity—and his own—to the obscene authority of quietude. Annihilate or be annihilated, Marlow. Exterminate all the brutes, or be exterminated oneself. Evidently it is one thing to know that most men's lives are insignificant and ridiculous, another to defend one's own. . . .

Marlow is so anxious to return to his normal economy of self that he tries to consign his whole Congo experience, together with its implied burden of demand, "to that oblivion which is the last word of our common fate" (XVI.155). But his taste of extremity will not yield to his apostate wish for simplicity and ease. It is precisely the principle of such experience as Marlow has had that it is autonomous, that its very memory is more compelling than the impalpable appeal of extinction. Thus, even as Marlow knocks on The Intended's door, even as he demands admission, as it were, to her uncomplicated sarcophagus of nonentity, his "expanded" consciousness makes a desperate gesture of revolt, a final, ungoverned appeal for the authority of life:

> I thought his memory was like the other memories of the dead that accumulate in every man's life; . . . but before the high and ponderous door, between the tall houses of a street as still and decorous as a well-kept alley in a cemetery, I had a vision of him on a stretcher, opening his mouth voraciously, as if to devour all the earth with all its mankind. He lived then before me; he lived as much as he had ever lived. . . . (XVI.155)

And with him lives Marlow's memory of passionate and particular life. With him lives unforgotten and undiminished Marlow's whole feeling for the "frightful realities" of sex and self, his whole ecstasy with unmediated being. Those "horned shapes" of long ago, that stirring "glow of fires"; Kurtz's "broken phrases," all "the tempestuous anguish of his soul." Try as he does, Marlow cannot dispose of the importunate claims of life. What little there is in him which needs perforce to Be will not let him:

> I rang the bell before a mahogany door on the first floor, and while I waited he seemed to stare at me out of the glassy panel—stare with that wide and immense stare embracing, condemning, loathing all the universe. I seemed to hear the whispered cry, "The horror! The horror!" (XVI.156)

Kurtz still acts here as Marlow's agent of opinion; and Marlow does "sum up" and judge by an hysterical hallucination. But however conceived, the judgment of censure Marlow imagines stands as an occasion of crisis in his life, and of climax in *Heart of Darkness*. Always before *Heart of Darkness* has understood Marlow earlier than he has understood himself: although he invariably discovers those failures of his attitude or action by which the novel defines him, Marlow never before has been able to perceive the inadequacy of one of his "steps" in time to struggle against it.[16] But here for the first time Marlow has comprehended, even imitated, Kurtz. For the first time he has achieved some knowledge of himself—achieved it, like Kurtz, in

16. One thinks, for example, of Marlow's earlier faith in arduous work. *Heart of Darkness* knows instantly what Marlow discovers in time: that all his palaver about engines and rivets represents a dreadful wish to avoid experience, a contemptible fear of choice. Here Marlow indicts himself. For the first time in the novel he perceives *with* the novel the full significance of a "step" which he is about to take, the consequences of a commitment which he feels himself bound to make.

time to use it, in time to identify and control "that inappreciable moment of time in which we step over the threshold
of the invisible" (XVI.151). By understanding as he has that
what he is *about* to do is "horrible," by understanding that
"all the universe" is contemptible, Marlow has described
for himself something of the openness and opportunity he
has admired about Kurtz's life. For, like Kurtz, Marlow has
compelled his life to submit to his own control, to yield to
the severe "threshold" of free choice. He has achieved an
authenticity of his own: like Kurtz, he has "kicked himself
loose of the earth" (XVI.144). Indeed, by so coherently
conceiving the consequences of what he is about to do,
Marlow at last establishes his life as a self, his right and
power to make, like Kurtz, an organized choice between
the opposed claims of opposite ways of being.

The novel's center of authority, then, has shifted—
has passed in this great moment of unresisted self-contempt from the dead Kurtz to the living Marlow. For the
first time in his life Marlow is not the victim of his novel's
opinion, but its source, agent, and hero.

But if he has opened his life, Marlow cannot save it.
It is the tragedy of *Heart of Darkness* that Marlow cannot
engage his "inappreciable moment" of choice, that he can
offer no more efficient struggle against his terrible taste for
dimness and death than to inveigh against himself in hysterical whispers of self-hatred and despair. "The horror!
The horror!" Fully certain that what he is about to do is
grievously wrong—believing, indeed, that he does not wish
to do it!—Marlow rings The Intended's bell, tells his
famous lies, perpetuates and thus enters into that absurd
woman's frightful compact with ignorance, vapidity, and
death. A "horror" indeed, Marlow manages this definitive

occasion of choice as he has all the others in his life—by shying from extremity, by stepping back from that "threshold of the invisible" which by any other name is character.

In his habitual way Marlow protests that he had no choice.[17] How, he pleads, could I *not* tell those lies? To disclose to that "guileless, profound, confident, and trustful" creature the brutal truth about her Kurtz, about human life, surely "would have been too dark—too dark altogether" (XVI.162). Maybe so, if Marlow's humanity were all that were at issue here. But what in fact has been at issue, as Marlow himself well knows, is Marlow's whole moral life, his final response of character to the great "enlargement" Kurtz and the Congo have worked upon the range of his assumptions and experience. His hedging notwithstanding, Marlow fully understands that he has been at Kurtz's edge, that he has involved himself in a primal and permanent choice between two modes of being, two versions of experience, two standards of self:

> I saw her and [Kurtz] in the same instant of time—his death and her sorrow—I saw her sorrow in the very moment of his death. Do you understand? I saw them together—I heard them together. She had said, with a deep catch of

17. As shall Jim, Marlow in fact tries to protest that he simply was not ready for his great test of character. He insists, that is, that there is no explaining how he came to interview The Intended; that this last occasion of his incertitude and infirmity—certainly the climactic moment of his moral life—was directed by a peculiarly hostile destiny, and in no way represented a fulfillment of need, or a gesture of character. He says: "I had no clear perception of what it is I really wanted. Perhaps it was an impulse of unconscious loyalty, or the fulfillment of one of those ironic necessities that lurks in the facts of human existence. I don't know. I can't tell. But I went" (XVI.155). He doesn't know. He can't tell. The only "ironic necessity" here is Marlow's apparently incorrigible need to blame the various catastrophes of his life upon anything else in the world but himself.

the breath, "I have survived" while my strained ears seemed to hear distinctly, mingled with her tone of despairing regret, the summing up whisper of his eternal condemnation.[18] (XVI.157)

The Intended or Kurtz. Her sorrow or his life; her frightened separation from experience or his desperate wish to be; her empty, institutional "survival" or his triumphant death.

Poor Marlow! "More than a year" after leaving the Congo (XVI.157) he is an unchanged man. Once again—once for all, conclusively—he has felt life to be impalpable, gray, less attractive than the undemanding release of endless nonentity and regret. No wonder he feels "a sensation of panic" (XVI.157). He has stepped over his threshold at last—has stepped with the prophetess of his kind "beyond the threshold of an eternal darkness" (XVI.159), beyond the bound of the stallion's appeal. Here, where life is soothing but dim, Marlow finally has his figurative character, his awful "crop of unextinguishable regrets." Here, terribly preserved from the demands and dues of a fiercer self, Marlow is free to struggle forever after the ecstasy and energy of that purer life he has refused. Free, too, to sum up and to judge the mode of unbeing he has affirmed; to regard with horror the closed shapes of his decision against life; to detest himself forever as "a trifle" (XVI.162) who feared to become either a monster or a saint.

It is Marlow's last gesture of integrity that he permits his narrative to end, like his moral life, in ellipses. He could do nothing else, for he leaves *Heart of Darkness* an emp-

18. Marlow's incoherence is excusable: he is about to make a dreadful confession, one to which language—it is one of the novel's themes—scarcely is adequate.

tied and helpless man. Mean, secretive, full of furious wrath against a self which he cannot change, Marlow leaves his novel not opened to experience but recoiling from it; not opened to human life but afraid of it, incapable of it, demonstrably opposed to it.

Eight

> If we are "ever becoming—never being" then
> I would be a fool if I tried to become this
> thing rather than that; for I know well that I
> will never be anything. (Garnett, 46)

What identity of self Marlow discovers in *Heart of Darkness* proceeds, then, from no normally human assembly of energies, functions, or joys, but from his extreme self-hatred: by detesting who he is, Marlow at last locates who he is. No doubt it is important to describe oneself, but obviously *this* sort of moral distinctness suggests only a theoretical value. For although it is true that other novels force their best people to feel painfully about themselves, they do so because they believe that self-contempt may provoke corrections of character, or changes of personality, or adjustments of difficulty. Marlow, though, gains nothing from his self-contempt. His awful abuse of himself does not lead to a freer culture of understanding, nor to a larger sentiment of existence, nor even to a deeper emotive power. He merely suffers. He is more particularized at the end of his novel than before his voyage to the Congo; but he is no more authoritative morally, and certainly he is less happy. His "enlargement" yields him more contempt for himself but not more character or life.

It is for this reason that *Heart of Darkness* ends so very suddenly. "Marlow ceased, and sat apart, indistinct and silent, in the pose of a meditating Buddha" (XVI.162). Marlow stops talking so abruptly and finally because in every sense which matters he *has* ceased. Reduced to one sensation of desperate contempt, no longer an affective creature, Marlow has become a sum of pain, a dim little duchy of suffering.[19] Indistinct, stilled, estranged from other men, himself, and all pleasurable life, he completes his career as he began it, in a desolate agony of isolation. In this we have the completed inflection of Conrad's own experience, of his own terror of life. For here Conrad has imagined that one cannot develop in moral consciousness and survive as a self; that all one's power of personality is less potent than the world's; that one's whole passion to live must yield at last to empty ellipses, to the weird, autistic postures of a moribund Bodhisattva. In this harshest moment of his most severe book, Conrad insists that one must leave the moral life as one enters it—stark, isolate, brilliantly actual not in identity but in pain.

Lest we mistake the grotesque significance of Marlow's discontinued human experience, Conrad extends *Heart of Darkness* for fifty more, frantically loded, words. The narrator takes up the novel's dropped voice not to fulfill some vague idea of structural harmony (he begins the

19. In this terrible autism Marlow establishes his community with Conrad's first figures of fiction. Like Almayer and Willems, Marlow has found life at once too lush and too bleak to endure; wearied, emptied, he discovers like the Dutchmen of Sambir that it is impossible to feel pleasure with the world. His suffering is more disturbing than either of theirs, though, because Marlow is a more gifted man than either Almayer or Willems. It signifies more to us that the brilliant and fascinating Marlow cannot survive the burdens of being human—just as in *Lord Jim* it shall mean so much to Marlow that Stein and Jim cannot.

book), but to complete its inhuman documentary of despair. Thus, although he is permitted only two lines in which to respond to Marlow's astonishing tale, the narrator is quick to announce that he shares in Marlow's pain—and that he is, therefore, a crucial character in *Heart of Darkness*, not merely its agent of transmission:

> I raised my head. The offing was barred by a black band of clouds, and the tranquil waterway leading to the uttermost ends of the earth flowed sombre under an overcast sky—seemed to lead into the heart of an immense darkness. (XVI.162)

Marlow's story has eroded all the narrator's first, uninformed serenity about men, life, the river, the world, himself (XVI.47). Now that he has heard *Heart of Darkness* the narrator feels what the novel expects we shall feel: that human life is in all things grim; that one is oneself unformed and unlovely, not deeply alive; that all the waterways and promontories of the world promise neither variety nor pleasure, but only "an immense darkness" of nonentity and despair. In their tonality of distress, their dreadful suggestion of fear and disgust, the narrator's last words define a completed sympathy with Marlow, an understanding of his misery so extreme as to imply communion with it.

Like Marlow, then, the narrator defines himself by his aversion to experience and his isolation from it. So, too, does *Heart of Darkness* define itself—and its tortured maker. "I know well that I will never be anything." Remedy or tragedy, *Heart of Darkness* is certainly autobiography, the most forbidding autobiography, I daresay, in English. (No other autobiography can have had less faith in the authority of the self!)

And yet, even if, in its shocking antipathy to human life, its fear that personality is aimless and unurged, *Heart of Darkness* cannot be thought to have freed Conrad from his own suffering, it may at least be supposed to have suggested an apparatus of accommodation. For if fitting out his own terrors as a recited fiction permitted Conrad to manage them, to endure them as sources of literature rather than as torments to peace, one may suppose that imagining *Heart of Darkness* preserved its author—perhaps even that it produced him. I am suggesting, that is, that Conrad resisted the materials of his existence by "narrating" them; that he survived his disorders of character by appropriating them for fiction and thus dismissing them, in one sense, from their primitive autonomy. By arrogating Conrad's pathology to itself, *Heart of Darkness* assumed, I think, the whole primacy of Conrad's misery—as if a despair so radical as his could propose itself as idea rather than experience. One cannot imagine that Conrad became happy by writing *Heart of Darkness*. But the issue for him in 1899 and 1900 obviously was not pleasure so much as sanity.

Chapter Seven

... I've fitted the pieces together, and there is enough of
them to make an intelligible picture.
(XXI.343)

An Intelligible Picture
Lord Jim

Conrad began *Lord Jim* during May or June of 1898, but in-
terrupted work on the novel in December 1898 to write
Heart of Darkness. He completed *Heart of Darkness* in February 1899 and returned to *Lord Jim* during the same
month.[1] The peculiar circumstance of their continuous
composition, taken with their shared use of Marlow as
both device and subject, narrator and character, suggests
that *Heart of Darkness* and *Lord Jim* are connected acts of
imagination, that the two novels are joined together in a
common impulse and project.

That impulse, as I have remarked about each of
Conrad's earlier works, is autobiographical: the novel is
chiefly interested in defining and sustaining the personality
of its author. *Lord Jim*, though, separates itself from—and
so concludes—the protracted process of self-elaboration
which Conrad initiated ten years before by beginning *Almayer's Folly*. For if *Lord Jim* produces as its landscape an
imagined universe fully as savage as that discovered in each

1. Cf. Baines, 210; 235.

of Conrad's earlier books, it as well develops a response to the earlier works' desperate situation, a mode of recovery from their crushing burden of disorder, loneliness, and pain. In this respect *Lord Jim* completes that era in Conrad's imagination of himself which I have tried to define in this study. More important, the novel "justifies" at last the personality which, together with *Almayer's Folly*, *An Outcast of the Islands*, *The Nigger of the "Narcissus,"* and *Heart of Darkness*, it so "coherently" establishes.

One

Marlow and Stein agree that "man is amazing, but he is not a masterpiece." By this they mean to suggest that, unlike other creatures, man cannot satisfy the requirements of his imagination. As Stein puts the matter, " 'Sometimes it seems to me that man is come where he is not wanted, where there is no place for him' " (XXI.208). " 'We want in so many different ways to be,' " he explains:

> "[The] magnificent butterfly finds a little heap of dirt and sits still on it; but man will never on his heap of mud keep still. He want to be so, and again he want to be so. . . . He wants to be a saint, and he wants to be a devil—and every time he shuts his eyes he sees himself as a very fine fellow—so fine as he can never be." (XXI.213)

One's "heart pain," Stein believes, is a function of one's power to achieve consciousness about oneself. " '. . . Because you not always can keep your eyes shut,' " he tells Marlow, " 'there comes the real trouble—the heart pain—the world pain. I tell you, my friend, it is not good for you to find you cannot make your dream come true, for the reason that you not strong enough are, or not clever enough. Ja!' " [2]

It is a mistake, as Stein thinks, for one to resist the limitations of the human condition. He tells Marlow—it is, oddly, the novel's most celebrated occasion—that the sensible and successful man submits to the inevitability of dissatisfaction and commits his energy to the pedestrian imperative of simple survival:

> "A man that is born falls into a dream like a man who falls into the sea. If he tries to climb out into the air as inexperienced people endeavour to do, he drowns—*nicht wahr?* . . . . No! I tell you! The way is to the destructive element submit yourself, and with the exertions of your hands and feet in the warm water make the deep, deep sea keep you up." [3] (XXI.214; Conrad's ellipsis)

Marlow consents to the injunction. What most is wanted in human life, he agrees, is not an unyielding assertion of individual appetite or need but an inexhaustible power of endurance—a power which he calls "the instinct of courage":

> I don't mean military courage, or civil courage, or any special kind of courage. I mean just that inborn ability to look temptations straight in the face—a readiness unintellectual enough, goodness knows, but without pose—a power of resistance, don't you see, ungracious if you like, but priceless—an unthinking and blessed stiffness before the outward and inward terrors, before the might of nature, and the seductive corruption of men. . . . (XXI.43)

2. XXI.213. Cf., too, XXI.217.

3. In fact Stein feels considerably less able to accommodate "the world pain" than he suggests here. By the end of his evening discussion with Marlow, indeed, he confesses that he does not know how one ought to live: " 'So if you ask me—how to be?' . . . His twitching lips uttered no word, and the austere exultation of a certitude seen in the dusk vanished from his face" (XXI.214).

This uncomplicated celebration of simple masculine probity invites mistrust. Modern readers are likely to react against an assumption which glorifies "stiffness" because it is an article of our shared persuasion that to suppress emotion is to inhibit the experience, and therefore the status, of the self. We normally maintain that those who could wish to circumscribe the range of human sensation secretly fear and despise life. But in their seemingly repressive moral attitudes Marlow and Stein do nothing but join themselves with the novel's mainstream of opinion. Captain Brierly, Captain Elliot, the French lieutenant—everyone of any established ethical authority in *Lord Jim* shares the two old friends' austere moral economy. And, indeed, there is nothing contemptible about the severe ethos with which *Lord Jim*'s fully situated people make communion. No one in the novel consciously wishes to restrict the experience of the self; they want rather to protect the self— and the community of selves—*from* experience. For the novel's people imagine other men and the outer world to be drastically dangerous. They respond in their endorsement of "unthinking and blessed stiffness" not to a brutal harshness of character, some fierce Murdstone delight in inhibition and repression, but to a universe which seems to each of them too perilous to support any less organized mode of being.

This impression of the universe is, of course, Conrad's own. It has shaped *Almayer's Folly, An Outcast of the Islands, The Nigger of the "Narcissus,"* and *Heart of Darkness,* and it forms the moral geography of *Lord Jim* as well. *Lord Jim,* indeed, makes programme of Conrad's terrified sense of other men's violence and iniquity. Time and again in its brief history the novel introduces episodes suggestive of the most gratuitous and terrible treachery, incidents of appalling and unpredictable reprobacy. The *Pat-*

na's swinish captain, the execrable Cornelius, Holy Terror Robinson, Sherif Ali, Rajah Tunku Allang, Gentleman Brown: *Lord Jim* is populated by a whole galaxy of chthonic creatures whose lives seem to represent a systematic crusade against human peace, solidarity, and dignity.

Nor is there anything, as one might say, "unnatural" about these people's dissoluteness. For in *Lord Jim,* as in each of Conrad's earlier novels, the universe itself seems organized in barely surreptitious, virtually animate opposition to human expectations and needs. As in each of his previous novels, Conrad in *Lord Jim* again imagines a geography of presented serenity which conceals enormously threatening and undivinable dangers; the novel's characters repeatedly are made to perceive their author's sense of "the suspended menace" at large "in the midst of the most perfect serenity" (XXI.96). The sun, for instance, appears to experience actual malice against men. It looks splendid but its splendor is "sinister." It is said not merely to shine with extraordinary intensity and heat but "under a serene sky" to have "killed all thought, oppressed the heart, withered all impulses of strength and energy" (XXI.15). Worse, the sun presumably is *pleased* to deplete men—as, evidently, it is pleased later in the book to "[dwarf] the earth into a mote of dust" (XXI.305), or as the night is pleased to settle "silently on all the visible forms, effacing the outlines, burying the shapes deeper and deeper, like a steady fall of implacable black dust" (XXI.306). Storms, too, operate in the novel as an instrument of the universe's vindictive malignancy. Evil deities of a sort, great winds strike the book's people as assaults deliberately directed against their irreducible impressions of peace, order, and personal primacy. Jim, for example, receives a gale at sea as an awesome attack upon his entire assumption of character:

> There was a fierce purpose in the gale, a furious ear-
> nestness in the screech of the wind, in the brutal tumult of
> earth and sky, that seemed directed at him, and made him
> hold his breath in awe. (XXI.7)

The malice of the universe often is more subtle in the novel, though, and therefore more dangerous. Thus, it is in the clearest weather, during the most serene hour of a ship's day, that the *Patna,* as if by "a special arrangement of a malevolent providence" (XXI.159), collides with a secreted hulk and in one instant shatters its crew's "great certitude of unbounded safety and peace" (XXI.17). The ship's crew is destroyed in its sense of world and self with baleful suddenness, as if the universe were organized by a principle of "burlesque meanness," or directed by an intention to perform upon all men "a fiendish and appalling joke," "a joke hatched in hell," "an utterly aimless piece of devilry" [4] (XXI.121; 108; 160). And the *Patna's* experience is far from episodic in *Lord Jim.* All men, Marlow tells us, must be wary of the gentle forms of life. All men must suspect those evenings "of freshness and starlight that would make the best of us forget that we are only on sufferance here and got to pick our way in cross lights, watching every precious minute and every irremediable step . . ." (XXI.35).

If, then, men in *Lord Jim* are unpredictably and sav-

---

4. At one point in his narrative Marlow goes so far as to suggest that the universe in fact *is* controlled in its malignancy; that the world is organized by a conscious intelligence which wages open contest against humankind. "It was all threats," Marlow tells us, "all a terribly effective feint, a sham from beginning to end, planned by the tremendous disdain of the Dark Powers . . ." (XXI.121). Conrad refers to the "Dark Powers" with some frequency in his fiction. The phrase seems to me more a freedom of speech, though, than an assumption of philosophy, a grim reflex of humor directed against the difficulty of being human.

agely mean to one another, if they often feel toward one another gratuitous and violent animosity, perhaps they take their cue from the malicious world in which they have their being—a world in which one is "tried more than is fair"; (XXI.124) a world which feels against one "the jeering intention of a spiteful and vile vengeance" (XXI.105), "a purpose of malice," an "unbridled cruelty . . . which means to smash, to destroy, to annihilate all [one] has seen, known, loved, enjoyed, or hated; all that is priceless and necessary . . ." [5] (XXI.11). It is this universe which men must organize themselves to anticipate and to oppose in *Lord Jim*, and which Marlow's obdurate moral code addresses. It is exactly *because* "the unexpected always happens" (XXI.95), as Marlow puts it, that he believes one steadfastly must maintain "an unthinking and blessed stiffness." It is because one cannot trust to the appearances of the world that, as Marlow believes, one must be able to trust to one's own, and to "the sovereign power enthroned in a fixed standard of conduct" (XXI.50). It is because "not one of us is safe" from "weaknesses that may lie hidden" (XXI.43) in the universe and in the self that, as he thinks, one must organize and perhaps even circumscribe the self. Marlow, Brierly, Elliot, the French lieutenant, even O'Brien, do not exalt sterility. They exalt, rather, what they take to be the protective power of a fixed moral assumption against the unfixed powers of the human personality and of the natural order which governs the personality. They want men, in a word, to be better than the world.

5. The description closely parallels Conrad's characterization of Donkin. (Cf. my p. 154.) Obviously Conrad responds here, as in *The Nigger*, to his own habitual sense of the natural order of things. It is to the point in this regard that the passage which I cite above is "spoken" not by Marlow but by *Lord Jim's* unidentified narrative consciousness: the "voice" more purely suggests Conrad's own than Marlow's can be said to do.

Two

The great question in *Lord Jim*, then—in all of Conrad's fiction—is, in Marlow's phrase, "How to live," in Stein's, "How to be!" (XXI.212; 213). It is a problem which is brought into particular focus not by anything which Marlow or Stein themselves precisely do, but by the behavior— or, perhaps, by the very appearance—of Jim, the likely ship's mate who cravenly abandons a presumably sinking tub one stinking night on the Red Sea.

Because of his participation in his community's forced and rather desperate faith in mute "stiffness," Marlow initially is able to experience an uncomplicated reaction to Jim's conduct and an only slightly more complicated response to Jim himself. At first hearing, Jim's desertion of the *Patna* seems to Marlow unambiguous and unforgivable. Like Brierly, O'Brien, the French lieutenant, Marlow begins by believing absolutely in the preserving, if unwritten, sanction of his craft's code, which seems to him less a sweet gesture of civilized men than a sort of extramundane ordination. With his scandalized brethren Marlow shares an assured contempt toward Jim's effort to qualify the authority of that necessary and absolute canon. As Brierly puts it, " 'We must preserve professional decency or we become no better than so many tinkers going about loose' " (XXI.68).

Unlike his coevals, though, Marlow cannot sustain for long the purity of his censure. In fact, Marlow understands quite early in the novel that he feels troubled less by that which Jim has done than by the discrepancy between Jim's conduct and his wholesome appearance. For it has been an article of Marlow's faith that one may extend trust to certain attitudes of carriage, that manner and physiognomy are moral qualities. At least in their sordid mien Jim's sordid shipmates "somehow fitted the tale" (XXI.41); but Jim does not. He *looks* so forthright, reliable, and safe. In Marlow's famous phrase, "He was one of us":

> I liked his appearance; I knew his appearance; he came from the right place; he was one of us. He stood there for all the parentage of his kind, for men and women by no means clever or amusing, but whose very existence is based upon honest faith, and upon the instinct of courage. . . . He was a youngster of the sort you like to see about you; of the sort you like to imagine yourself to have been; of the sort whose appearance claims the fellowship of these illusions you had thought gone out. . . . (XXI.43; 128)

To Jim "on the strength of a single glance" Marlow "would have trusted the deck":

> And, by Jove! it wouldn't have been safe. There are depths of horror in that thought. He looked as genuine as a new sovereign, but there was some infernal alloy in his metal. . . . I couldn't believe it. I tell you I wanted to see him squirm for the honour of the craft. (XXI.45–46)

As it happens it is Marlow who most must squirm. For in his integrity he is quick to understand that Jim has exposed—exploded—the authority of his "craft." That craft, after all, supposes itself capable of recognizing infernal alloys. Failing that, it purports to neutralize such "alloys," to impart upon the weak an artificial capacity for steadfastness and resolve, to supply to the unfortunate an unearned "genuineness." Marlow understands that if his ethos so abjectly can fail so "promising a boy," that "if this sort can go wrong like that" (XXI.40), Jim in some respects is correct to insist as peremptorily as he does that the universe admits of no firm supports—that no "fixed standard of conduct" can be proof against either the militant aggressiveness of the natural world or the shocking peccancy of the human mind.

"There are depths of horror in that thought" alone. What more unsettles Marlow, though, is his growing suspicion that his own "stiffness" perhaps is untrustworthy, his gradual perception that "if this sort can go wrong" so, certainly, can he.[6] Marlow never fully admits, as Jim wants him to do,[7] that he should himself have abandoned the *Patna.* But this residual confidence cannot diminish his sense of personal "horror," for by argument and example Jim does convince him that conceivably he might do almost anything else. " 'Nobody, nobody is good enough' " (XXI.319), Marlow eventually confesses. One's "moral identity," he acknowledges at last, ". . . [is] a convention, only one of the rules of the game, nothing more . . ." [8] (XXI.81).

6. It is in part to allay this fear that Marlow commits such an extravagant supply of energy and attention to Jim—as if by involving himself so intensely in Jim's situation he may discover circumstances which can justify the "boy's" behavior, and thus salvage the authority of "the craft." Marlow himself proposes this sense of his conduct: "Was it for my own sake that I wished to find some shadow of an excuse for that young fellow whom I had never seen before, but whose appearance alone added a touch of personal concern to the thoughts suggested by the knowledge of his weakness—made it a thing of mystery and terror—like a hint of a destructive fate ready for us all whose youth—in its day—had resembled his youth? I fear that such was the secret motive of my prying" (XXI.51). Marlow has other, less conscious "motives," to which I shall return.

   Brierly, of course, cannot defend *himself* against the personal implications of Jim's failure. (Cf. XXI.58–62.)

7. Cf. XXI.81; 92; 106; 135.

8. Cf., too, XXI.197; 222; 225. On several occasions Marlow seems to confess that about his own past he has much to justify—if not simply to suppress. Cf. XXI.34; 41; 88.

Three

If this be so, how is one to live? If not in accordance with a "fixed standard of conduct," how is one to be? As his previously untested investment in "the steadfastness of men" (XXI.121) deteriorates, Marlow increasingly supposes that a human being more appropriately may be judged by the quality of his consciousness than by the propriety of his behavior. "Moral identity," he begins to assume, is knowable more by the complexity of one's sensibility than by the stolidity of one's comportment.

So it is that, as he is deprived by the events of the novel of his faith in "the instinct of courage," Marlow learns to direct his judgment against those characters in *Lord Jim* who seem to him deficient in feeling, observation, or perception. Thus, of all the novel's villains and degenerates he most unreservedly contemns those men "to whom the whole of life is like an after-dinner hour with a cigar; easy, pleasant, empty . . ." (XXI.35). Jim's father, for example, suggests himself as an insignificant and foolish prater, full of "little thoughts about faith and virtue" (XXI.341). In their systematic inauthenticity the novel's tourists seem to Marlow revolting, if vaguely comic (XXI.77–8; 87; 100). Cornelius strikes him as "a sinister pantaloon," "vermin-like" (XXI.307; 323). Chester and Robinson appear "phantasmal and extravagant" (XXI.174). The Rajah Allang seems "dirty, little, used-up, old . . . wizened grimy" (XXI.228). The Sultan of Patusan "is an imbecile youth with two thumbs on his left hand" (XXI.227).

Marlow comes to believe, indeed, that such fatuousness as this is nothing less than deliberate, that most men experience as the chief impulse of their life the *desire* to avoid sensation.[9] He first indicts his direct audience (XXI.34–35), but goes on to accuse us all of succumbing to an arid and cowardly revulsion from affectual existence:

> The desire of peace waxes stronger as hope declines, till at last it conquers the very desire of life. Which of us here has not observed this, or maybe experienced something of that feeling in his own person—this extreme weariness of emotions, the vanity of effort, the yearning for rest? (XXI.88)

It seems to Marlow that, seen from this point of view, particularly "fixed standards of conduct" express the covert urge to neutralize experience, the secret and manipulative wish to protect the self against test or potentially painful investment of feeling. Thus, as he is expanded in his own ethical consciousness by his increasing sympathy for Jim's, Marlow feels himself estranged in an especially intense and discomforting way from the novel's harbingers of fixed opinion. The French lieutenant appears to him to be marked less by courage or moral authority than by "stolid glibness" (XXI.139). Brierly seems filled with "self-satisfaction" (XXI.58). The autonomically heroic Bob Stanton suggests himself as "a naughty youngster fighting with his mother" (XXI.150). In each of the communicants of his former faith Marlow principally detects "the soft spot, the place of decay, the determination to lounge safely through existence" (XXI.13).

To the degree that he disestablishes the novel's other men Marlow finds himself compelled to endow and to celebrate Jim. For it seems to him that, if Jim has failed the first Marlovian "standard of conduct," he from the first triumphantly survives the other. Jim, after all, precisely re-

9. Perhaps it is this assumption which permits Marlow to suppose, extremely, that ". . . those who do not feel do not count" (XXI.222).

fuses to be a "lounger": he always engages the world, presses his arc, meets and contests that sad "desire of peace" to which, as Marlow believes, everyone else accedes. Whatever else he has done, Jim seems to Marlow "fine in the wildness of his unexpressed, hardly formulated hope" (XXI.153) that one may have one's will and way with the brutally depersonalizing universe. "The thing is that," as Marlow puts it, "in virtue of his feeling [Jim] mattered" (XXI.222):

> He had the gift of finding a special meaning in everything that happened to him. . . . I affirm that he had achieved greatness, . . . greatness as genuine as any man ever achieved. (XXI.304–5; 225; 244)

Like Achilleus, Jim is able to say about his life, " 'I am satisfied . . . [Conrad's ellipsis] nearly. . . . I can stand it' " (XXI.306). In this respect he, at least, establishes himself in "imperishable reality" (XXI.216); he seems to Marlow the one being who has "come nearest to rising above the trammels of earthly caution" [10] (XXI.277):

> I had made up my mind that Jim, for whom alone I cared, had at last mastered his fate. He told me he was satisfied . . . nearly. [Conrad's ellipsis] This is going further than most of us dare. I—who have the right to think myself good enough—dare not. Neither does any of you here, I suppose? (XXI.324–25)

Four

The chief victim of Marlow's altered "ideal of conduct" (XXI.121) obviously is Marlow himself. As his rela-

10. No doubt it is as an expression of this conviction that Marlow so often describes Jim as accumulating about himself all of the world's "sunshine" and "light". Cf. XXI.173; 177; 229; 265; 336.

tionship with Jim progresses Marlow feels radically cen-
sorious toward himself, more at odds with his own
"cautious" mode of being than with that of any other man.
For he feels increasingly certain that, as measured against
Jim's, his own experience is without quotient. Jim always
has believed in the absolute authority of personality—"believed," as Marlow confesses, "where I had already
ceased to doubt" (XXI.153). "Worn and clouded," "overcome by a profound and helpless fatigue" (XXI.32; 132),
Marlow cannot trust or enjoy or even acknowledge his own
"special meaning." It seems to him, indeed, that he has no
particularity or power, that he is cold at his core, stark,
sterile, deeply and sadly insincere. He remarks:

> As to me, I have no imagination. . . . I felt I had done
> nothing. And what is it that I had wished to do? I am not
> sure now. . . . I remained strangely unenlightened. I was
> no longer young enough to behold at every turn the mag-
> nificence that besets our insignificant footsteps. . . . After
> all, what did *I* know? (XXI.223; 317; 185; 134; Conrad's em-
> phasis)

Marlow fears, this is to say, that because he has risked
nothing and understood nothing, he has achieved nothing.
He fears that by substituting his tepid "ideal of conduct"
for the primal exigencies of free experience, his "sheltering conception of light and order" (XXI.313) for the threatening hazards of absolute personality,[11] he has, like Brierly,
"almost cheated his life of its legitimate terrors" (XXI.64).
Perhaps—and only perhaps—Marlow may be thought to be
a more reliable man than Jim. But he seems to himself less
actual than his friend, less authentic in his sensation of ex-

11. It is important to remark the fact that Marlow never underestimates
the price which Jim pays for his splendid authenticity. Cf., for example,
XXI.100; 153.

istence.[12] He never has abandoned a sinking ship; but he has abandoned, as he believes, the exalted project and exacting pleasures of a life that is genuinely human.

It is for this reason that by the end of his narrative Marlow acknowledges Jim not only as a friend but as a savior of sorts:

> [Jim] had startled me out of a dream of wandering through empty spaces whose immensity had harassed my soul and exhausted my body. . . . I felt a gratitude, an affection, for that straggler whose eyes had singled me out, keeping my place in the ranks of an insignificant multitude. How little that was to boast of, after all! (XXI.132; 334)

Considered from this point of view, Jim in his "sheer truthfulness" (XXI.393) legitimizes not only his own existence but Marlow's as well. "I'd lost all confidence in myself" (XXI.154), Marlow confesses. If Jim cannot return his older friend to his happily exploded sense of gratitude and ease, he *can* stir and excite him, permit him access to significance and particularity. It seems to the "harassed" and "exhausted" Marlow a magnificent gift.

Five

It is precisely from this point, though, that one feels there to be something computational about Marlow's relationship with Jim, a subtle taint of manipulation and use where once, perhaps, there had been simple generosity. As their intimacy progresses, that is, Marlow appears to

12. At one point in his narrative Marlow directly acknowledges his inferiority to Jim. "I was the irreproachable man," he remarks, ". . . but [Jim's] selfishness had a higher origin, a more lofty aim" (XXI.153).

divine in Jim not a man in need of aid but a system of help for his own pain, an instrument of recovery from his own instinction of vapidity and squalor.

At the least there develops an increasingly co-optative tone about Marlow's responses to Jim. After all, he begins his account of their association by remarking that originally he had felt merely an "interest" (XXI.32) in Jim, a gratuitous "curiosity" (XXI.42; 76) about his character. Soon, though, the quality of Marlow's "interest" suggests a more extreme investment, an indelicate hint of usurpation in place of that initial spontaneous sympathy. Thus, as he meets with Stein he not entirely ironically refers to Jim as both a "toy"—"one of those flat wooden figures that are worked by a string" (XXI.184)—and "a specimen" [13] (XXI.211). And in a moment of radical self-exposure he goes on to define the full reach of his acquisitive, of his virtually taxonomic, interest in his "distinct" and "touching" (XXI.177; 223) friend:

> I could see in his glance darted into the night all his inner being carried on, projected headlong. . . . [Jim] began to pace the room, reminding me by the set of his shoulders, the turn of his head, the headlong and uneven stride, of that night when he had paced thus, confessing, explaining—what you will—but, in the last instance, living—living before me. . . . (XXI.83; 235)

13. Marlow is capable of yet less pleasant attitudes toward other men. About the dying Brown, for example, he remarks: "I had to bear the sunken glare of his fierce crow-footed eyes if I wanted to know; and so I bore it" (XXI.344). Later he adds: "He died during the night, I believe, but by that time I had nothing more to learn" (XXI.346). Certain of his impulses about Jim are disturbing enough, to be sure. Marlow reports, for instance, that he and Stein "avoided pronouncing Jim's name as though we had tried to keep flesh and blood out of our discussion, or he were nothing but an erring spirit, a suffering and nameless shade" (XXI.215).

In the end, then, Jim so attracts and compels Marlow because Marlow imagines that he actually can *attach* himself to Jim, that he can seize upon Jim's emotive authenticity and make part of it his own. "The views he let [Marlow] have of himself," of his splendidly actual "inner being," seem to Marlow so redolent with expressiveness, sincerity, and reality that he thinks to affiliate himself with their quality, to link himself by sympathy—if not by mere proximity—with his friend's heroic genuineness.

Six

The essential device and gesture of this interesting strategy is the narrative act itself. For Marlow believes that it is principally by organizing, interpreting, and recording Jim's experience that he can associate himself with it. If, that is, it be Jim who actually makes "the conquest of love, honour, men's confidence" (XXI.226), it is Marlow who perceives that fact and publicizes its implications. If it be Jim, the pioneering partner, who lives in "unconscious subtlety" (XXI.235), it is Marlow who makes his subtlety usable by raising it to vibrant consciousness. It seems to Marlow, therefore, that his narrative simultaneously permits Jim to claim the full significance and quality of his "greatness" and permits Marlow himself to become coadjutant with it. It seems to Marlow that by comprehending and advertising Jim's adventure he at once salvages his partner's delicacy from obscurity and meaninglessness and establishes a vantage point for his own.

It is for this reason that, in one of the most important passages in Conrad's early fiction, Marlow feels able to assert, ". . . [Jim's] is a victory in which I had taken my part." He goes on to declare:

I am telling you so much about my own instinctive feelings
and bemused reflections because there remains so little to
be told of him. He existed for me,[14] and after all it is only
through me that he exists for you. I've led him out by the
hand; I have paraded him before you. (XXI.224)

"I," "I've," "I"; "my," "me," "me." The man who had
demeaned himself as illegitimate and insignificant appears
to have developed a use for—and an interest in—his "own
instinctive feelings and bemused reflections." The man
who had loathed and reviled himself seems to have discovered a lovely potential in the contemplative devices of his
"exhausted" character, a way of making himself suppose,
as had Jim, that his own quietistic "existence is necessary—
you see, absolutely necessary—to another person"
(XXI.304).

The narrative act, then, seems to Marlow both to establish and to justify his existence.[15] Certainly his recital
promises to preserve his life's most intense, as one might
say, his most "romantic" experience. For it has been in his
association with Jim that, as he remarks, the most "tremu-
lous, subdued, and impassioned note . . . had come in
[his] way" (XXI.283); it has been in his association with Jim
that Marlow most has felt himself to possess "a special
meaning," to be in his own right "touched" (XXI.309) and
"wonderful" (XXI.315). By narrating Lord Jim, by describing
his partner's story and his own "part" in it, Marlow finds

14. It is possible to suggest that Marlow uses the preposition "for" in a
curious way here. It seems to me that at least in part he intends to suggest
that Jim conducts his life on behalf of Marlow—that he "existed" for the
sake of enlivening Marlow's "exhausted" sensibility. If this be so, Marlow
should seem to possess at once a more selfish and a more social imagination than any other character in literature.

15. I have used Conrad's personal vocabulary deliberately: for Marlow's
achievement of certitude and serenity obviously establishes the ground
for Conrad's own. I shall return to the point.

himself able to regain and to perpetuate that sensation of authority, that movement of personality, which his intimacy with Jim had provoked autonomously. By reconstructing his cherished past as an organized narrative Marlow finds himself able to resurrect "the whole real thing" which otherwise should have "left behind the detailed and amazing impression of a dream" (XXI.318). By arresting in language the moments of his own "greatness" he rescues for use in the present "the sounds, the visions, the very savour of the past . . ." (XXI.338). By describing his association with Jim as a composed and ordered tale Marlow recovers in both a semantic and an emotional context his entire consciousness of its quality, reproduces in both language and sensation its bold and not again *experientially* discoverable "truthfulness." [16] "I can easily picture [Jim] to myself," he reports. "I remember the smallest details; . . . I can testify . . ." (XXI.84; 332; 405).

Seven

More than personal "testimony," though, is at issue in this ambitious enterprise. For Marlow's idea of himself is almost wholly at the mercy of his listeners—of his own certifying partners. Should he be unable to make his audience

16. Marlow had believed in Patusan, it will be recalled, that one could not achieve so much as this. Jewel's voice, he remarked then, "had the power to drive me out of my conception of existence, out of that shelter each of us makes for himself to creep under in moments of danger, as a tortoise withdraws within its shell. . . . But still—it was only a moment: I went back into my shell directly. One *must*—don't you know? . . ." (XXI.313; Conrad's emphasis). Perhaps one must "withdraw" in this way. But by narrating the events of *Lord Jim* Marlow produces a way repeatedly to perform that expansion—that creation—of himself which he had discovered in Patusan.

perceive his experience with Jim in its full particularity and force, he cannot, as he believes, entirely reclaim it—nor feel it to be established in perfect signification and durability. So it is that, in another of the novel's important moments, he remarks of his impressions in Patusan:

> All I had lately seen, all I had heard, and the very human speech itself, seemed to have passed away out of existence, living only for a while longer in my memory, as though I had been the last of mankind. . . . This was, indeed, one of the lost, forgotten, unknown places of the earth; I had looked under its obscure surface; and I felt that when to-morrow I had left it for ever, it would slip out of existence, to live only in my memory till I myself passed into oblivion. I have that feeling about me now; perhaps it is that feeling which has incited me to tell you the story, to try to hand over to you, as it were, its very existence, its reality—the truth disclosed in a moment of illusion. (XXI.323)

Obviously Marlow refers here less to Patusan or his responses to Patusan than to his character itself: as I have remarked, it is chiefly his own sensibility which Marlow finds "one of the lost, forgotten, unknown places of the earth." By describing "the story" of his decisive experience, though, by treating his life as a tellable tale, Marlow hopes to hold, as it were to entrust to others, his character's "very existence, its reality." In this sense, perhaps, he imagines that he can make of "a moment of illusion" a lifetime—or more—of tangible, irrefutable "truth."

If this be a brave strategy, it is as well a deeply dangerous one. As Marlow acknowledges, he has tried "to hand over" to his audience the foundation of his identity. Should he fail to earn the belief and trust of his listeners he shall risk not merely their boredom but his own collapse as an organized and sensible personality. It is for this reason that Marlow feels there to be so much at stake in his uses of language. Words have no arcane function for this extraordinary seaman because, as I have suggested, at stake for Marlow in his power to make others understand his communications is nothing less than his power to be. No wonder, then, he is so frantic after precision of expression, literalness of effect:

> I am trying to interpret for you into slow speech the instantaneous effect of visual impressions. . . . All this, as I've warned you, gets dwarfed in the telling. I can't with mere words convey to you the impression. . . . This is my impression and it is all I can give you. . . . Try as I may for the *success* of this yarn I am missing innumerable shades—they were so fine, so difficult to render in colourless words . . . I have given up expecting those last words, whose ring, if they could only be pronounced, would shake both heaven and earth. (XXI.48; 272; 308; 96; 225; my emphasis)

"The *success* of this yarn." Unless he can describe exactly the full nuance of his moments of former feeling, Marlow feels that he must lose them forever—and so lose himself. As he puts the matter, ". . . Should I let [my life with Jim] slip away into the darkness I would never forgive myself" [17] (XXI.180).

17. Marlow's anxiety is compounded by the fact that he cannot trust fully to the responsiveness of his audience. He remarks at one point in the narrative: " 'Frankly, it is not my words that I mistrust but your minds. I could be eloquent were I not afraid that you fellows had starved your imaginations to feed your bodies' " (XXI.225). His concern seems well-founded; he is forced to write to his unnamed correspondent: "You alone have showed an interest in [Jim] that survived the telling of his story . . ." (XXI.338). Marlow is not always convinced, though, of the legitimacy of language; " '. . . for words also,' " he once declares, " 'belong to the sheltering conception of light and order which is our refuge' " (XXI.313) from the burdens of full authenticity.

Perhaps, then, Marlow, unlike Jim, cannot "dare" to say that he has become "satisfied . . . nearly." His satisfaction, after all, is still at issue as he leaves the novel and must again be placed at issue each time that he tells his story. Yet, it seems to me that in *Lord Jim* Marlow does achieve a "victory," or at least a "greatness," akin to his partner's "extraordinary success" (XXI.416). For Marlow, too, has had the courage and skill to attempt an accommodation with the universe and with himself. Like Jim, Marlow refuses to be "not worth having" (XXI.413). Like Jim, Marlow undertakes "to prove his power in another way" from that given to most men, and thus to "conquer the fatal destiny itself" (XXI.410) of his own self-loathing. At the least, as he remarks about Jim, Marlow's seemingly depleted "spirit seemed to rise above the ruins of his existence" (XXI.410). And why should it not? Out of materials far less promising than even his partner's, he manages to create for himself an approach to "that full utterance which," as he declares, "through all our stammerings is of course our only and abiding intention" (XXI.225).

In Marlow's case that utterance, if not full, seems fully serviceable. "My information was fragmentary," he exults, "but I've fitted the pieces together, and there is enough to make an intelligible picture" (XXI.343). This is to say that in his inspired discovery of the uses of language Marlow assembles not simply a novel but "an intelligible picture" of a personality. By narrating *Lord Jim* he collects from among all the incoherence of his unpleasure and unbeing "something of me—the best" (XXI.205). Out of the most meager and fragmented resources and with the offered assistance of no one Marlow shapes himself as a man whom he can bear to be. For the first time in his life he frees himself from the bleak oppressiveness of the outer world and the sad ravages of his own aberrant psychology.

Perhaps he cannot join that community discovered by other novelists' characters, the community of the fully peaceful and the fully free. No one in Conrad's fiction, though, is permitted to achieve quite so much as this.

Eight

Obviously at work here for Conrad, who, after all, is Marlow's narrator, is a crucial gesture of *self*-reconciliation: it has been my point in this study that what Marlow does in literature Conrad hoped to do in life, that what Marlow achieves in fiction Conrad wished to achieve as a maker of fiction. Just as Marlow recovers from his fear that he has no character by producing a linguistic or a narrative self, so Conrad, by telling Marlow's tale, by attaching himself to Marlow as Marlow attaches himself to Jim, may be thought at last to have produced and secured a serviceable personality of his own.[18] At the least Conrad may be said to have established in *Lord Jim*—together with his earlier novels—an explanation of his life's chief ambition and procedure. For if he no more than Marlow or Jim could achieve in his novels "that full utterance" or "those last words," he did produce for his own use the terms of that external justification for which he so long had searched. " 'I don't want to excuse myself,' " he has Jim say, " 'but I would like to explain—I would like somebody to understand—somebody—one person at least! You! Why not you?' " (XXI.81).

By 1900, to be understood by "somebody"—by us,

18. It may be appropriate here to recall Conrad's description of his relationship as a novelist with William Charles Olmeijer, the prototype for Kaspar Almayer. Cf. my p. 53–54.

indeed—proposed itself to Conrad as both an acceptable apparatus of character and an acceptable system of sanction. The twin impulses—to establish "an intelligible picture" of himself and to legitimize the picture by his readers' comprehension of its integuments—for the rest of his life offered itself to Conrad as a bulwark against his "awful vision" (XXI.100) and a defense against his mind's "unreasonable forces" (XXI.88). Thus, as he began the second era of his career as a novelist Conrad felt able to say, in however ironic a way, that like Marlow and Jim he, too, was "satisfied . . . nearly." To Garnett, who always had understood something of his anxiety and sorrow, he wrote:

> I admit I stood [in *Lord Jim*] for a great triumph and I have only succeeded in giving myself utterly away. Nobody'll see it, but you have detected me falling back into my lump of clay I had been lugging up from the bottom of the pit, with the idea of breathing big life into it. And all I have done was to let it fall with a silly crash. . . .
>
> I've been satanically ambitious but there's nothing of a devil in me, worse luck. The *Outcast* is a heap of sand, the *Nigger* a splash of water, *Jim* a lump of clay. A stone, I suppose, will be my next gift to the impatient mankind—before I get drowned in mud to which even my supreme struggles won't give a simulacrum of life. Poor mankind! Drop a tear for it—but look how infinitely more pathetic I am! This pathos is a kind of triumph no criticism can touch. Like the philosopher who crowed at the Universe I shall know when I am utterly squashed. This time I am only very bruised, very sore, very humiliated.
>
> This is the effect of the book upon me; the intimate and personal effect. Humiliation. Not extinction. Not yet. All of you stand by me so nobly that I must still exist. (Garnett, 171–72)

Anyone who reads widely in Conrad's correspondence will recognize the letter's excitement and hope. The self-mockery notwithstanding—Conrad never freed himself from *that* idiom—the letter is all alive with a sense of opportunity and renewal almost unique for him. "Not extinction. Not yet." Far from it: during the next ten years of his life Conrad worked with the greatest power of his life. (Perhaps, like Jim, he "could no more stop telling now than he could have stopped living by the mere exertion of his will" [XXI.100].) And if he could not live during that decade in anything like perfect equanimity and repose, he did manage largely to preserve "the belief in himself snatched from the fire" (XXI.272), "the big life" he had breathed into "the lump of clay" which had been himself. Like the lights flickering from the deserted *Patna,* he sent into the world volume after volume of his continuing "simulacrum of life," as if to say to more established men, " 'I am here—still here. . . .' " As he remarks in *Lord Jim,* "What more can . . . the most forsaken of human beings say?" (XXI.136).

Conrad's personal achievement in *Lord Jim* was as "immense," then, as that of his characters. As he has Marlow say of Jim, he created for himself in the novel "a seal of success upon his words, . . . conquered ground for the soles of his feet, [gained] the blind trust of men . . ." (XXI.272). The edifice which Conrad erected in his spectacularly difficult way, this "simulacrum of life," doubtless was less one of personality than of performance. But this was his courage: like Marlow, like Jim, he was willing to have his character at any hazard, to chance his whole identity upon his own continuing authority as an author and upon our intelligence as readers.[19] In this regard one dares say

19. Conrad always was frank about both the totality of his risk and its desperate psychic cost. The letters which I have cited and his lifelong bouts with temper, self-loathing, illness, and doubt comprise a terrible testi-

that no other novelist ever can have invested so much in his work as Conrad habitually did in his. Certainly no other novelist can have been more at the mercy of—or more empowered by—his sovereignty with language. The fullest measure of Conrad's success with this appalling, albeit self-defined, burden is the fact that against all odds he remained sane. Or perhaps it is rather the fact that after completing *Lord Jim* he for the most part ceased to write covert autobiography of the kind I have tried to define in this study; the fact that Conrad felt released enough by having written fiction about himself to extend his attention more directly to the psychology and the society of others.

This is to say that after writing *Lord Jim* Conrad at last became able to satisfy Thaddeus Bobrowski's most difficult injunction. "From the blending of the blood in [the] two excellent races in your worthy person," Bobrowski had written to Conrad in 1880, "should spring a character whose endurance and wise enterprise will cause the whole world to be astonished! " (Baines, 66).[20] As, fifty years after his death, Conrad increasingly seems to us our century's most important novelist, I think it inevitable that we shall learn to regard him as our most interesting as well. It is true that we are not yet so "astonished" by Conrad's "endurance and wise enterprise" as we ought to be. But as we are led by the quality of the fictions which those energies produced to investigate the personality which controlled

---

mony to the constancy of his incertitude and worry. In this connection, see especially Conrad's letter of 12 October 1899 to Edward Sanderson. (LL,I.281–84). It should be remarked, too, that Conrad's two most intimate friends were exquisitely aware of the fragility—and of the remarkableness—of Conrad's achievement in this regard. Cf. the extraordinary exchange between Garnett and Cunninghame Graham (Watts, 212–14).

20. Najder prints a slightly different version of Bobrowski's letter. Cf. Najder, p. 67.

them, we cannot fail to become excited by the extremity of Conrad's will to identify and to justify himself. To be sure, an author's private struggle for coherence and peace—the century's struggle—is not a traditional subject for criticism. In Conrad's case, though, as his guardian implied before the fact, the literature is otherwise incomprehensible.

Selected Bibliography

Works by Conrad

Complete Works. 26 vols. Garden City, New York: Doubleday, Page and Company, 1925.

Conrad to a Friend: 150 Selected Letters from Joseph Conrad to Richard Curle. Ed. Richard Curle. New York: Doubleday, Doran and Company, 1928.

Conrad's Polish Background: Letters to and from Polish Friends. Ed. Zdzisław Najder, tr. Halina Carroll. London: Oxford University Press, 1964.

Joseph Conrad: Letters to William Blackwood and David S. Meldrum. Ed. William Blackburn. Durham: Duke University Press, 1958.

Joseph Conrad: Life and Letters. Ed. G. Jean-Abruy. 2 vols. Garden City, New York: Doubleday, Page and Company, 1927.

Joseph Conrad's Letters to Cunninghame Graham. Ed. C. T. Watts. Cambridge, Eng.: The University Press, 1969.

Joseph Conrad's Letters to His Wife. Preface by Jessie Conrad. London: privately printed by *Bookman's Journal*, 1927.

Letters from Joseph Conrad, 1895–1924. Ed. Edward Garnett. Indianapolis: Bobbs-Merrill Company, 1928.

Letters of Joseph Conrad to Marguerite Poradowska, 1890–1920. Tr. and ed. John A. Gee and Paul J. Sturm. New Haven: Yale University Press, 1940.

Works about Conrad

Allen, Jerry. *The Sea Years of Joseph Conrad.* Garden City, New York: Doubleday, 1965.

Anderson, Quentin. Introduction to *Lord Jim.* New York: Washington Square Press, 1963.

Baines, Jocelyn. *Joseph Conrad: A Critical Biography.* London: Weidenfeld and Nicolson, 1959.

Bradbrook, Muriel C. *Joseph Conrad: Poland's English Genius.* Cambridge, Eng.: The University Press, 1941.

Brown, Douglas. "From *Heart of Darkness* to *Nostromo:* An Approach to Conrad." *The Pelican Guide to English Literature,* vol. 7. Baltimore: Penguin Books, 1964.

Conrad, Borys. *My Father: Joseph Conrad.* London: Calder & Boyars, 1970.

Conrad, Jessie. *Joseph Conrad and His Circle.* London: Jarrolds, 1935.

———— *Personal Recollections of Joseph Conrad.* London: privately printed by Strangeways, 1924.

———— *Joseph Conrad as I Knew Him.* Garden City, New York: Doubleday, Page and Company, 1926.

Curle, Richard. *The Last Twelve Years of Joseph Conrad.* London: Sampson Low, Marston, 1928.

Fleishman, Avrom. *Conrad's Politics: Community and Anarchy in the Fiction of Joseph Conrad.* Baltimore: The Johns Hopkins Press, 1967.

Ford, Ford Madox. *Joseph Conrad: A Personal Remembrance.* Boston: Little, Brown, and Company, 1924.

Gordan, John. *Joseph Conrad: The Making of a Novelist.* Cambridge: Harvard University Press, 1940.

Guerard, Albert J. *Conrad the Novelist.* Cambridge: Harvard University Press, 1958.

Hay, Eloise Knapp. *The Political Novels of Joseph Conrad.* Chicago: University of Chicago Press, 1963.

Hewitt, Douglas. *Conrad: A Reassessment.* Cambridge, Eng.: Bowes and Bowes, 1952.

Kimbrough, Robert, ed. *Heart of Darkness.* Rev. ed. New York: W. W. Norton, 1971.

Leavis, F. R. *The Great Tradition: George Eliot, Henry James, Joseph Conrad.* New ed. London: Chatto & Windus, 1960.

Lohf, Kenneth A., and Eugene P. Sheehy. *Joseph Conrad at Mid-Century: Editions and Studies, 1895–1955.* Minneapolis: University of Minnesota Press, 1957.

Meyer, Bernard C., M.D. *Joseph Conrad: A Psychoanalytic Biography.* Princeton: Princeton University Press, 1967.

Miller, J. Hillis. *Poets of Reality: Six Twentieth Century Writers.* Cambridge: Belknap Press, 1965.

Morf, Gustav. *The Polish Heritage of Joseph Conrad.* Sampson Low, Marston, 1950.

Moser, Thomas. *Joseph Conrad: Achievement and Decline.* Cambridge: Harvard University Press, 1957.

———, ed. *Lord Jim.* New York: W. W. Norton, 1968.

Owens, Guy, Jr. "A Note on *Heart of Darkness.*" *Nineteenth-Century Fiction,* XII (September, 1957), 168–69.

Reid, B. L. *The Man from New York: John Quinn and His Friends.* New York: Oxford University Press, 1968.

Roussel, Royal. *The Metaphysics of Darkness.* Baltimore: The Johns Hopkins Press, 1971.

Russell, Bertrand. *Portraits from Memory.* New York: Simon and Schuster, 1936.

——— *Autobiography.* 3 vols. New York: Simon and Schuster, 1967–69.

Said, Edward W. *Joseph Conrad and the Fiction of Autobiography.* Cambridge: Harvard University Press, 1966.

——— Introduction to *Three Novels by Joseph Conrad.* New York: Washington Square Press, 1970.

Sherry, Norman. *Conrad's Eastern World.* Cambridge, Eng.: Cambridge University Press, 1966.

Stallman, R. W., ed. *The Art of Joseph Conrad: A Critical Symposium.* East Lansing: Michigan State University Press, 1960.

Stewart, J. I. M. *Joseph Conrad.* New York: Dodd, Mead, 1968.

Tanner, Tony. *Conrad: Lord Jim* ("Studies in English Literature"). London: Edward Arnold, 1963.

Trilling, Lionel. *Beyond Culture.* New York: Viking Press, 1965.

Warren, Robert Penn. Introduction to *Nostromo.* New York: Modern Library, 1951.

Woolf, Virginia. *The Common Reader*. New York: Harcourt, Brace & World, 1967.

Zabel, Morton Dauwen. *Craft and Character in Modern Fiction*. New York: Viking Press, 1957.

———— Introduction to *Lord Jim*. Boston: Houghton Mifflin, 1958.

———— Introduction to *The Portable Conrad*. New York: Viking Press, 1969.

Index

282   Index